Kathryn Armstrong

The White Ribbon Cook Book

A collection of original and revised recipes in cookery and housekeeping

Kathryn Armstrong

The White Ribbon Cook Book
A collection of original and revised recipes in cookery and housekeeping

ISBN/EAN: 9783744785303

Printed in Europe, USA, Canada, Australia, Japan

Cover: Foto ©Lupo / pixelio.de

More available books at **www.hansebooks.com**

Economy and Wealth
Temperance and Health in the Household

The White Ribbon Cook Book

A COLLECTION OF ORIGINAL AND REVISED
RECIPES IN COOKERY AND
HOUSEKEEPING

EDITED BY
KATHRYN ARMSTRONG

CHICAGO:
THE WOMAN'S TEMPERANCE PUBLISHING ASSOCIATION
THE TEMPLE

PREFACE

The recipes in this volume have been most carefully selected and are the result of practical experience, all of them having been tested by myself or by other practical housekeepers. I am under obligations to many friends in America and in Europe, and I wish to extend thanks specially to those women in all parts of the world, interested in the cause of temperance, who have sent contributions. I trust that they and all who may have occasion to use this little book will be satisfied with my effort to prove that wine, brandy and spirituous liquors of any kind may be dispensed with, and that no culinary requirement necessitates the introduction of these poisons into any household.

K. A.

...Contents...

Introductory	7
Boiling	8
Roasting	9
Broiling	9
Frying	10
Cooking	11
Soups	14
Fish	29
Oysters, Shellfish, etc	40
Poultry and Game	46
Meats	58
Beef	59
Pork	66
Veal	68
Mutton	73
Curries	79
Gravies	84
Sauces	87
Stocks	96
Vegetables	98
Salads	119
Pickles	126

CONTENTS

Eggs 130
Catsups, etc.................... 137
Forcemeats..................... 140
Bread and Cakes................ 142
Pastry 173
Dessert........................ 210
Home-made Candies............ 212
Ice-Cream, Ices, etc............ 221
Preserves...................... 229
Canned Fruits, Jellies, etc..... 240
Dairy Dishes................... 253
Beverages..................... 255
Sick-room Cookery............. 261

THE WHITE RIBBON
Cook Book

FROM the richest to the poorest, the selection and preparation of food often becomes one of the chief objects in life. The resources of every family may be greatly increased by the knowledge of what may be called trifling details, and refinement in the art of cookery depends much more on the *manner* of doing a thing than on the cost attending it. To cook well is immensely more important to the middle and working classes than to the rich, for they who live by the "sweat of their brow," whether mentally or physically, must have the requisite strength to support their labor. Every wife, mother or sister should be a good plain cook. If she has servants she can direct them, and if not, so much the more must depend upon herself.

An old saying, to be found in one of the earliest cookery books — "First catch your hare," etc.—has more significance than is generally supposed. To catch your hare well, you must spend your income judiciously. This is the chief thing. In our artificial state of society, every income, to keep up appearances, has at least half as much more to do as it can afford. In the selection of provisions the *best* is generally the *cheapest*. Half a pound of good meat is more nutritious than three times the amount of inferior. As to vegetables, buy them fresh. Above all, where an income is small and there are many to feed, be careful that all the nourishment is retained in the food that is purchased. This is to be effected by careful cooking. Cleanliness is an imperative condition. Let all cooking-utensils be clean and in order. Uncleanliness produces disorder, and disorder confusion. In the cooking of meat by any process whatever, remember, above all, to cook the juices *in* it, not *out* of it.

Boiling.

In boiling, put the meat, if fresh, into cold water, or, if salt, into luke-warm. Simmer it very gently until done. It is a general rule to allow a quarter of an hour to every pound of meat; but in this, as in everything else, judgment must be used according to the bone and shape of the joint, and according to the taste of the eaters. All kinds of meat, fish, flesh and fowl, should be boiled very slowly, and the scum taken off just as boiling commences. If meats are allowed to boil too fast they toughen, all their juices are extracted, and only the fleshy fiber, without sweetness, is left; if they boil too long they are reduced to a jelly, and their nourishing properties are transferred to the water in which they are boiled. Nothing is more difficult than to boil meat exactly as it should be; close attention and good judgment are indispensable.

Roasting.

In roasting meat the gravy may be retained in it by pricking the joint all over with a fork and rubbing in pepper and salt. Mutton and beef may be underdone; veal and pork must be well cooked. Young meat generally requires more cooking than old; thus lamb and veal must be more done than mutton and beef. In frosty weather meat will require a little more time for cooking. All joints for roasting will improve by hanging a day or so before cooking.

Broiling.

Broiling is the most nutritious method of cooking mutton and pork chops, or beef and rump steaks, kidneys (which should never be cut open before cooking), etc. Have the gridiron clean, and put over a clear fire; put the meat on it; "keep it turned often." This last is a common direction in books, but the reason why is never stated: it is to keep the gravy in the meat. By letting the one side of a steak be well done before turning, you will see the red gravy settled on the top of the steak, and so the meat is hard and spoiled. This is cooking the gravy out, instead of keeping it in to nourish the consumer. Never stick the fork in the meaty part; you will lose gravy if you do. Be sure to turn often, and generally the chop or steak is done if it feels firm to the fork; if not done, it will be soft and flabby.

Frying.

Although very bad for chops or steaks, the frying-pan is indispensable for some things, such as veal cutlets, lamb chops (sometimes), fish, pancakes, etc. Most meats and fish are usually fried with egg and bread crumbs. The frying-pan must be kept clean. This is very essential, as the dirt that sticks to the pan absorbs the fat, prevents the meat browning and turns it black. Have a clear, brisk fire, for the quicker meat is fried the tenderer it is. According to what is to be fried, put little or much fat in the pan; fish and pancakes require a considerable quantity. The fat must always *boil* before putting the meat into it; if not, it coddles. For veal cutlets a little butter is best and most economical, as it helps to make the gravy. Some cooks have a few slices of bacon with cutlets or liver; the fat from this, if the bacon be not rank, will do very nicely; and if the meat be well flavored and fried quickly, and some nice gravy made to it, few persons would know the difference. Some like thickened and some plain gravy to these fried meats; some a large quantity, others very little; all these must be accommodated. To make these gravies, have ready a little burnt sugar to brown with; empty the pan of the fat, if it be, as is most likely; too rank to use; put warm water in the pan; mix very smoothly sufficient flour and water to thicken it to taste; into this put as much butter as you like to use (a little will do, more will make it richer); pepper and salt it sufficiently; stir it very smoothly into the pan while the water is only warm; stir it well until it boils, and brown it with the burnt sugar to your taste. Care must be taken, after the gravy boils, not to let it boil fast for any length of time, as all *thickened* gravies, hashes, etc., boil away very fast and dry up; neither must it stand still in the pan; a whitish scum then settles on the top and spoils the appearance of it.

N. B.—For all frying purposes be particular that the pan is thoroughly hot before using.

Cooking Time-Table.

Baking Meats.

Beef Sirloin—Rare, 8 minutes for each pound; well-done, 10 to 15 minutes for each pound.

Beef Ribs or Rump—10 to 15 minutes for each pound.

Beef Fillet—20 to 25 minutes.

Lamb—Well done, 15 minutes for each pound.

Mutton—Rare, 10 to 12 minutes for each pound; well done, 15 to 18 minutes for each pound.

Pork—Well done, 25 to 30 min. for each pound.

Veal—Well done, 18 to 20 min. for each pound.

Braised Meat—$3\frac{1}{2}$ to 4 hours.

Chickens—Weighing from 3 to 5 pounds, 1 to $1\frac{1}{2}$ hours.

Turkeys—Weighing from 9 to 12 pounds, 3 to $3\frac{1}{2}$ hours.

Fish—Of average thickness, weighing from 6 to 8 pounds, 1 hour.

Cake and Pastry.

Sponge Cake—45 to 55 minutes.
Plain Cake—20 to 45 minutes.
Cookies—10 to 12 minutes.
Gingerbread—20 to 30 minutes.
Plum Pudding—$2\frac{1}{4}$ to 3 hours.
Tapioca or Rice Pudding—1 hour.
Bread Pudding—65 minutes.
Pies with two crusts—30 to 40 minutes.
Graham Rolls—$\frac{1}{2}$ hour.
Wheat Rolls—10 to 18 minutes.
Bread—40 to 60 minutes.
Biscuit—10 to 18 minutes.

Boiling.

Beefsteak—Cut $1\frac{1}{2}$ inches thick, 5 to 8 minutes.
Beefsteak—1 inch thick, 3 to 5 minutes.
Mutton Chops—8 to 10 minutes.
Chickens—18 to 25 minutes.
Fish—Thin, 4 to 8 minutes.
Fish—Thick, 10 to 15 minutes.
Ham—7 to 10 minutes.

Boiling Fish.

Bass—10 minutes for each pound.
Bluefish—10 minutes for each pound.
Fresh Cod or Haddock — 6 minutes for each pound.
Halibut—In square, 15 minutes for each pound.
Salmon—In square, 15 minutes for each pound.
Small Fish—6 to 8 minutes for each pound.
Oysters—3 to 4 minutes, or until the edges curl.

Boiling Meats.

Veal—2 or 3 hours.
Beef—3 or 4 hours.
Mutton—2 or 3 hours.

Ham—5 to 5½ hours.
Sweetbreads—20 to 25 minutes.
Chickens—1 to 1½ hours.
Fowls—2 to 3 hours.
Tongue—2 to 3 hours.

Vegetables.

String Beans—1½ to 2 hours.
Shell Beans—1 to 2 hours.
Cauliflower—30 to 40 minutes.
Cabbage, New—30 to 45 minutes.
Corn, Young—5 to 10 minutes.
Carrots—50 to 60 minutes.
Asparagus—15 to 18 minutes.
Onions—35 to 45 minutes.
Oyster Plant—40 to 60 minutes.
Peas—15 to 20 minutes.
Potatoes—Boiled, 20 to 30 minutes.
Potatoes—Steamed, 30 to 45 minutes.
Turnips—35 to 50 minutes.
Parsnips—35 to 45 minutes.

SOUPS

THE true economy of soups lies in the fact that so many things which might otherwise be wasted may be utilized in making them. In households where expenditure is not so much a consideration, it may be deemed expedient always to purchase fresh meat for the sole purpose of making soup, but, in such instances, the soup could certainly not be regarded as an *economical* addition to a dinner. Still, where Economy *must* rule, the resources from which she may draw a tureen of good soup, without having recourse to the butcher, are ample. Almost everything that is used as food may be converted into soup. Scraps of meat, bread, vegetables, rice, sago, spare milk, and, better still, bones left from the meat after cooking, may, with a little ingenuity, be made into excellent, nourishing soup.

The basis of all good soup is *stock*. This may be made from meat or bones and flavored with vegetables. Let it be borne in mind that no good stock can be made the day it is required for soup. It should be made the previous day, strained into a basin, and allowed to stand until required, when the fat, which would render the soup so objectionable, will have cooled on the top and may be taken off entirely. The stock may then be used as the basis of any kind of soup.

In making stocks or soups care must be taken to simmer gently, *not boil*, or they will be found wanting both in flavor and nourishment. The lid of the stock-pot must be kept tightly closed, or there will be considerable waste during the long time which the contents must of necessity simmer. It will be necessary to remove the lid a few times in order to take off the scum as it rises.

When preparing the stock, all the meat used should be cut into small pieces, and the bones broken or crushed. Cold water and salt should be added, and the whole brought very gradually to simmering point, the vegetables being added after the stock has been well skimmed.

On no account must stock be left in an iron stock-pot any length of time, or it will contract a very unpleasant flavor. It must be poured into an earthenware vessel and remain uncovered. To those about to purchase a stock-pot we would recommend an earthenware rather than an iron one as being more cleanly and not necessitating the emptying out of the stock when finished.

To Color Soups—To obtain a green color pound spinach leaves and add the juice obtained to the stock. For a red color use tomatoes, without the skins and seeds. For amber grate a carrot and mix with the soup, and for a rich brown use burnt sugar or burnt onions.

Macaroni Soup—Five cents' worth of bones, 1 tablespoonful salt and peppercorns, 1 good-sized turnip and 4 leeks, 2 carrots, 4 onions, 2 cloves, 1 blade of mace, 1 bunch of herbs, (marjoram, thyme, lemon-thyme and parsley), $\frac{1}{4}$ lb. macaroni.

Time required, about $2\frac{1}{2}$ hours. Break up the bones and put them into a stewpan with cold water enough to cover them and 1 quart more.

When on the point of boiling put in a tablespoonful of salt to help the scum to rise, then take the turnip, peel it and cut it in quarters; then take 2 carrots, wash and scrape them; take also 4 leeks, wash and shred them up finely; now take 4 onions, peel them and stick 2 cloves into them; then skim the soup well and put in the vegetables, add a blade of mace and a teaspoonful of peppercorns, then allow soup to simmer for $2\frac{1}{2}$ hours, then take $\frac{1}{4}$ lb. of macaroni, wash and put in a stewpan with plenty of cold water and a little salt. Allow it to boil until tender, then strain off the water and pour some cold water on, to wash the macaroni again; then cut in small pieces and it is ready for the soup. When the soup is ready for use strain it over the macaroni.

Milk Soup—4 potatoes, 2 leeks or onions, 2 oz. butter, pepper, $\frac{1}{4}$ oz. salt, 1 pint milk, 3 tablespoonfuls tapioca.

Put 2 quarts of water into a stewpan, then take 4 potatoes, peel and cut in quarters, take also 2 leeks, wash well in cold water and cut them up; when the water boils put in potatoes and leeks, then add the butter, salt and pepper to taste, Allow it to boil to a mash, then strain the soup through a colander, working the vegetables through also; return the pulp and the soup to the stewpan, add one pint of milk to it and boil; when boiling sprinkle in by degrees tapioca, stirring all the time; then let it boil for 15 minutes gently.

Spring Vegetable Soup—2 lbs. shin of beef, 2 lbs. knuckle of veal, a little salt, 2 young carrots, 1 turnip, 1 leek, $\frac{1}{2}$ head of celery, 1 cauliflower, 1 gill of peas, $\frac{1}{4}$ saltspoonful of carbonate of soda.

Cut the meat from the bone—do not use the fat; break the bones in halves; do not use the marrow. Put the meat and bones into a stockpot with five pints of cold water, a teaspoonful of salt will assist the scum to rise, boil quickly and remove scum as it rises, then simmer gently 5 hours. Cut carrots and turnips in slices; the head of celery and leek wash well and cut in squares; cut the cauliflower in sprigs after washing. One hour before serving add vegetables; the sprigs of cauliflower can be put in 15 minutes before serving. Put one gill of peas, a teaspoonful of salt, a quarter of a saltspoonful of soda into boiling water and boil 15 minutes, then put peas in tureen and put soup over them.

Good Gravy Soup—1 lb. beef, 1 pound veal, 1 lb. mutton, 6 quarts water, 1 crust of bread, 1 carrot, 1 onion, a little summer savory, 4 cloves, pepper and a blade of mace.

Cut the meat in small pieces and put into the water, with the crust of bread toasted very crisp. Peel the carrot and onion, and, with a little summer savory, pepper, 4 cloves and a blade of mace, put in the stewpan. Cover it and let it stew slowly until the liquid is reduced to 3 qts. Then strain it, take off the fat, and serve with sippets of toast.

Scotch Mutton Broth—2 qts. of water, neck of mutton, 4 or 5 carrots, 4 or 5 turnips, 3 onions, 4 large spoonfuls of Scotch barley, salt to taste, some chopped parsley.

Soak a neck of mutton in water for an hour; cut off the scrag, and put it into a stew-pot with two quarts of water. As soon as it boils skim it well, and then simmer it an hour and a half; then take the best end of the mutton, cut it into pieces (two bones in each), take some of the fat off, and put in as many as you think proper; skim the moment the fresh meat boils up, and every quarter of an hour afterwards. Have ready 4 or 5 carrots, the same number of turnips, and 3 onions, all cut, but not small, and put them in soon enough to get quite tender; add 4 large spoonfuls of Scotch barley, first wetted with cold water. The meat should stew three hours. Salt to taste, and serve all together. Twenty minutes before serving put in some chopped parsley. It is an excellent winter dish.

A Roast Beef and Boiled Turkey Soup—Bones of a turkey and beef, 2 or three carrots, 2 or 3 onions, 2 or 3 turnips, ½ doz. cloves, pepper, salt, tomatoes, 2 tablespoonfuls of flour, some bread.

The liquor that the turkey is boiled in, and the bones of the turkey and beef, put into a soup-pot with 2 or 3 carrots, turnips and onions, ½ dozen cloves, pepper, salt and tomatoes, if you have any; boil it 4 hours, then strain all out. Put the soup back into the pot, mix 2 tablespoonfuls of flour into a little cold water; stir it into the soup; give it one boil. Cut some bread dice-form, lay it in the bottom of the tureen, pour the soup on it, and color with a little soy.

White Soup—3 potatoes, 3 leeks, or a few green onions, 3 quarts water or stock, a small teacupful sago, 1 pint milk, 2 oz. butter.

Boil the potatoes and onions in the stock until quite tender, then mash them through a sieve with a little of the stock. Return the whole to the saucepan, add the milk. Sprinkle in the sago gradually, stirring well. When the sago has boiled clear and tender, stir in the butter and serve. If water be used instead of stock, ½ teaspoonful of salt should be added with the potatoes and leeks, and pepper to taste.

Greek Soup—4 lbs. lean beef, 1 lb. lean mutton, 1 lb. veal, 4 oz. lean ham, 4 carrots, 4 onions, 1 head celery, a little soy, a few allspice and a few coriander seeds, some pepper and salt, 10 quarts water.

Cut up the beef, mutton and veal into small pieces, and throw into a stewpan with 10 quarts of cold water; add a little salt, and then place on the stove to boil; take off the scum, add a little cold water, and take off the second scum; then cut up the carrots, onions and celery and throw in the pot; add a little more salt, a few allspice, and coriander seeds; let it simmer 6 hours, color the soup with a little soy, and strain it through a fine cloth; take off any fat that may be on the soup with a sheet of paper; before sending to table boil the soup, and place in the tureen a little fried lean ham cut into small pieces.

Giblet Soup—3 sets of ducks' giblets, 2 lbs. beef, some bones, shank bones of two legs of mutton, 3 onions, some herbs, pepper and salt, carrots, 3 quarts water, $\frac{1}{4}$ pint cream, 1 oz. butter, 1 spoonful flour.

Thoroughly clean 3 sets of ducks' giblets, cut them in pieces, and stew with 2 lbs. of beef, some bones, the shank bones of 2 legs of mutton, 3 small onions, some herbs, pepper and salt to taste, and carrots, for 3 hours in 3 quarts of water. Strain and skim, add $\frac{1}{4}$ pint of cream mixed with one ounce of butter kneaded with a spoonful of flour, and serve with the giblets. (Only the gizzard should be cut.)

Potato Soup — 2 lbs. potatoes, a pinch of celery seed, a sprig of parsley, 2 quarts white stock, pepper and salt to taste.

Boil or steam the potatoes very dry, mash them very finely with a fork, and add them gradually to the boiling stock. Pass through a sieve, add the seasoning, and simmer 5 minutes, adding 1 oz. of butter and ½ pint of milk. Serve with fried bread or toast.

Oyster Soup a la Reine—2 or 3 doz. small oysters, some pale veal stock, mace, cayenne, 1 pint boiling cream.

Two or 3 dozen small oysters to each pint of soup should be prepared. Take the beards and simmer them separately in a little very pale veal stock 30 minutes. Heat 2 quarts of the stock, flavor with mace and cayenne, and add the strained stock from the oyster beards. Simmer the fish in their own liquor, add to it the soup and 1 pint of boiling cream. Put the oysters in a tureen, pour over the soup and serve. If not thick enough thicken with arrowroot or butter mixed with flour.

Chicken Soup (Brown)—1 or 2 fowls, a bunch of herbs, 1 carrot, 1 onion, 2 oz. lean ham, 2 oz. butter, pepper and salt, 2 quarts good stock, and a little roux, a few allspice, a little grated nutmeg and mace.

Cut up the carrot and onion, and fry in 2 oz. of good butter, a nice light brown; add the ham and fowls cut up small, taking care to break up the bones with a chopper, add the stock, and boil until the fowl is cooked to rags; thicken with a little roux, add the allspice and mace and a little grated nutmeg, color with a little soy, add seasoning to taste. Serve with the soup some plain boiled rice.

Beef Gravy Soup—Some beef water, 2 oz. salt to every gallon of water, 4 turnips, 2 carrots, some celery, 4 young leeks, 6 cloves, 1 onion, ½ teaspoonful peppercorns, some savory herbs.

Various parts of beef are used for this; if the meat, after the soup is made, is to be sent to the table, rump steak or the best parts of the leg are generally used, but if soup alone is wanted, part of the shin with a pound from the neck will do very well. Pour cold water on the beef in the soup pot and heat the soup slowly, the slower the better, letting it simmer beside the fire, strain it carefully, adding a little cold water now and then, put in 2 oz. of salt for every gallon of water, skim again, and put in four turnips, two carrots, some celery, 4 young leeks, 6 cloves stuck into an onion, half a teaspoonful of peppercorns, and some savory herbs; let the soup boil gently for six hours; strain.

Milk Soup with Vermicelli—Salt, 5 pints boiling milk, 5 oz. fresh vermicelli.

Throw a small quantity of salt into 5 pints of boiling milk, and then drop lightly into it 5 oz. of good fresh vermicelli; keep the milk stirred as this is added, to prevent its gathering into lumps, and continue to stir it very frequently from 15 to 20 minutes, or until it is perfectly tender. The addition of a little pounded sugar and powdered cinnamon makes this a very palatable dish. For soup of this description, rice, semolina, sago, cocoa-nut, sago and macaroni may all be used, but they will be required in rather smaller proportions to the milk.

Green Pea Soup—4 lbs. beef, ½ pk. green peas, 1 gal. water, ½ cup rice-flour, salt, pepper and chopped parsley.

Four lbs. beef, cut into small pieces, ½ pk. green peas, 1 gallon water, ½ cup of rice-flour, salt, pepper and chopped parsley; boil the empty pods of the peas in the water 1 hour before putting in the beef. Strain them out, add the beef, and boil slowly for 1½ hour longer; ½ hour before serving, add the shelled peas, and 20 minutes later, the rice-flour with salt, pepper and parsley. After adding the rice-flour, stir frequently, to prevent scorching. Strain into a hot tureen.

Celery Soup—The white part of 3 heads of celery, ½ lb. rice, 1 onion, 1 quart stock, 2 quarts milk, pepper and salt, and a little roux.

Cut up the celery and onions very small, boil them in the stock until quite tender, add the milk and the rice, and boil together until quite a pulp, add pepper and salt and a little roux, strain through a fine hair sieve or a metal strainer, and boil a few minutes, taking care it does not burn. Serve some small croutons or fried bread with it.

Tomato Soup—4 lbs. tomatoes, 2 onions, 1 carrot, 2 quarts of stock or broth, pepper and salt and a little roux, 2 oz. fresh butter.

Cut up the onions and carrot, place them in a stewpan with the butter, and lightly fry them. Take the seeds out of the tomatoes, then put them in the stewpan with the fried onions and carrot, add the stock, pepper and salt, and let them boil for 1 hour, occasionally stirring them; add a little roux to thicken the soup, and strain through a fine hair sieve. Serve the soup very hot, and send to the table with it some small pieces of fried bread, sprinkled with chopped parsley.

Tomato Soup without Meat—1 can tomatoes, 2 large onions, ½ pint milk, 1 tablespoonful flour, 2 tablespoonfuls butter, salt, pepper.

Take 1 can of tomatoes, press through the colander and set on the fire where it will stew gently. Slice 2 large onions very thin and add to the tomatoes. Let it stew ½ hour, then add ½ pint of milk, 1 tablespoonful of flour rubbed in 2 of butter, and salt and pepper to taste. Let it boil 3 minutes, when it is done. Serve with bits of toasted bread.

Soup a la Dauphine—6 lbs. of lean beef, 4 carrots, 2 turnips, 4 onions, 1 head celery, 4 oz. lean ham, pepper and salt, a little soy, 2 bay leaves, a bunch of herbs, a few allspice, 2 blades of mace, 5 qts. water.

Cut up the onions, carrots, turnips and celery into small pieces, and lay in the bottom of a large stewpan; cut up the 6 lbs. of lean beef, and lay on the top of the vegetables, sprinkle a little salt over it, and cook over the fire (taking care it does not burn) for 2 hours; add 5 qts. of water, and bring it to the boil; take off the fat and scum, add a little more cold water, and throw in 3 blades of mace, 2 bay leaves, a bunch of herbs, 4 oz. of lean ham cut up very fine, and a few allspice, color a light brown with a little soy, and simmer for 5 hours, and then strain through a fine cloth, and with a sheet of paper take off any floating fat; boil again, and before serving throw in the soup some green taragon leaves and a little chervil.

Julienne Soup—1 carrot, 1 turnip, 1 stick of celery, 3 parsnips, 2 or 3 cabbage leaves, butter, lettuce, 1 handful of sorrel and chervil, stock, salt and pepper.

Cut in very small slices a carrot, a turnip, a stick of celery, 3 parsnips, and 2 or 3 cabbage leaves, put them in a saucepan with butter, and give them a nice color, shaking the saucepan to prevent them from sticking to the bottom, then add a lettuce and a handful of sorrel and chervil torn in small pieces, moisten these with stock and leave them on the fire for a few minutes, then boil up, add the whole of the stock and boil gently for 3 hours; season with salt and pepper.

Mrs. President Harrison's Clear Soup—4 lbs. lean beef, 4 qts. water, 1 teaspoonful celery seed, 2 small onions, 2 small carrots, 1 bunch parsley, 6 blades mace, 16 whole cloves, the whites of 4 eggs, salt and pepper to taste.

Cut the beef in pieces of the size of a walnut, taking care not to leave a particle of fat on them. Pour on it the water and let it boil up 3 times, skimming well each time; for if any of the grease is allowed to go back into the soup it will be impossible to get it clear. Scrape the carrots, stick 4 cloves firmly into each onion, and put them in the soup. Then add the celery seed, parsley, mace, pepper and salt. Let this boil until the vegetables are tender, then strain through a bag, return to the soup-pot, and stir in the well-beaten whites of the eggs. Boil until the eggs gather to one side, skim off, and color a delicate amber by burning a dessertspoonful of brown sugar and stirring it into the soup until sufficiently colored. Wash the bag in warm water, pour the soup through again, and serve.

Clear Soup—1 quart brown stock, ¼ lb. very lean beef, 1 onion, 1 carrot, 2 whites of eggs.

Carefully remove the fat from the meat, chop it fine and put it in a basin of cold water, just stirring it to separate it. Let it stand 5 minutes, then pour it into a saucepan with the vegetables cut in pieces, the whites and broken shells of the eggs, and the stock; whilst heating over the fire, whisk well until it begins to rise, when cease, and let it boil 2 minutes. Cover closely and let it stand quietly until there is a thick crust on top, then strain through a jelly bag or soup-cloth. Vegetables cut into small strips, or wafers, and boiled for 10 minutes, may be added before serving.

Barley Soup—½ pint pearl barley, 1 qt. white stock, the yolk of 1 egg, 1 gill cream, ½ pat fresh butter, bread.

Boil half a pint of pearl barley in a quart of white stock till it is reduced to a pulp, pass it through a hair sieve, and add to it as much well-flavored white stock as will give a purée of the consistency of cream; put the soup on the fire, when it boils stir into it, off the fire, the yolk of an egg beaten up with a gill of cream; add half a pat of fresh butter, and serve with small dice of bread fried in butter.

A Delicate and Delicious Soup—Three carrots, 2 turnips, 2 onions, 3 leeks, 1 stick of celery, 2 oz. butter, a little mutton broth, seasoning to taste.

Cut up the vegetables small and fry them in the butter till tender and of a light brown color. Add enough to keep them from burning, and stew them for an hour. Then rub through a sieve with a little more broth. Stew for a few minutes longer; salt and cayenne to taste.

If properly done the soup will be as thick as cream.

Onion Soup—Water that has boiled a leg or neck of mutton, 1 shank bone, 6 onions, 4 carrots, 2 turnips, salt.

Into the water that has boiled a leg or neck of mutton put the carrots and turnips and shank bone, and simmer 2 hours, then strain it on six onions, first sliced and fried a light brown, simmer 3 hours, skim carefully, and serve. Put into it a little roll or fried bread.

Eel Soup—3 lbs. eels, 1 onion, 1 oz. butter, 3 blades mace, 1 bunch sweet herbs, $\frac{1}{4}$ oz. pepper-corns, salt, 2 tablespoonfuls flour, $\frac{1}{4}$ pt. cream, 2 qts. water.

Wash the eels, cut them into thin slices and put them in the stewpan with the butter; let them simmer for a few minutes, then pour the water to them, and add the onion cut in small slices, the herbs, mace and seasoning. Simmer till the eels are tender, but do not break the flesh. Remove them carefully, mix flour smoothly to a batter with the cream, bring it to a boil, pour over the eels, and serve.

Asparagus Soup—Twenty-five heads of asparagus, 1 qt. stock, 1 tablespoonful flour, 1 oz. butter, sugar, pepper and salt, some spinach greening, 1 pat of fresh butter or 1 gill of cream, small dice of bread.

Put 25 heads of asparagus in a saucepan with a qt. of stock, free from fat, let them boil till quite done; remove the asparagus, pound it in a mortar, then pass it through a sieve; mix a tablespoonful of flour and 1 oz. of butter in a saucepan on the fire; add a little sugar, pepper and salt, quantity sufficient for the asparagus pulp, and the stock in which the asparagus was originally boiled; let the whole come to a boil, then put in a little spinach greening, and lastly a pat of fresh butter, or stir in a gill of cream. Serve over small dice of bread fried in butter.

Cream of Asparagus Soup—One bundle asparagus, 1 qt. milk, butter, flour.

Wash the asparagus, cut it into pieces, put in a saucepan, cover with 1 pt. of boiling water, boil gently for ¾ of an hour, remove the tips and put aside until wanted; press the remaining part through a colander, using the water in which it was boiled; put 1 qt. of milk into a double boiler; rub together one large tablespoonful of butter and two tablespoonfuls of flour; stir this carefully into the milk; stir constantly until smooth and partly thick. If, by any carelessness, it should look the slightest lumpy, put it through a sieve, return to the double boiler, and add the asparagus that has been pressed through the colander. Season to taste with salt and pepper, add the asparagus tips, and as soon as the whole is smoking hot, serve. You can not fail, unless you allow the mixture to stand, then the vegetable will separate from the milk and give it a curdled appearance.

Cream of Tomato Soup—One pt. can tomatoes, 1 qt. milk, parsley, mace, butter, flour, bay leaf, sugar, soda.

To the tomatoes add a sprig of parsley, a blade of mace and a bay leaf, and stew together for 15 minutes. Rub together 1 tablespoonful of butter and 2 tablespoonfuls of flour; add to 1 qt. boiling milk and stir constantly until it thickens. When ready to use the soup, press the tomatoes through a sieve and add 1 teaspoonful of sugar and ¼ teaspoonful of soda, then the boiling milk. It must not go on the fire after the tomatoes and milk are mixed, or it will curdle.

Mulligatawney Soup—One chicken (or 3 rabbits), 3 small onions, butter, curry powder, ½ lemon, cloves.

Cut up a good-sized chicken as for a fricassee; cut 3 small onions in slices, put a tablespoonful of butter in a frying-pan, add the chicken and onion, and stir till a nice brown; mix well with these a tablespoonful of curry powder, 4 whole cloves, the juice of ½ a lemon, and salt to taste. Put all in the soup kettle with 2 qts. of water, bring slowly to a boil, skim and let it simmer gently for 2 hours. Three rabbits may be used in place of the chicken, if preferred.

Corn Soup—One can green corn, 1 pt. milk, flour, butter, 1 egg.

Take one can of green corn and put it on the back of the stove with 2 qts. of hot water; let it cook gently ½ hour, then put where it will cook more rapidly. When the corn is tender, put in 1 pt. of milk, season to taste, let it boil up, then add 2 tablespoonfuls of flour mixed with 3 of butter. If you like you may, after removing the soup from the fire, stir in one well-beaten egg, beating rapidly to prevent curdling.

Bean Soup—One qt. dried white beans, a cup milk or cream, butter, soda.

Soak 1 qt. of dried white beans over night. In the morning, drain; add 2 qts. of water; when it comes to the boiling point, pour off and add 2 qts. of fresh boiling water, also about $\frac{1}{4}$ of a teaspoonful of soda. Boil until the beans are soft; then press through a sieve and return it to the kettle. Add salt and pepper to taste and a cup of cream or a cup of milk and a bit of butter. If still too thick, add more milk. Crackers buttered and browned in the oven or squares of bread browned in butter are nice to serve with this.

Oyster Soup—Fifty oysters, 1 pt. milk, a blade of mace, 1 tablespoonful butter, 1 teaspoonful flour, powd. cloves, salt, pepper, chopped parsley.

Put in a stewpan a pint of milk, a blade of mace, with a heaping tablespoonful of butter; put in another stewpan the juice from 50 oysters; place them on the stove. When the milk begins to boil thicken it with a heaping teaspoonful of flour previously mixed with milk; then stand it back on the range where it does not boil. When the scum begins to rise on the top of the oyster juice skim it off; then add a pinch of powdered cloves and some salt and black pepper. When it begins to boil pour it into the stewpan with the milk, stirring gently, so it does not curdle or lump. Then turn in the oysters. Let them boil about 1 minute or until the edges curl; then turn into a soup tureen, where you have previously placed a tablespoonful of chopped parsley. Serve at once.

FISH

FRESH water fish have often a muddy smell and taste. To take this off soak the fish in strong salt and water after it is nicely cleaned, then dry and dress it. The fish must be put in the water while cold and set to do very gently, or the outside will break before the inner part is done. Crimp fish should be put into boiling water, and when it boils up put a little cold water in, to check extreme heat, and simmer it a few minutes. Small fish nicely fried, covered with egg and crumbs, make a dish far more elegant than if served plain. Great attention should be paid to the garnishing of fish. Use plenty of horse-radish, parsley and lemon. If fish is to be fried or broiled it must be wrapped in a clean cloth after it is well cleaned. When perfectly dry, wet with an egg (if for frying) and sprinkle the finest bread crumbs over it; then, with a large quantity of lard or dripping, boiling hot, plunge the fish into it and fry a light brown; it can then be laid on blotting-paper to receive any grease. Butter gives a bad color; oil fries the finest color for those who will allow for the expense. Garnish with raw or fried parsley, which must be thus done: When washed and picked throw it again into clean water; when the lard or dripping boils, throw the parsley into it immediately from the water, and instantly it will be green and crisp, and must be taken up with a slice. If fish is to be broiled, it must be seasoned, flavored and put on a gridiron that is very clean, which, when hot, should be rubbed with a piece of suet to prevent the fish from sticking. It must be broiled on a very clear fire and not too near, or it may be scorched.

Cod's Head and Shoulders (to Boil) — One cod's head and shoulders, salt water, 1 glass of vinegar, horseradish.

Wash and tie it up, and dry with a cloth. Salt the water, and put in a glass of vinegar. When boiling, take off the scum; put the fish in, and keep it boiling very briskly about ½ hour. Parboil the milt and roe, cut in thin slices, fry, and serve them. Garnish with horseradish; for sauce, oysters, eggs, or drawn butter.

Stewed Codfish in Brown Sauce — Slice the fish, take off the skin and fry quickly a fine brown, lift it out and place in a stewpan with boiling brown gravy; add the juice of a lemon and some salt. Stew the fish gently until it begins to break, lift it on a hot dish, stir into the gravy 1½ oz. of butter with 1 teaspoonful of flour and a little mace. Boil the sauce 1 minute, pour it over the fish and serve.

Salmon Croquettes — The contents of 1 can of salmon from which the oil has been poured and which has been shredded fine, 1 cupful of fine bread crumbs, 1 egg and cayenne pepper to taste; mix well, make into balls, dip first into beaten egg and then into bread crumbs or cracker dust; fry in plenty of boiling lard and drain on coarse brown paper before serving. Garnish the dish with parsley and, if you like, slices of lemon.

Salt Cod — Cod, vinegar (1 glass), parsnips, cream, butter, flour.

Soak and clean the piece you mean to dress, then lay it all night in water, with a glass of vinegar. Boil it enough, then break it into flakes on the dish; pour over it parsnips boiled, beaten in a mortar, and then boiled up with cream and a large piece of butter rubbed with a little flour. It may be served as above with egg sauce instead of the parsnip, and the root sent up whole; or the fish may be botled and sent up without flaking, and the sauces as above.

Cod's Roes — One or more cod's roes, $1\frac{1}{2}$ oz. of butter, 2 eggs, 1 teaspoonful of salt, 1 pinch of cayenne pepper, 1 grate of nutmeg, 1 dessertspoonful of tomato sauce or vinegar.

Boil 1 or more cod's roes, according to size, till quite set and nearly done. Take them out of the water, and when cold cut them into slices $\frac{3}{4}$ of an inch thick. Now put into a small stewpan $1\frac{1}{2}$ oz. of butter; when made liquid over the fire, take it off and stir into it the yolks of 2 eggs, a small teaspoonful of salt, a pinch of cayenne pepper, a grate of nutmeg, and a dessertspoonful of tomato or Mogul sauce, or the vinegar from any good pickle. Mix all well together and stir it over the fire for 2 or 3 minutes to thicken. Dip the slices of cod's roe in this sauce to take up as much as they will, lay them in a dish, pour over them any of the sauce that may be left, put the dish into the oven for 10 minutes, and send to table very hot.

Codfish Balls—Equal quantities of potatoes and boiled codfish, 1 oz. butter, 1 egg.

Equal quantity of mashed potatoes and boiled codfish minced fine; to each $\frac{1}{2}$ lb. allow 1 oz. of butter and a well-beaten egg; mix thoroughly. Press into balls between 2 spoons; drop into hot lard, and fry till brown.

Salt Salmon (to Souse) — One salt salmon, cayenne, whole allspice, a little mace, cold vinegar.

Wash a salt salmon, and cover it with plenty of clean water. Let it soak 24 hours, but be careful to change the water several times. Then scale it, cut it into 4 parts, wash, clean, and put on to boil. When half done change the water; and when tender, drain it, put it in a stone pan, sprinkle some cayenne, whole allspice, a few cloves and a little mace over each piece; cover with cold vinegar. This makes a nice relish for tea.

Fish Pie—Any remains of cold fish, such as cod or haddock. Clear the fish from the bones, put a layer of it in a pie-dish, sprinkle with pepper and salt, then put a layer of bread crumbs, some grated nutmeg and chopped parsley. Repeat this until the dish is quite full, pour in some white sauce, cover with a layer of bread crumbs or mashed potatoes. Bake $\frac{1}{4}$ to $\frac{1}{2}$ an hour.

Salmon (Fried, with Anchovy Sauce)—Some thin slices from the tail end of a salmon, anchovy sauce, flour, bread crumbs, eggs, water, a little roux, a little cayenne pepper, lard.

Scrape the scales off the tail end of a salmon, cut in thin slices, dip them in flour, then in 2 eggs whisked up with a tablespoonful of water and a tablespoonful of anchovy sauce, then dip them in bread crumbs, and fry in boiling lard for 8 or 10 minutes; dish them up on a napkin in a nice heap, and sprinkle a little chopped parsley over them, and serve in a sauceboat some sauce.

Salmon (Dressed, Italian Sauce)—Two slices about 3 in. thick of good salmon, 2 onions, 1 carrot, 1 shallot, 2 gherkins, a few preserved mushrooms and a few capers, 3 oz. of butter, a little chopped parsley, 1 tablespoonful of anchovy sauce, and a pint of good stock, and a little roux.

Fish. 33

Cut up 2 onions and 1 carrot into thin slices, and lay them in the bottom of a baking-dish with a little pepper and salt and 1 oz. of butter; lay the slices of salmon on the top of the vegetables, cover them with buttered paper, and bake for 35 minutes in a warm oven; when cooked, serve with sauce made as follows: Cut up 1 shallot very fine, and lightly fry in 2 oz. of butter; throw in a little chopped parsley, 2 gherkins chopped fine, and a few capers and mushrooms, cut up very fine, and 1 pt. of good stock, a little roux to thicken, and one tablespoonful of anchovy sauce and a little pepper; boil these ingredients together for 30 minutes, lift the salmon carefully onto a dish (taking care no onion or carrot hang to it), pour the boiling sauce over it and serve very hot.

Perch and Tench — Put them into cold water, boil them carefully and serve with melted butter and soy. Perch is a most delicate fish. They may be either fried or stewed, but in stewing they do not preserve so good a flavor.

Trout and Grayling (to Fry) — Scale, gut, and wash well; then dry them, and lay them separately on a board before the fire, after dusting some flour over them. Fry them of a fine color with fresh dripping; serve with crimp parsley and plain butter. Perch and tench may be done the same way.

Perch and Trout (to Broil) — Split them down the back, notch them two or three time across, and broil over a clear fire; turn them frequently, and baste with well salted butter and powdered thyme.

Mackerel—Boil, and serve with butter and fennel.

To broil them, split, and sprinkle with herbs, pepper and salt; or stuff with the same, crumbs and chopped fennel.

Potted: Clean, season, and bake them in a pan with spice, bay leaves and some butter; when cold, lay them in a potting-pot, and cover with butter.

Pickled: Boil them, then boil some of the liquor, a few peppers, bay leaves, and some vinegar; when cold, pour it over them.

Mackerel (Pickled, called Caveach)—Six mackerel, 1 oz, of pepper, 2 nutmegs, a. little mace, 4 cloves, 1 handful of salt.

Clean and divide them; then cut each side into three, or, leaving them undivided, cut each fish into five or six pieces. To six large mackerel, take nearly an ounce of pepper, 2 nutmegs, a little mace, 4 cloves and a handful of salt, all in the finest powder. Mix, and, making holes in each piece of fish, thrust the seasoning into them; rub each piece with some of it; then fry them brown in oil; let them stand till cold, then put them into a stone jar and cover with vinegar; if to keep long, pour oil on the top. Thus done, they may be preserved for months.

Mullet with Tomatoes—One-half doz. red mullet, pepper, salt and chopped parsley, 5 or 6 tablespoonfuls of tomato sauce.

Butter a baking dish plentifully, lay on it side by side ½ doz. red mullet, sprinkle them with pepper, salt and chopped parsley, then add about 5 or 6 tablespoonfuls of tomato sauce. Cover the whole with a sheet of well-oiled paper, and bake for about ½ hour.

Soles—If boiled, they must be served with great care to look perfectly white, and should be well covered with parsley. If fried, dip in egg, and cover them with fine crumbs of bread; set on a frying-pan that is just large enough, and put into it a large quantity of fresh lard or dripping, boil it, and immediately slip the fish into it; do them of a fine brown. Soles that have been fried are very nice when cold with oil, vinegar, salt and mustard.

Soles au Gratin—Soles, a little stock, 1 lemon, a little anchovy, pepper and salt, bread crumbs, a small piece of butter, and a little vinegar.

Place a sole in an oval tin baking-dish, lay on the top a piece of butter, and round it the juice of ½ a lemon and a little anchovy sauce, a teaspoonful of vinegar and a little pepper, and then bake it for 15 minutes in a hot oven; when nearly cooked sprinkle some bread crumbs over it and color the top with a salamander. Serve in the tin it was baked in, with a little chopped parsley on the top.

Sturgeon (Fresh)—Sturgeon, egg, bread crumbs, parsley, pepper, salt.

Cut slices, rub egg over them, then sprinkle with crumbs of bread, parsley, pepper, salt; fold them in paper, and broil gently. Sauce: butter, anchovy and soy.

Turbot en Mayonnaise—Some fillets of turbot, oil, tarragon vinegar, salt and pepper, eggs, cucumbers, anchovies, tarragon leaves, beets, capers, aspic jelly.

Cut some fillets of cooked turbot into moderate-sized round or oblong pieces, carefully taking off the skin and extracting all bones. Place these pieces of fish into a bowl, with a dressing made of oil, tarragon vinegar, salt and pepper. As soon as the fish is well flavored with this seasoning, arrange the pieces round a dish like a crown. Place a circle of chopped hard-boiled eggs, tiny pickled cucumbers, anchovies, tarragon leaves, beetroot and capers round the dish, and then arrange a wall of aspic jelly round the edge of the dish. Fill up the center of the crown of the fish with good mayonnaise sauce.

Turbot au Gratin (a nice Dish for Luncheon) — Cold cooked turbot, anchovy sauce, a little stock, cayenne pepper, 2 oz. butter, a little flour and some bread crumbs.

Place a piece of butter, about 2 oz., in a stewpan and melt it on the fire; add a little flour, then a little anchovy sauce and a little cayenne pepper; stir these well together and then drop in the sauce any cold turbot you may have left from dinner the evening before, place some of the turbot out of the sauce in large patty pans, and cover it with bread crumbs and bake it in a hot oven; if the top does not get brown enough, heat a salamander and finish off that way. Serve the patty pans upon a napkin or paper.

Smelts (to Fry) — Smelts, egg, bread crumbs, lard.

They should not be washed more than is necessary to clean them. Dry them in a cloth, then lightly flour them, but shake it off. Dip them into plenty of egg, then into bread crumbs, grated fine, and plunge them into a good pan of boiling lard; let them continue gently boiling, and a few minutes will make them a bright yellow-brown. Take care not to take off the light roughness of the crumbs, or their beauty will be lost.

Eel Pie — One or two eels, seasoning, gravy, gelatine.

Cut up 1 or 2 eels and stew gently until tender in a little good brown gravy, seasoned to taste;

when done enough, strain the gravy through muslin, add gelatine and pour over the fish. A few sprigs of parsley placed about the mould will much improve the appearance.

Eels (to Boil) — Clean, cut off the heads, and dry them. Joint them into suitable lengths, or coil them on your fish-plate; boil them in salted water. Use drawn butter and parsley for sauce.

Haddock with Tomatoes — One dried haddock, 1 onion, 1 oz. butter, 1 ripe tomato, pepper, parsley.

Soak a dried haddock in plenty of cold water for half a day, drain off the water and replace it with boiling water; when the haddock has been in this for 2 hours, take it out, carefully remove all the bones and skin, and break the meat into flakes; slice a moderate-sized onion, put it into a saucepan with 1 oz. of butter; as soon as the onion is soft, add one ripe tomato, cut into slices; after a couple of minutes add the flesh of the haddock, a sprinkling of pepper and some finely minced parsley; shake the saucepan on the fire, until the contents are thoroughly heated, then draw it aside, to be kept warm till the time for serving.

Fish Croquettes—Remnants of turbot, brill, haddock, or salmon, butter, pinch of flour, some milk, pepper, salt, nutmeg, parsley.

From some remnants of boiled turbot, brill, haddock, or salmon, pick out the flesh carefully, and mince it, not too finely; melt a piece of butter in a saucepan, add a small pinch of flour and some hot milk; stir on the fire until the mixture thickens, then put in pepper, salt, and a little grated nutmeg, together with some finely-chopped parsley, and, lastly, the minced fish. As soon as the whole is quite hot, turn it out on a dish to get cold, then fashion and finish the croquettes as in the first recipe.

Halibut (Boiled) — Halibut, salted water.

Allow the fish to lie in cold salt water for an hour. Wipe dry in a clean cloth and score the skin, then put into the fish-kettle with cold salted water sufficient to cover it. Let it come slowly to the boil, and allow from $\frac{1}{2}$ to $\frac{3}{4}$ of an hour for a piece weighing 4 or 5 lbs. When ready, drain, and serve with egg sauce.

Halibut (Baked) — Halibut, a little butter, salt and water, a tablespoonful of walnut catsup, a dessertspoonful of Worcestershire sauce, the juice of a lemon, a little brown flour.

A piece of halibut weighing 5 or 6 lbs., lay in salt water for 2 hours. Wipe in a clean cloth and score the skin. Have the oven tolerably hot, and bake about 1 hour. Melt a little butter in hot water and baste the fish occasionally. It should be of a fine brown color. Any gravy that is in the dripping-pan mix with a little boiling water, then stir in the walnut catsup and Worcestershire sauce, the juice of the lemon, and thicken with the brown flour (the flour should be mixed with a little cold water previously), give one boil and serve in sauce-boat.

Baked Herrings or Sprats — Herrings, allspice, salt, black pepper, 1 onion and a few bay-leaves, vinegar.

Wash and drain without wiping them; season with allspice in fine powder, salt, and a few whole cloves; lay them in a pan with plenty of black pepper, 1 onion, and a few bay-leaves; add vinegar enough to cover them. Put paper over the pan, and bake in a slow oven. If you like throw saltpetre over them the night before, to make them look red. Gut, but do not open them.

Fish Chowder — Two lbs. solid fish-shreds, ½ lb. salt pork, 4 onions, 10 potatoes, salt and pepper, 2 tablespoonfuls farina, milk.

Take ½ lb. fat salt pork, cut into slices, and fry out well. Slice four large onions and fry in the pork fat until they are a light brown. Stir constantly to prevent burning, and thus make the chowder better. Put this into a pot with 3 qts. of boiling water and let it boil 20 minutes. Skim out the pieces of pork and onion and add 10 potatoes, sliced, not too thin, and boil 20 minutes. Then add 2 lbs. of solid fish-shreds and boil 10 minutes if the fish is not cooked. Add salt and pepper to taste. When cooked stir in slowly a thickening made of 2 tablespoonfuls of farina mixed in cold milk, and let it boil up once only. Put the pot back on the fire, and after letting it stand a few moments skim off the scum which will rise to the top, and serve.

Planked Shad — Secure a handsome, thick oak board, and have some holes bored, with stout wooden pegs to fit; spread the dressed fish open on the board, securing it with the pegs. Rest the end of the plank in a shallow pan and set all before a clear fire; put a little salt and water in the pan and baste the fish often, adding when it is nearly done a tablespoonful of melted butter and half as much walnut catsup. If the board is handsome serve the shad on it, but it can be laid on a hot dish and the gravy, with a little walnut catsup added, poured over. Serve with pickled walnuts.

OYSTERS, SHELLFISH, ETC.

Lobsters (Potted) — Lobsters, mace, white pepper, nutmeg, salt and butter.

Half boil them, pick out the meat, cut it into small pieces, season with mace, white pepper, nutmeg and salt, press close into a pot, and cover with butter, bake ½ hour; put the spawn in. When cold, take the lobster out, and put it into the pots with a little of the butter. Beat the other butter in a mortar with some of the spawn, then mix that colored butter with as much as will be sufficient to cover the pots, and strain it. Cayenne may be added if approved.

Lobster Croquettes — Lobster, pepper, salt, powdered mace, bread crumbs, 2 tablespoonfuls of butter, egg, biscuit, parsley.

To the meat of a well-boiled lobster, chopped fine, add pepper, salt, and powdered mace. Mix with this one quarter as much bread crumbs, well rubbed, as you have meat; make into pointed balls, with 2 tablespoonfuls of butter melted; roll these in beaten egg, then in biscuit powdered fine, and fry in butter or very nice sweet lard. Serve dry and hot, and garnish with crisped parsley. This is a delicious supper dish or entrée.

Crabs (Hot) — One good-sized crab, pepper, salt, bread crumbs, milk, cream, or oiled butter, parsley.

For this, 1 good-sized crab or 3 or 4 small ones may be used. The meat must be picked from the claws and the soft inside from the body; season with pepper and salt, add a small quantity of bread crumbs, and moisten with milk, or, better still, a few spoonfuls of cream or oiled butter. When well mixed, put it into the large shell, strewing fresh bread crumbs over the top, and sprinkling some oiled butter over these; let it remain in the oven just long enough to get hot through and to be a nice golden-brown color. It should be served very hot on a napkin garnished with parsley.

Crabs (Boiled) — Crabs, salt water, sweet oil.

Boil them in salt and water 20 minutes; take them out, break off the claws, wipe the crabs, throw away the small claws, and crack the large ones and send to table. Rub a little sweet oil on the shells.

Oysters on Toast—Drain the liquor from a qt. of oysters; cut each into 4 pieces, and strain through coarse muslin back into the sauce. When it boils again, dip out a small cupful and keep it hot. Stir into that left on the range a liberal teaspoonful of butter rolled in a scant teaspoonful of cornstarch. In another vessel heat $\frac{1}{2}$ cup of milk. Stir the oysters into the thickened liquor; season with pepper and salt, and cook, after they are scalding hot, 5 minutes before adding the milk. Line a hot platter with neat slices of crustless toast, buttered, wet with the reserved liquor, and cover with the oysters.

Oysters (Stewed) — Oysters, a piece of mace, some lemon peel, a few white peppers, cream, butter, and flour.

Open and separate the liquor from them, then wash them from the grit; strain the liquor, and put with the oysters a piece of mace and lemon peel, and a few white peppers. Simmer them very gently, and put some cream, and a little flour and butter. Serve with sippets.

Oysters (Stewed) — Liquor from 2 qts. of oysters, one teacupful of hot water, salt, pepper, 2 tablespoonfuls of butter, 1 cupful of milk.

Drain the liquor from 2 qts. of firm, plump oysters; mix with it a small teacupful of hot water, add a little salt and pepper, and set over the fire in a saucepan. Let it boil up once, put in the oysters, let them boil for 5 minutes or less —not more. When they "ruffle," add two tablespoonfuls of butter. The instant it is melted and well stirred in, put in a large cupful of boiling milk, and take the saucepan from the fire. Serve with oyster or cream biscuits, as soon as possible. Oysters become tough and tasteless when cooked too much or left to stand too long after they are withdrawn from the fire.

Oyster Sausages — One doz. large oysters, ½ lb. rump steak, a little seasoning of herbs, pepper and salt.

Chop all fine, and roll them into the form of sausages.

Angels on Horseback—Oysters, bacon.

Trim the beards from as many oysters as may be required, wrap each in a very thin shaving of fat, streaky bacon (cold boiled bacon is the best); run them one after the other onto a silver skewer, and hold them over a toast in front of a clear fire until the bacon is slightly crisp; serve on the toast immediately.

Escalloped Lobster — Select lobsters that are rather above the medium size; plunge them in boiling water for half an hour. When cool enough to handle, split in two and remove the entrails; cut the meat into dice, being careful to pick out all the meat from the claws. Prepare in a farina kettle a pint of rich gravy made from equal parts of cream and milk, thickened with a heaping tablespoonful of flour, creamed with 2 tablespoonfuls of butter. Season well with salt, cayenne pepper and a tiny pinch of grated nutmeg; add the lobster to the sauce thus made, place in a buttered baking-dish, cover with bread crumbs; place in a hot oven for 10 minutes to brown.

Barbecued Oysters—Drain a dozen large oysters, dust them over with pepper and cut an equal number of thin slices of bacon of about the same size. First put a slice of bacon and then an oyster and bacon and so on, alternating, on an iron skewer, taking care not to crowd them, and roast in a very hot oven until the bacon begins to crisp. Serve hot in a covered dish.

Panned Oysters—Select large, fat oysters, split and toast round crackers, and spread in the bottom of a pan; drain the liquor from the oysters, put in a saucepan and set on the stove to boil; skim, and season with pepper, salt and a little butter; moisten the toasted crackers with hot liquor, and lay the oysters over; spread with bits of butter and set in a hot oven for 15 minutes.

Scalloped Oysters—Butter a baking-dish; fill it with alternate layers of rolled crackers and oysters; over each layer of oysters spread bits of butter and dash pepper—not salt, as it will shrivel them. Heat the liquor of the oysters, add to it 1 teacupful of cream, season to taste and pour over the oysters. Set in a moderate oven and bake nearly an hour.

Oysters (Fried)—Carefully dry in a clean cloth a dozen large oysters. In a bright frying-pan put 2 heaping tablespoonfuls of good butter, and as soon as this comes to a boil throw in the oysters and whip them out with a strainer as soon as they begin to curl up, and serve immediately. Oysters cooked in this manner are delicious, but the butter must be heated to the point when the blue smoke hovers over the pan. To 3 well-beaten eggs add $\frac{1}{2}$ pt. of oyster juice, a teaspoonful of salt and black or cayenne pepper, according to taste. Work into this a gill of sweet oil, until the whole becomes a batter. On a bed of cracker dust on the table lay your oysters, then take them one by one by the beard, dip them in the mixture and then in the bread crumbs. Repeat this three or four times, first in the egg mixture, then in the bread crumbs. Place each oyster on the table by itself. Do not pile one on top of the other or they will become heavy. Now fry in a pan of hot butter and serve on a hot dish.

Oysters (Roast) — Take a dozen large oysters, wash them clean and place them on the coals of a bright fire. As soon as the shells open, pour the juice into a hot soup-plate, remove the oysters from the shells with a knife, put them in the plate with a lump of butter and serve while hot. Oysters treated in this manner retain more of their flavor and are easier digested than when cooked in any other way.

Oysters (Stewed) — To a pint of milk add the juice of 25 oysters, a teaspoonful of salt, pepper according to taste. Let it boil for 1 or 2 minutes, then add your oysters and a generous lump of butter.

Oyster Patties — Make a rich paste, roll it out ½ in. thick, then turn a teacup down on the paste, and, with the point of a sharp pen-knife, mark the paste lightly round the edge of the cup. Then with the point of the knife make a circle about ½ in. from the edge; cut this circle half way through. Place them on tins, and bake in a quick oven. Remove the center, and fill with oysters seasoned and warmed over the fire.

Oyster Omelet — Six eggs, whites and yolks beaten separately; 1 tablespoonful of cream, ½ teaspoonful of corn starch wet with the cream, a saltspoonful of salt and a dust of pepper; a dozen fine oysters broiled.

Beat yolks well, adding the cream and cornstarch; stir in the stiffened whites lightly; have ready a tablespoonful of butter in a frying-pan, hissing hot, but not browned. Pour in the omelet, and as soon as it sets at the edges, loosen with a knife and shake gently with a uniform motion from side to side, until the center is almost set. The oysters should have been broiled before you began the omelet. To do this, roll them in fine cracker-crust, salted and peppered, broil quickly over a clear fire, transfer to a hot dish, put a bit of butter on each, and cover and keep hot while the omelet is cooking. When this is done, line one-half of it, as it lies on the pan, with the oysters, fold the other over dexterously and reverse the frying-pan quickly upon the heated dish in which it is to be served.

POULTRY AND GAME

IN choosing ducks, be careful to secure those with plump bodies and thick and yellowish feet, and, to insure their being tender, it is advisable to let their hang a day or two. In choosing turkeys, the hens are preferable for boiling on account of their whiteness and tenderness.

Partridges in perfection will have dark-colored bills and yellowish legs; the time they should be kept entirely depends upon the taste of those for whom they are intended, as what some people consider delicious, to others would be disgusting and offensive.

Rabbits when young have smooth and sharp claws.

In selecting a goose, choose one with a clean white skin, plump breast and yellow feet. Charcoal is considered as an admirable preventive for decomposition.

Chicken Patties—Cold chicken, milk, flour, pepper, salt and butter, puff paste.

Mince cold chicken, and stir it into a white sauce, made of milk thickened with flour and flavored with pepper, salt and butter; line small patty pans with puff paste, bake first, and then fill with the mixture, and set in a hot oven for a few minutes to brown.

Fowl (to Boil)—For boiling, choose those that are not black-legged. Pick them nicely, singe, wash and truss them. Flour them, and put them into boiling water. Serve with parsley and butter, oyster, lemon, liver or celery sauce.

Fowls (Roast)—Butter, flour, gravy, lemon-juice, sausages, bacon.

Fowls require constant attention in dredging and basting, and the last ten minutes let butter rolled in flour be stuck over them in little bits, and allowed to melt without basting. The gravy for fowls should always be thickened, and slightly flavored with lemon juice. Sausages or rolled bacon should be served on the same dish, and white mashed potatoes should always be handed with poultry.

Chicken Cutlets (with Rice) — A teaspoonful of rice, some good stock, 1 onion, salt and pepper, some cold ham and chicken, egg, bread-crumbs.

Boil a teacupful of rice in some good stock, and pound it in a mortar with an onion that has been cooked in butter, with salt and pepper. Pound separately in equal portions cold ham and chicken; form this into cutlets; cover them with egg and bread-crumbs and fry. Serve with a sharp sauce.

Chicken a la Jardiniere — 2 young chickens, butter, 1 onion, some savory herbs, carrots, turnips, onions, beef stock, mushrooms, 2 cabbages, some heads of asparagus, pepper, sugar.

Put two young chickens in a saucepan with some butter, a large onion chopped up, some savory herbs, some salt and sufficient water; the chickens should be dropped in the mixture when it is boiling, and left in the saucepan until the liquid is reduced by half; cut up in good shapes some carrots and turnips, some whole onions skinned and blanched, and put them in a saucepan with some butter, some beef stock, some mushrooms, two very young cabbages and some heads of asparagus; season with salt, pepper, and a little sugar; cook very gently, and fifteen minutes before serving add a piece of butter kneaded with flour. Serve with vegetables well arranged around the dish.

Chicken Rissoles—Some remnants of fowls, ham and tongue, butter, a pinch of flour, white pepper, salt, nutmeg, parsley, eggs, a few drops of lemon-juice, flour, water, 3 pinches of sugar.

Mince very finely some remnants of fowls, free from skin, add an equal quantity of ham or tongue, as well as a small quantity of truffles, all finely minced; toss the whole in a saucepan with a piece of butter, mixed with a pinch of flour; add white pepper, salt, and nutmeg to taste, as well as a little minced parsley; stir in off the fire the yolks of one or two eggs beaten up with a few drops of lemon-juice, and lay the mixture on a plate to cool. Make a paste with some flour, a little water, two eggs, a pinch of salt, and two or three of sugar; roll it out to the thickness of a penny piece, stamp it out in round pieces three inches in diameter; put a piece of the above mince on each, then fold them up, fastening the edges by moistening them with water. Trim the rissoles neatly with a fluted cutter, dip each one in beaten-up egg, and fry a golden color in hot lard.

Chicken (Jellied)—A chicken, 1 oz. of butter, pepper and salt, ½ packet of gelatine.

Boil the chicken until the water is reduced to a pint; pick the meat from the bones in fair-sized pieces, removing all gristle, skin and bone. Skim the fat from the liquor, add an ounce of butter, a little pepper and salt, and half a packet of gelatine. Put the cut-up chicken into a mould, wet with cold water; when the gelatine has dissolved pour the liquor hot over the chicken. Turn out when cold.

Chicken Loaf—A chicken, 2 oz. of butter, pepper, salt, egg.

Boil a chicken in as little water as possible until the meat can easily be picked from the bones; cut it up finely, then put it back into the saucepan with two ounces of butter, and a seasoning of pepper and salt. Grease a square china mould and cover the bottom with slices of hard-boiled egg; pour in the chicken, place a weight on it, and set aside to cool, when it will turn out.

Chicken Croquettes — Breast of a roast fowl, tongues, truffles, butter, flour, stock, parsley, pepper, salt, nutmeg, eggs, lemon-juice, parsley.

The breast of a roast fowl, two parts; of boiled tongue, one part, and of truffles, one part; mince all these very finely, and mix them together. Melt a piece of butter in a saucepan, stir a little flour into it, then put in the above mixture, and moisten with a small quantity of stock; add some finely minced parsley, pepper, salt, and nutmeg to taste. Stir it on the fire for a few minutes, then stir in it, off the fire, the yolks of one or two eggs beaten up with the juice of a lemon and strained. Spread out this mince (which should be pretty stiff) on a marble slab, and when it is nearly cold fashion it into small portions in the shape of balls or of cones. Dip each in a beaten-up egg, and then roll it in very fine baked bread-crumbs; repeat this operation after the lapse of an hour, and after a similar interval fry the croquettes in hot lard to a golden color. Serve on a napkin, with plenty of fried parsley.

Pressed Chicken — Two chickens, boiled until the meat leaves the bones easily, then pull to pieces and chop fine, letting the liquor in which they were cooked boil down until only a cupful remains. Add about one-half as much chopped ham as chicken; roll two soda crackers, pour the stock over, seasoning highly. Mix well together, put in a deep, long pan, pressing down hard with the hand. Fold a cloth several times, put over the top, and put on a weight. It will slice nicely if prepared the day before using.

Braised Chicken — Draw and prepare a chicken as for roasting. Truss it without filling and place in a baking-pan over ½ of a small carrot and 1 onion, chopped fine, 4 cloves, 1 sprig of parsley and a little salt and pepper. To this add 1 pint of rich meat stock, cover closely and bake in a quick oven for 1½ hours. Then dish the fowl and place it where it will keep hot. Put one tablespoonful of butter in a frying-pan, let it brown and rub smooth in it one tablespoonful of flour; add to this the liquor in which the chicken was braised and then twelve mushrooms, chopped fine. Stir this continually until it boils.

Wild Duck (Roast) — Duck, bread-crumbs, carrot, pepper and salt, sage and onions, currant jelly, 1 pinch of cayenne, browned flour.

Before roasting, parboil with a small carrot peeled and put inside. This will absorb the fishy taste. If you have no carrot at hand, an onion will have the same effect, but unless you mean to use onion in the stuffing a carrot is preferable. When parboiled, throw away the carrot or onion, lay in fresh water for half an hour, stuff with bread-crumbs seasoned with pepper, salt, sage and an onion, and roast till brown and tender, basting half the time with butter and water, then with drippings. Add to the gravy, when you have taken up the duck, one tablespoonful of currant jelly and a pinch of cayenne. Thicken gravy with browned flour and serve in a tureen.

Quail Pie — Puff paste, salt pork or ham, 6 eggs, butter, pepper, 1 bunch parsley, juice of 1 lemon.

Clean and dress the birds, loosen the joints, but do not divide them; put on the stove to simmer, while you prepare puff paste. Cover a deep dish with it, then lay in the bottom some shreds of pork or ham, then a layer of hard boiled eggs, a little butter and pepper. Take the birds from the fire, sprinkle with pepper and minced parsley. Squeeze lemon juice upon them, and upon the breasts of the birds a few pieces of butter rolled in flour. Cover with slices of egg, then shred some ham and lay upon this. Pour in a little of the gravy in which the quails were parboiled, and put on the lid. Leave a hole in the middle and bake a little over 1 hour.

Rabbit Pie—Two rabbits, ¼ lb. fat pork, 4 eggs, pepper, butter, a little powdered mace, a few drops of lemon juice, puff paste.

Cut a pair of rabbits into ten pieces, soak in salt and water half an hour and simmer until half done, in enough water to cover them. Cut a quarter of a pound of pork into slices, and boil four eggs hard. Lay some pieces of pork in the bottom of the dish, the next a layer of rabbit. Upon this spread slices of boiled egg and pepper and butter. Sprinkle, moreover, with a little powdered mace, a few drops of lemon juice upon each piece of meat. Proceed in this manner until the dish is full, the top layer being pork. Pour in water in which the rabbit was boiled; when you have salted it and added a few lumps of butter rolled in flour, cover with puff paste, make a hole in the middle and bake for 1 hour. Cover with paper if it should boil too fast.

Rabbit (Stewed)—One rabbit, dripping or butter, flour, 6 onions.

Cut a rabbit in pieces, wash in cold water, a little salted. Prepare in a stewpan some flour and clarified dripping or butter; stir it until it browns. Then put in the pieces of rabbit, and keep stirring and turning until they are tinged with a little color; then add 6 onions, peeled but not cut up. Serve all together in a deep dish.

A German Dish—A tender fowl, salt, pepper, mace, flour, yolk of 1 egg, hot lard, liver, gizzard, parsley.

Quarter a tender fowl, season the pieces with pepper, salt and mace; flour, and then dip them in the beaten-up yolk of an egg; fry a golden color in hot lard; dish them, garnished with the liver and gizzard fried separately, and with fried parsley. Serve either with a salad garnished with hard-boiled eggs or tomato sauce.

Giblets (to Stew) — Salt and pepper, butter, 1 cup of cream, 1 teaspoonful of flour.

Treat them as directed for giblet-pie (under the head "Pies"); season them with salt and pepper, and a very small piece of mace. Before serving give them one boil with a cup of cream, and a piece of butter rubbed in a teaspoonful of flour.

Pigeons—May be dressed in many ways. The flavor depends very much on their being cropped and drawn as soon as killed. No other bird requires so much washing. Pigeons left from dinner the day before may be stewed or made into a pie; in either case care must be taken not to overdo them, which will make them stringy. They need only be heated up in gravy, made ready, and force-meat balls may be fried and added, instead of putting a stuffing into them. If for a pie, let beefsteaks be stewed in a little water, and put cold under them, and cover each pigeon with a piece of fat bacon, to keep them moist. Season as usual.

Pigeons (Roast) — Should be stuffed with parsley, either cut or whole, and seasoned within. Serve with parsley and butter. Peas or asparagus should be dressed to eat with them.

Turkey (to Roast) — The sinews of the legs should be drawn, whichever way it is dressed. The head should be twisted under the wing; and in drawing it take care not to tear the liver, nor let the gall touch it. Put a stuffing of sausage-meat, or, if sausages are to be served in the dish, a bread stuffing. As this makes a large addition to the size of the bird, observe that the heat of the fire is constantly to that part; for the breast is often not done enough. A little strip of paper should be put on the bone to hinder it from scorching while the other parts roast. Baste well and froth it up. Serve with gravy in the dish, and plenty of bread-sauce in a sauce-tureen. Add a few crumbs and a beaten egg to the stuffing of sausage-meat.

Roast Turkey — Plain force-meat, 1 turkey, bacon, butter, salt, pork sausages, gravy.

Pluck, singe, draw, wipe thoroughly and truss a fine turkey; stuff it with plain force-meat, pack it up in some thin slices of fat bacon, and over that a sheet of buttered paper; put in oven, basting frequently with butter. A quarter of an hour before it is done, remove the paper and slices of bacon. Sprinkle with salt just before serving. Garnish with pork sausages, and serve with a tureen of gravy. Time of roasting, 2 or 3 hours, according to size.

Partridge—Dress 1 doz. nice partridges; put them in a baking-pan with 1 lb. good butter, a small teacupful vinegar, 1 teaspoonful water, 2 pods red pepper, $\frac{1}{2}$ teaspoonful ground black pepper, and salt to suit your taste. Put the pan into the stove, which must be hot enough to cook them at once; ¾ of an hour is generally sufficient. When the birds are brown all over, which they will be if you have basted them diligently as you turned them, set the pan on the top of the stove, pour in at once 1 quart of fresh sweet cream, adding ½ teacupful of grated biscuit crumbs; stir well to keep from burning, and serve in a few minutes on a warm platter.

To Cook Ducks—Prepare as many ducks as you wish for a meal and cut them up as you would to stew. Cover with cold water and let it come to a boil, then pour off the water, adding a fresh supply. Boil until tender, season with pepper and salt, then, pouring off the water, fry brown in butter. This is a splendid dish; the parboiling takes out all the wild taste which ducks usually have. Old prairie chickens may be treated in the same way.

Roast Goose—Prepare the goose the same as a chicken. Fill with potato or onion stuffing, being careful not to fill it too full, as this dressing will always swell in cooking. Place it in a baking-pan with 1 cupful of water and 2 teaspoonfuls of salt. Bake in a quick oven, allowing 25 minutes for each pound, basting it frequently. When the goose has been roasting an hour, cool the oven and finish the roast at a moderate heat. Goslings may be cooked in the same manner, allowing 15 minutes to each pound.

Potato Stuffing for Geese or Ducks—Mix together 2 cupfuls hot mashed potatoes, 1 teaspoonful salt, 1 teaspoonful onion juice, 4 tablespoonfuls of cream, ¼ teaspoonful black pepper, 1 tablespoonful chopped parsley, 1 tablespoonful butter and the yolks of 2 eggs. Beat until light.

Truffle and Chestnut Stuffing—One lb. fat bacon, 2 shallots, 1 lb. chestnuts, ½ lb. truffles, pepper, salt, spices, thyme, marjoram.

Mince 1 lb. of fat bacon and a couple of shallots, give them a turn on the fire in a saucepan; then put in 1 lb. of chestnuts, boiled and peeled, and ½ lb. of truffles, both cut up in moderate-sized pieces; add pepper, salt and spices to taste; also a little powdered thyme and marjoram. Give the mixture another turn or two on the fire, and it is ready.

Truffle Sauce—Rub a saucepan with a shallot, melt a piece of butter in it, add a very small quantity of flour and the trimmings of the truffles chopped coarsely; moisten with some good stock free from fat, and season with pepper, salt and the least piece of nutmeg. Let the sauce simmer about 10 minutes, and it is ready.

To Boil a Turkey—Pick, singe, draw and wash it. Truss it by drawing the legs in under the skin; fasten them with a piece of tape round the joints, and tie it round the rump. Make a stuffing of bread-crumbs, pepper and salt, or of chopped oysters, and put it where the crop was taken out. Boil slowly for 2 hours, take off the tape, and serve with either oyster, celery or plain white sauce.

Chestnut Sauce (for Roast Turkey)—Remove the outer skin from a number of chestnuts (carefully excluding any that may be the least tainted), put them to boil in salted water with a handful of coriander seeds, and a couple of bay leaves. When thoroughly done, remove the outer skin, and pound the chestnuts in a mortar, adding a little stock (free from fat) now and then. When a smooth paste is obtained, fry an onion in butter to a light color, add the chestnut paste and sufficient stock to get the sauce of the desired consistency; add salt and pepper to taste, pass through a hair sieve, and serve.

Roast Haunch of Venison — Butter, salt, flour and water.

Trim the joint neatly, wipe it well with a cloth, rub it over with butter, and sprinkle it with salt; then wrap it up in a sheet of buttered kitchen paper. Make a paste with flour and water, roll it out to the thickness of about half an inch, wrap the joint in this, and close up all the openings carefully by wetting the edges of the sheet of paste; lastly, pack up the haunch into a sheet of well buttered paper, put in the oven for about three hours, basting occasionally, then remove the paste and paper coverings, baste the haunch plentifully with butter, and when nearly done dredge some flour over it and some salt. Serve on a hot water dish.

Breast of Venison (Stewed) — One onion, 1 carrot, a bundle of sweet herbs, a few cloves, pepper and salt, common stock, butter, 1 tablespoonful of flour, 1 squeeze of lemon.

Remove the bones and skin, roll it up and tie it with a string in the shape of a round of beef, put it into a stewpan with an onion and carrot, sliced, a bundle of sweet herbs, a few cloves and pepper and salt to taste, add common stock sufficient to come up to the piece of venison, cover up the stewpan and let the contents simmer gently for about three hours, turning the meat occasionally; when done strain as much of the liquor as will be wanted for sauce, into a saucepan containing a piece of butter, previously melted and well mixed with a tablespoonful of flour, stir the sauce on the fire until it thickens, then add a squeeze of lemon; pour it over the meat in a dish and serve.

Wild Ducks (Stewed) — Pepper, salt, flour, butter, gravy made of the giblets, neck, and some pieces of veal, 1 shallot, 1 bunch of sweet herbs, ½ cup of cream or rich milk in which an egg has been beaten, brown flour, one tablespoonful of wine, juice of half a lemon.

Prepare to parboil for ten minutes. Lay in cold water for half an hour. Cut into joints, pepper, salt and flour them. Fry a light brown in some butter. Put them in a stewpan and cover with gravy made from the giblets, necks, and some pieces of veal. Add a minced shallot, bunch of sweet herbs, salt and pepper. Cover and stew for half an hour or until tender, take out the duck, skim the gravy and strain; add half a cup of cream, or some rich milk in which an egg has been beaten, thicken with brown flour, and add the juice of half a lemon. The lemon juice must be beaten in slowly, or the cream may curdle. Boil up and pour over the ducks and serve.

MEATS

IN purchasing beef secure meat of a deep red color, with the fat mingled with the lean, giving it a mottled appearance. The fat will be firm, and the color resembling grass butter. The smaller the breed, so much sweeter the meat. It will be better for eating, if kept a few days. Veal, lamb and pork (being white meat) will not keep more than a day or two.

BEEF — For roasting, the sirloin and rib pieces are the best. The chief object is to prevent the escape of the juices, and if you are roasting in an oven, it is a very good plan to throw a cup of *boiling* water over the meat when it is first put in the oven. This will prevent the escape of the juices for a while, and will thoroughly warm through the meat.

MUTTON — Choose this by the fineness of its grain, good color, and firm white fat. It is not the better for being young; if of a good breed and well-fed, it is better for age; but this only holds with wether-mutton; the flesh of the ewe is paler, and the texture finer. Ram-mutton is very strongly-flavored; the flesh is of a deep red, and the fat is spongy.

LAMB — Observe the neck of a fore-quarter; if the vein is bluish it is fresh; if it has a green or yellow cast it is stale. In the hind-quarter, if there is a faint smell under the kidney, and the knuckle is limp, the meat is stale. If the eyes are sunken, the head is not fresh. Grass-lamb comes in season in April or May, and continues till August. House-lamb may be had in great towns almost all the year, but is in highest perfection in December and January.

PORK — Pinch the lean, and if young it will break. If the rind is tough, thick, and cannot easily be impressed by the finger, it is old. A thin rind is a merit in all pork. When fresh, the flesh will be smooth and cool; if clammy, it is tainted. What is called measly pork is very unwholesome, and may be known by the fat being full of kernels, which in good pork is never the case. Pork fed at still-houses does not answer for curing any way, the fat being spongy. Dairy-fed pork is the best. A sucking pig, to be eaten in perfection, should not be more than three weeks old, and should be dressed the same day it is killed.

VEAL — Veal should be perfectly white; if purchasing the loin, the fat enveloping the kidney should be white and firm. Veal will not keep so long as older meat, especially in hot or wet weather. Choose small and fat veal. It is in season from March to August.

Beef-Steak Pudding—½ lb. of flour, 6 oz. of beef suet, 2½ lbs. of rump or beefsteak, pepper and salt, 1 doz. oysters, ¼ pint of stock.

Chop the suet finely, and rub it into the flour with your hands, sprinkling a little salt, then mix with water to a smooth paste; roll the paste to an eighth of an inch; line a quart pudding basin with the paste; cut the steak into thin slices, flour them, and season with pepper and salt; put the oysters and the liquor that is with them into a saucepan and bring it to the point of boiling; then remove from the fire, and strain the liquor into a basin; then cut off the beards and the hard parts, leaving only the soft, roll the slices of steak, filling the basin with the meat and oysters; pour in the stock and liquor from the oysters. Cover with paste and boil three hours.

N. B.—Be sure the water is boiling before putting the pudding in.

Fillets of Beef (with Olives)—A piece of rump steak, pepper, salt, olives, onions, flour, stock, sauce.

Cut a piece of rump steak into slices $3/8$ of an inch thick, and trim them into shape. Melt plenty of butter in a baking-tin, lay the fillets of beef in this, and let them stand in a warm place for an hour or so; then sprinkle them with pepper and salt, and fry them in some very hot butter, turning them to let both sides color. Stone a quantity of olives and parboil them. Fry some onions a brown color in butter, add a little flour, and, when that is colored, as much stock as you want sauce, pepper, salt and spices to taste. Let the sauce boil, then strain it, add the olives, and serve when quite hot, with the fillets in a circle round them.

Grenadins of Beef—Rump steak, lard, bacon fat, rich stock of gravy, onions, turnips, butter, flour, milk, pepper, salt and nutmeg.

Cut some rump steak in slices a little more than half an inch thick, trim them all to the same size in the shape of cutlets, and lard them thickly on one side with fine lardoons of bacon fat. Lay them out, the larded side uppermost, into a flat pan, and put into it as much highly-flavored rich stock or gravy as will come up to the grenadins without covering them. Cover the pan and place it in the oven to braise gently for an hour. Then remove the cover, baste the grenadins with the gravy, and let them remain uncovered in the oven till the larding has taken color; they are then ready. Take equal quantities of carrots and turnips cut into the shape of olives. Boil all these vegetables in salted water, then melt a piece of butter in a saucepan, add a tablespoonful of flour, stir in sufficient milk to make a sauce, add pepper, salt and a little grated nutmeg. Put all the vegetables into this sauce, of which there should be just enough to hold them together; toss them gently in it till quite hot. Dress them in the middle of a dish, round them dispose the grenadins in a circle, and, having removed the superfluous fat from their gravy, put this round the grenadins, and serve.

Beefsteak Pie—Forcemeat, 2 oz. of fat bacon, 2 oz. of bread crumbs, parsley, thyme, a small onion, mushrooms, seasoning for forcemeat, salt, pepper and nutmeg, 2 eggs, a tender rump-steak, shallot, gravy.

Make some forcemeat with 2 oz. of fat bacon, 2 oz. of bread crumbs, a little chopped parsley, thyme, a small onion and some mushrooms; add seasoning of salt, pepper and nutmeg, pound in mortar, moistening with the yolks of 2 eggs. Take a tender rump steak or the under cut of a sirloin of beef, cut it in thin slices, season with salt, pepper and a little shallot. Roll each slice like a sausage with some forcemeat inside, border a pie dish, put in the beef and forcemeat, fill it up with good gravy, flavored with Harvey sauce. Cover with puff paste; bake in a moderate oven. Make a hole in the top, and add some reduced gravy.

Fillets of Beef (a la Chateaubriand)—A piece of sirloin of beef, pepper, salt, oil.

A piece of the under cut of the sirloin of beef; trim off the fat neatly, and the skin next to it; cut it across the grain into slices $1\frac{1}{2}$ in. thick, sprinkle them with pepper, dip them in oil, and broil over a clear fire, sprinkle with salt, and serve very hot in a dish garnished with potatoes *sautées au beurre*. For potatoes *sautées au beurre* see receipt under "Vegetables."

Corn Beef — Four gal. of fresh water, ½ lb. of coarse brown sugar, 2 oz. of saltpetre, 7 lbs. of common salt.

Put 4 gal. of fresh water, ½ lb. of coarse brown sugar, 2 oz. saltpetre, 7 lbs. of common salt into a boiler, remove the scum as it rises, and, when well boiled, leave it to get cold. Put in the meat in the pickle, lay a cloth over it, and press the meat down with bricks or any weight.

Beef Cake (Cold Meat Cookery) — To each lb. of cold roast meat allow ¼ lb. of bacon or ham, a little pepper and salt, 1 bunch of minced savory herbs, 2 eggs.

Have your meat underdone and mince very finely, add the bacon, which must also be well minced; mix together, stir in the herbs and bind with 2 eggs; make into square cakes about ½ inch thick, fry in hot dripping, drain on blotting paper, and serve with gravy poured round.

Beef Croquettes — One cupful cold beef, chopped fine, 1 cupful mashed potatoes, 2 tablespoonfuls finely minced parsley and 1 onion; season to taste; then add 1 well-beaten egg and mix thoroughly. Mould into balls, dip first in bread crumbs, then into beaten egg; fry in plenty of hot lard until a delicate brown. Eat very hot.

Bubble and Squeak (Cold Meat Cookery) — A few thin slices of cold boiled beef, a little butter, small cabbage, 1 sliced onion, pepper and salt to taste.

Fry the beef gently in the butter, place on a flat dish, and cover with fried greens. Savoys may be used. Boil until tender, press in colander, mince and then put in frying-pan with butter and sliced onion, and a little salt and pepper.

Roast Bullock's Heart—One bullock's heart, ¼ lb. suet, 6 oz. bread crumbs, ¼ pt. of milk, 1 tablespoonful of chopped parsley, 1 dessertspoonful of chopped mixed herbs, ¼ lb. of dripping or butter, 1 pt. of gravy or beef-tea. For the sauce: One small onion, a dessertspoonful of flour, salt and pepper, butter the size of an egg, a large spoonful of mushroom catsup.

Wash the heart in salt water, taking care to remove all the blood; wash in second water and dry with a clean cloth; be careful to dry it thoroughly; chop the suet as finely as possible, mix with some bread crumbs the suet, parsley, herbs, salt and pepper; lastly, put in the milk, then proceed to fill all the cavities of the heart with the stuffing; take a piece of paper, grease it well with butter or dripping, place this over the cavities and tie it on tightly with string; put 1 oz. of dripping into the pan, and baste the heart occasionally; when gravy boils, cut up the onion, sprinkling with pepper and salt, and add to the gravy; allow it to stew gently until about 5 minutes before the heart is done; skim occasionally; when done strain the liquor; into another saucepan put the butter, and allow it to melt a minute or two; then add the flour and mix smoothly together; then pour in slowly the liquor, stirring until it boils and thickens. Then dish up, remove paper, and add to the sauce the mushroom catsup. Immediately pour this sauce round the heart and serve.

Stuffed Steak — Take a good-sized steak — either round or flank will do—slash until tender. Have ready a dressing made of bread crumbs well seasoned, with bits of butter and onion or parsley chopped through it. Spread the steak with this, roll and tie firmly. Brown 3 tablespoonfuls of flour in your pan, work in a little butter and thin with cold water. Put the steak in the pan, and baste frequently as it bakes in a moderate oven.

Beef Omelet — Three lbs. of beefsteak, ¾ lb. of suet, salt and pepper, a little sage, eggs, 6 Boston crackers.

Three lbs. of beefsteak, ¾ lb. of suet, chopped fine; salt, pepper, and a little sage, 3 eggs, 6 Boston crackers rolled; make into a roll and baste.

Beef (Stewed)—One tablespoonful of butter, 2 sliced onions, 12 whole cloves, allspice, ½ teaspoonful salt, ¼ teaspoonful of black pepper, 1 pt. of cold water, 2 or 3 lbs. of tender beef, a little flour, a few sprigs of sweet basil.

In a stewpan place a large tablespoonful of butter, in which fry until quite brown two sliced onions, adding, while cooking, 12 whole cloves; ditto allspice; ½ teaspoonful of salt, and half that quantity of black pepper; take from the fire, pour 1 pt. of cold water, wherein lay 2 or 3 lbs. of tender lean beef cut in small, thick pieces; cover closely, and let all stew gently 2 hours, adding, just before serving, a little flour thickening. A few sprigs of sweet basil is an improvement.

Irish Stew —Cut three pounds of the neck of beef into small pieces, put in a saucepan and cover with half a gallon of boiling water, add a teaspoonful of salt, 2 sliced onions and 3 or 4 pepper-corns, and simmer gently for 3 hours. Pare and quarter half a dozen potatoes, add to the meat, and cook half an hour longer; thicken with the beaten yolk of an egg and a tablespoonful of butter rolled in flour.

Meats. 65

Hamburg Steak—This is a nice way to cook Hamburg steak: Chop fine 1 pound of round steak, add 2 small onions, chopped fine, and pepper and salt to taste. Flour your hands, take two tablespoonful of the mixture and make into small, flat cakes. Have a large lump of butter very hot in your frying-pan, drop in the cakes and fry brown on either side. Some people make a gravy by adding a couple teaspoonfuls of flour to the butter in the pan, stirring in half a pint of cold water, with salt and pepper, and letting it boil up.

Hash—Put 1½ teacups of boiling water into a saucepan, and make a thin paste with a teaspoonful of flour and a tablespoonful of water. Stir and boil it for 3 minutes. Add half a teaspoonful of black pepper, rather more of salt, and 1 tablespoonful of butter. Chop cold beef into fine hash, removing all tough, gristly pieces; put the meat into a tin pan; pour over it the gravy above mentioned, and let it heat ten minutes or so, but not cook. If preferred, add equal quantity of chopped boiled potatoes, and if you have the gravy of yesterday's dinner, you may use it instead of the made gravy, and you will need less pepper and salt and butter.

Beef Tongue—If it has been dried and smoked before it is dressed it should be soaked over night, but if only pickled, a few hours will be sufficient. Put it in a pot of cold water over a slow fire for an hour or two before it comes to a boil; then let it simmer gently for from three to four hours, according to its size; ascertain when it is done by probing it with a skewer. Take the skin off, and before serving surround the root with a paper frill.

Jellied Tongue—Boil until done one large beef's tongue, saving a pint of the liquor;

remove the skin, allow it to get perfectly cold and slice as for the table. In half a pint of water dissolve thoroughly two ounces of gelatine; carefully take from a teacupful of browned veal gravy all the grease, stir in a small tablespoonful of sugar, one tablespoonful of burned sugar to color the jelly, and three tablespoonfuls of vinegar, then the liquor in which the tongue was boiled; mix in well the dissolved gelatine, then a pint of boiling water; strain through a jelly bag. As soon as it begins to set, pour a little jelly into the bottom of the mould, add a layer of tongue, then more jelly, until it is full; set in a cold place. When wanted, dip the mould an instant into hot water, and turn the contents into a dish, which should be garnished with lettuce leaves, nasturtium flowers or sprigs of celery.

PORK

Pork Pie—¼ lb. of lard, 1 lb. of pork (leg or loin), seasoning, 1 lb. of flour and an egg, ½ glass of cold water.

Put the lard and water into rather a large saucepan; place upon the fire and allow to boil (take care it does not boil over, or it will catch fire). Cut the pork into pieces about an inch square; when the lard and water are quite boiling pour into the middle of the flour and mix with a spoon. When the paste is cool enough knead it well, it must be rather stiff; cut off a quarter of the paste, and the remainder mould into the shape of a basin, pressing it inside; shape it evenly all round, it should be about ⅓ inch in thickness; dip the pieces of pork in cold water, seasoning well with pepper and salt, then place in the mould of paste as closely as possible. If liked, a little chopped sage can be sprinkled over the pork; then take the rest of the paste, roll it, and cut to the size of the top of the mould, taking care to have it the same size as the inside; break an egg and divide the yolk from the white; with a paste-brush dip into the white of egg and brush the edge of the paste; then place this on the top of the pie, pressing the edges well. Any trimmings of paste that are left cut into little leaves, dip into the white of egg, and stick them on top of the pie; then wet the pie all over with the yolk of the egg and bake for about 2 hours.

Pork (Hashed)—Some remnants of cold roast pork, pepper and salt to taste, 2 onions, 2 blades of mace, 1 teaspoonful of flour, 1 teaspoonful of vinegar, 2 cloves, ½ pint of gravy.

Take the onions, chop and fry them a nice brown; then take the pork and cut it into thin slices, seasoning with pepper and salt to taste, and add these to the rest of the above ingredients; stew it for about half an hour gently, and serve with sippets of toasted bread.

Sucking Pig (Roast)—Pig, 3 oz. of breadcrumbs, 18 sage leaves, pepper and salt, tablespoonful of butter, salad oil to baste with, tablespoonful of lemon juice, ½ pint of gravy.

Stuff the pig with finely grated bread-crumbs, minced sage, pepper and salt, and a tablespoonful of butter. Take care these are well blended. After stuffing the pig sew up the slit neatly, truss the legs back, to allow the inside to be roasted, put in oven, and directly it is dry have ready some butter tied in a piece of thin cloth, and rub the pig with this in every part. Continue this operation several times while roasting; do not allow the pig to burn in any part. Then take ½ pint of gravy, 1 tablespoonful of lemon juice, and the gravy that flowed from the pig; pour a little of this over the pig, and the remainder send to the table in a tureen. Instead of butter for basting many cooks use salad oil, as this makes the crackling crisp. Before dishing cut off the head and part the body down the middle, and lay on the dish back to back. Take care that it is sent to table *very* hot, and serve with apple sauce. It will take about 2 hours for a small pig to roast.

Pork Cheese—About 2 lbs. of cold roast pork, a dessertspoonful of chopped-up parsley, 5 sage leaves, pepper and salt, a bunch of savory herbs, 2 blades of mace, a little nutmeg, ½ teaspoonful of minced lemon peel, sufficient gravy to fill the mould.

Cut the pork into pieces, but do not chop; there should be about ¼ of fat to 1 pound lean; sprinkle with pepper and salt, pound the spices thoroughly and mince as finely as possible the parsley, sage, lemon peel and herbs; then mix all this nicely together. Place in mould and fill with gravy. Bake a little over an hour. When perfectly cold turn out.

To Boil a Ham—Let it soak in cold water for 24 hours before putting it on the fire, cover it with cold water and boil slowly. When it can be easily probed with a skewer lift it out and take off the skin, boiling it again for 1 hour. Leave it in the water it is boiled in till quite cold, when grate burnt bread over it and trim with frills of cut paper.

VEAL

Roast Veal (Stuffed) — Eight oz. of bruised bread crumbs, 4 oz. of chopped suet, shallot, thyme, marjoram and winter savory, 2 eggs, salt and pepper.

To 8 oz. of bruised crumbs of bread add 4 oz. of chopped suet, shallot, thyme, marjoram and winter savory, all chopped fine; 2 eggs, salt and pepper to season; mix all these ingredients into a firm, compact kind of paste, and use this stuffing to fill a hole or pocket which you will have cut with a knife in some part of the piece of veal, taking care to fasten it in with a skewer. A piece of veal weighing 4 lbs. would require rather more than an hour to cook it thoroughly before a small fire.

Veal (Stewed) — Two qts. of water, 1 peeled onion, a few blades of mace, a little salt, ¼ lb. of rice, butter, chopped parsley.

Break the shank bone, wash it clean, and put it into 2 qts. of water, 1 onion peeled, a few blades of mace and a little salt; set over a quick fire, and remove the scum as it rises; wash carefully ¼ lb. of rice, and when the veal has cooked for about an hour skim it well and throw in the rice; simmer for ¾ of an hour slowly; when done put the meat in a deep dish and the rice around it. Mix a little drawn butter, stir in some chopped parsley, and pour over the veal.

Veal and Ham Pie — Forcemeat balls, 1 or 2 eggs, ham and veal, mushrooms, gravy, pie crust, jelly, onions, herbs, lemon peel, salt, cayenne, parsley, whites of eggs.

Cut some thin slices off the leg or neck of veal, free them from skin and gristle, lard them well, and season with salt and pepper. Have some eggs boiled hard and thin slices of ham. Make some forcemeat balls with fat bacon, the trimmings of the veal, chopped onions, parsley and sweet herbs, grated lemon peel, salt, cayenne, and pounded mace. Pound all in a mortar, and bind with 1 or 2 eggs. Line a pie with good paste, and fill it with layers (not too close), first one of ham, then one of veal, of forcemeat balls, of the eggs (cut in halves), and so on; a few mushrooms may be added; put in some gravy; lastly, a layer of thin bacon, and cover all with tolerably thick crust, glaze. Bake for about 4 hours in a moderate oven. Make a hole in the top, and insert some good savory jelly — made with an ox or calf's foot, knuckle of veal, and trimming of bacon and ham well flavored with onions, more herbs and lemon peel, and cleared with the whites of egg. Leave till quite cold, then it can be cut with a sharp knife into slices.

Veal Pudding—Slice boiled veal about ½ an inch in thickness; butter a pudding dish and have ready 2 cupfuls of boiled rice; put first a layer of rice, then one of meat; season to taste, and add, if you like, a little chopped sage. Beat 1 egg into 1 cupful of milk; add a little salt and pour over the pudding; bake ¾ of an hour.

Veal Cake—One-half lb. veal cutlets, 1 rasher of ham, 2 hard-boiled eggs, a little veal stuffing, and ½ oz. of gelatine.

Cut the eggs into slices and arrange them at the bottom and sides of a pie-dish. Cut the veal and ham into rather small pieces; arrange them in layers, with a little stuffing and egg between, and a small quantity of water, pepper and salt. Cover with a plain crust, in which make two holes. Bake very slowly for 2 hours. Before it is done have ready the gelatine dissolved in ½ teacupful of boiling water, with pepper and salt. Pour this into the holes in the crust. Shake it down well, to mix together. Turn out when cold.

Veal (Marbled)—Spice, butter, tongue and veal.

Meats. 71

Some cold roasted veal, season with spice, beat in a mortar; skin a cold boiled tongue, cut up and pound it to a paste, adding to it nearly its weight of butter; put some of the veal into a pot, and strew in lumps of the pounded tongue; put in another layer of the veal and then more tongue; press it down and pour clarified butter on top; this cuts very prettily like veined marble. White meat of fowls may be used instead of veal.

Veal Scallop — Pepper and salt, crackers, milk and gravy from meat, 2 eggs, butter.

Chop some cold roast or stewed veal very fine; put a layer on the bottom of a pudding dish well buttered; season with pepper and salt; next have a layer of finely-powdered crackers; wet with a little milk or some of the gravy from the meat. Proceed until the dish is full; spread over all a thick layer of cracker-crumbs, seasoned with salt and wet into a paste with milk and 2 beaten eggs. Stick pieces of butter all over it, cover closely, and bake half an hour; then remove the cover and bake long enough to brown nicely. Do not get it too dry.

Veal Cutlets—Four lbs. of the best end of the neck of veal, $\frac{1}{2}$ teaspoonful of minced thyme, rind of a small lemon, 1 bunch of parsley, 1 tablespoonful of butter, 1 teaspoonful of lemon juice, 1 egg, pepper and salt, bread-crumbs, $\frac{1}{2}$ lb. of bacon.

To shape the cutlets, saw off the end of the rib bone, saw off the chine bone also, which lies at the back of the cutlets; then form the cutlets to a neat shape. Mince thyme and lemon rind and parsley as finely as possible; melt the butter, and add these ingredients to it; add also the egg, pepper and salt, and beat all up together; then rub very finely some crumbs of bread; dip each cutlet into the mixture, then cover with bread-crumbs; when the gridiron is perfectly warm arrange the cutlets upon it. Have the fire nice and bright, but do not allow them to cook too fast or the bread-crumbs will burn before the cutlets are cooked through; allow them to brown nicely on both sides; about 10 minutes will be the time. Serve on a wall of mashed potatoes in a circle; fill the center of dish with rolls of bacon and with a nice brown sauce. (See "Sauces.")

For Rolls—Cut some neat slices of bacon, roll them up and run a skewer through each; place this in the oven for about 5 minutes, then remove the skewer and arrange in center of dish.

Veal Croquettes—Boil 1½ lbs. of veal—or use that left from roast. Mince very fine, add two eggs, ½ cup of rolled crackers, salt and pepper. Make into small balls or cakes, roll in flour and fry in butter, or put in wire basket and fry in lard. Serve on napkin.

Hashed Calf's Head (a la Poulette)—Calf's head, 1 oz. of butter, 2 tablespoonfuls of flour, ½ pint of white stock, a few button mushrooms, white pepper and salt to taste, 2 eggs, juice of a lemon, parsley.

Cut the remnants of a boiled head into uniform pieces the size of half an apple. Melt in a saucepan 1 or 2 ounces of butter, according to the quantity of meat to be hashed; amalgamate with it 1 or 2 tablespoonfuls of flour, then stir in ½ pint, more or less, of white stock. Stir well, then add a few button mushrooms, white pepper and salt to taste, and let the sauce boil for 10 minutes. Put the saucepan by the side of the fire, and lay the pieces of calf's head in it; let them get hot slowly, but not boil. Just before serving stir in off the fire the yolks of two eggs, beaten up with the juice of a lemon, and strained; also a small quantity of either tarragon or parsely very finely minced.

Veal (Braized Loin of)—Veal, 2 oz. of butter, 1 carrot, 1 onion, a little parsley, sweet herbs, a leaf or two of basil, a bay leaf, a crust of bread toasted brown, a little flour, and a little stock.

About 2 oz. of butter, 1 carrot, 1 onion, a little parsley, sweet herbs, a leaf or two of basil, and a bay leaf; brown a large crust of bread and put it in a stewpan with the above things, and fry them until they are brown; then flour the meat and brown it well, putting it back in the saucepan; add a little stock, and baste it in the gravy till done, and keep turning the meat. Simmer 4 pounds for 3 or 4 hours.

MUTTON

Mutton Cutlets—This is an entrée always ready to hand, but it must be carefully and neatly prepared. A dish of well-dressed mutton cutlets is truly "a dish to put before a king;" whereas greasy, fat, gristly meats, called for the nonce cutlets, offend the taste of the least fastidious. The first thing to attend to is the cutting and trimming of the cutlets neatly. Take a piece of the best end of the neck of mutton, saw off the bones short, remove gristle and fat, cut the cutlets about one-third of an inch in thickness, shape and trim them neatly, beat them with a cutlet bat dipped in water, and then proceed to cook them by any of the following recipes:

Pepper, salt, and broil them over a brisk fire; serve them with mashed or *sautée* potatoes in the center of the dish.

Season as above, and before broiling dip them in oil or oiled butter. Serve with—

Soubise Sauce—Peal and blanch 4 onions, cool in water, drain, put them in a stewpan with enough water or white stock to cover; add some cayenne, bay leaf, a little mace, a small piece of ham or bacon; keep the lid closely shut and simmer gently until tender; take them out, drain them thoroughly, press through a sieve or tammy cloth, add ½ pt. of bechamel sauce made thus: Put in a stewpan a little parsley, 1 clove, a small piece of bay leaf, sweet herbs, and 1 pt. of white stock freed from fat; when boiled long enough to extract the flavor of the herbs, etc., strain it, boil up quickly till reduced to half the quantity; mix a tablespoonful of arrowroot with ½ pt. of milk or cream, pour on the reduced stock and simmer for 10 minutes.

A Dainty Dish—For a dainty dish of cold meat, boil a leg of lamb in water enough to cover, to which add a handful of cloves and whole allspice and a stick or two of cinnamon. Let it stand in the water in which it was boiled to become cold. Slice very thin. Beef can be cooked in the same style.

Mutton Pudding—2 lbs. of the chump end of the loin, weighed after being boned; suet crust (proportions—6 oz. of suet to each lb. of flour); 1 tablespoonful of minced onion, pepper and salt.

Cut the meat into thin slices, sprinkling with pepper and salt. For the suet crust use the above proportions of flour and suet, mixing with a little salt and pepper, milk or water, to the proper consistency. Line your dish with the crust, lay in the meat, *nearly* fill the dish with water; add the minced onion and cover with the crust.

Irish Stew (Mutton) — 2 lbs. thick mutton cutlets, 4 lbs. potatoes, 1 onion, pepper and salt, ½ pint of water.

Prepare the potatoes as for boiling, cut them in halves. Slice the onion very thinly. Place a layer of potatoes at the bottom of the stewpan, then a layer of cutlets, and a sprinkling of onion, pepper and salt; then another layer of potatoes and so on until all is used up. Pour in the water, cover the pan closely and simmer gently for 2 hours.

Mutton (Boned Leg of, Stuffed) — A leg weighing 7 or 8 pounds, 2 shallots, forcemeat.

Make forcemeat, to which add the minced shallots. Get the butcher to take the bone from the mutton, as he can do it without spoiling the skin; if very fat, cut off some of it. Fill up the hole with the forcemeat, then sew it up to prevent it falling out, tie up neatly and roast about 2½ hours or a little longer. When ready to serve, remove the string and serve with a good gravy.

Lamb (Stewed) — A breast of lamb, 1 tablespoonful of salt, 1 qt. of canned peas, 1 tablespoonful of wheat flour, 3 tablespoonfuls of butter, pepper to taste.

Cut the scrag, or breast of lamb, in pieces, and put in a stewpan with water enough to cover it. Cover the stewpan closely and let it simmer or stew for fifteen or twenty minutes; take off the scum, then add a tablespoonful of salt and a quart of canned peas; cover the stewpan and let them stew for half an hour; work a small tablespoonful of wheat flour with three tablespoonfuls of butter, and stir it into the stew; add pepper to taste; let it simmer together for ten minutes.

Lamb Chops — A little butter, a little water, enough potatoes to fill a small dish, 1 teacupful of cream.

Lamb chops are excellent cooked this way: Put them in a frying-pan with a very little water, so little that it will boil away by the time the meat is tender; then put in lumps of butter with the meat and let it brown slowly; there will be a brown, crisp surface, with a fine flavor. Serve for breakfast with potatoes cooked thus: Choose the small ones and let them boil till they are tender; drain off the water, and pour over them, while still in the kettle, at least one teacupful of cream; mash them smoothly in this.

Shoulder of Mutton (Boiled with Oysters) — A little pepper, a piece of mace, about 2 dozen oysters, a little water, an onion, a few peppercorns, about ½ pint of good gravy, a tablespoonful of flour and butter.

Hang it some days, then salt it well for two days; bone it, and sprinkle it with pepper and a piece of mace pounded; lay some oysters over it, and roll the meat up tight and tie it. Stew it in a small quantity of water, with an onion and a few peppercorns, till quite tender. Have ready a little good gravy, and some oysters stewed in it: thicken this with flour and butter, and pour over the mutton, when the tape is taken off. The stewpan should be kept covered.

Sweetbreads — Half boil them, and stew them in a white gravy; add cream, flour, butter, nutmeg, salt and white pepper. Or do them in brown sauce seasoned. Or parboil them, and then cover them with crumbs, herbs and seasoning, and brown them in a Dutch oven. Serve with butter and mushroom catsup or gravy. N. B.—If there is no oven at hand, they may be toasted before the fire upon a toasting fork.

Fried Sweetbreads — After they are parboiled and cold, split in halves and cut into pieces as large as very large oysters, wipe dry and dip in beaten egg, then in fine cracker crumbs; fry in hot lard or butter same as oysters; sprinkle with salt before dipping in egg. Serve hot; garnish with parsley.

Sweetbreads (Larded) — A couple of sweetbreads, a few strips of bacon, onions, carrots, sweet herbs, pepper, salt, spice to taste, a small quantity of rich stock.

Trim a couple of sweetbreads, soak them half an hour in tepid water, then parboil them for a few minutes, and lay them in cold water; when quite cold take them out, dry them, and lard them quickly with fine strips of bacon. Put a slice of fat bacon in a stewpan with some onions, carrots, a bunch of sweet herbs, pepper, salt, and spices to taste, and a small quantity of rich stock; lay the sweetbreads on this, and let them gently stew till quite done, basting the top occasionally with the liquor. When cooked, strain the liquor, skim off superfluous fat, reduce it almost to a glaze, brown the larded side of the sweetbreads with a salamander, and serve with sauce over them.

Kidneys (a la Brochette) — Plunge some mutton kidneys in boiling water; open them down the center, but do not separate them; peel and pass a skewer across them to keep them open, pepper, salt, and dip them into melted butter, broil them over a clear fire on both sides, doing the cut side first; remove the skewers, have ready some maître d'hotel butter, viz.: butter beaten up with chopped parsley, salt, pepper, and a little lemon juice. Put a small piece in the hollow of each kidney, and serve very hot.

Stewed Kidneys — 4 kidneys, $\frac{1}{2}$ a small onion, 1 oz. butter, 3 teaspoonfuls of flour, pepper and salt to taste.

Cut the kidneys in small pieces, and roll them in flour; chop the onion small, and fry with the pieces of kidney in the butter until brown. Then add the pepper, salt, and enough cold water to cover them, and stew very gently for an hour. Thicken with the flour a few minutes before done, and serve very hot.

CURRIES.

MOST people have a liking for a really good curry; but how very rarely it is to be obtained in America, unless at the house of some one who has passed a good many years in India. The dish miscalled a curry is frequently set before people, but too often as far as possible removed from the real and appetizing *plat* which a good Indian cook will send to table. The meat is tough, has most likely been boiled instead of gently simmered, the sauce, or thick gravy, is hot enough in all conscience, but it tastes only of curry powder of an inferior kind; the rice is a sloppy mess, and the result is a fiery, leathery sort of indigestible hash, instead of a sweet, acid, highly but agreeably flavored, perfectly cooked and digestible dish, fit to set before a prince. Any cook, of whatever nationality, who has really mastered the art of stewing properly, that is, very gently and slowly, can cook a curry; the real difficulties lie in procuring good curry powder or curry paste.

Curry Powder — 1 lb. pale turmeric seed, ¼ lb. cumin seed, ¼ lb. black pepper, ½ lb. coriander seed, 2 oz. cayenne pepper, ¼ lb. Jamaica ginger, 10 oz. caraway seed, ¼ oz. cardamines.

Purchase the ingredients of a first-class druggist. Additional heat can be obtained, by those who like very hot curries, if red Chile powder be added according to taste. Mix together all the ingredients well powdered, and place before the fire or in the sun, stirring occasionally. Keep in well corked bottles.

Indian Curry—2 large tablespoonfuls of curry powder, a dessertspoonful of salt, the same of black pepper, 4 onions, ¼ lb. butter, 1½ lbs. meat, ½ pint of milk, lemon juice or Chile vinegar.

Two large tablespoonfuls of curry powder, a dessertspoonful of salt, the same of black pepper. Fry and chop very fine four onions, then moisten the curry powder with water, and put it in a stewpan, with all the above ingredients, and a quarter of a pound of butter. Let it stew for twenty minutes, stirring all the time to prevent burning, then add one and a half pounds of cold or fresh meat, or any fowl or rabbit, cut into short, thick pieces, without fat, add half a pint of milk or good stock to make the curry thick. Boil all up at once, and let it stew gently for three or four hours. When ready add lemon juice or Chile vinegar.

Curried Rabbit—1 rabbit, ¼ lb. butter, 1 apple, 2 onions, 2 tablespoonfuls curry powder, ¼ pint of cream, 1 pint stock, 1 lemon, a saltspoonful of salt.

Melt the butter over the fire, peel and chop the onions as finely as possible, then put them into the melted butter to fry a light brown. After the rabbit has been properly prepared for cooking, wash well and dry in a cloth, cut in pieces of equal size. After straining the butter from the onions, return the former to the stewpan, put in pieces of rabbit, and allow to fry for ten or fifteen minutes, turning occasionally. Peel and core the apple, and chop as finely as possible. When the meat is done add to it two tablespoonfuls of curry powder and the salt, stirring for five minutes, then add the fried onion, chopped apple and a pint of good stock. Allow to simmer for two hours, at the end of the time add the cream, squeeze the juice from the lemon into the stewpan. It is then ready to serve.

N. B.— Veal or chicken can be used, if preferred.

Curry of Mutton — Mutton, 1 onion, butter the size of an egg, curry powder, a little salt, a cup of cream.

Slice a medium-sized onion, and put it with a large lump of butter in a saucepan; let it cook slowly for five minutes. Cut the mutton in neat pieces; sprinkle curry powder over them, also a little salt, and just before putting in the saucepan pour a part of a cup of sweet cream over them. Let this all simmer gently for half an hour, so that the ingredients will become thoroughly mixed.

A Dry Malay Curry — A cauliflower, 2 onions, a sour apple, a pint of shrimps, slices of cold mutton, 2 oz. butter, a large tablespoonful of curry powder, a lemon, a small teaspoonful of salt.

Pick a cauliflower into small pieces and well wash them; chop two onions and one sour apple, pick a pint of fresh boiled shrimps, cut some slices of cold mutton about half an inch thick, knead two ounces of butter with a large tablespoonful of curry powder, and a small teaspoonful of salt. Put the butter, onions and apple into a stewpan, and fry till brown, then add the cauliflower and shrimps. Shake the saucepan frequently, and let it simmer for an hour and a half, adding the slices of mutton towards the end of the time, that they may be heated through. Finally, add the juice of a lemon. Place the slices of mutton round the dish with the cauliflower, etc., in the middle. Serve very hot, with a separate dish of boiled rice.

Curried Lobster — Lobster, cream, rice.

Take the flesh of a lobster (or a tin of lobster does very well for this dish), make curry gravy with plenty of cream; pour into a saucepan with the lobster, warm it just to boiling point; serve with rice round.

Boiled Rice for Curry — Put the rice on the stove in cold water, and allow it to come to a boil for a minute or two. Strain, dry and put in stewpan without lid at the back of the stove, to allow the steam to evaporate; shake into dish very hot; a few drops of lemon juice put in directly after it boils will make the grains separate better.

Curried Eggs — 6 eggs, 2 onions, butter, a tablespoonful of curry powder, 1 pint of broth, a cup of cream, arrowroot.

Slice the onions and fry in butter a light brown, add curry powder, and mix with the broth, allowing to simmer till tender; then put in cream, and thicken with arrowroot; simmer for five minutes, then add 6 hard-boiled eggs, cut in slices.

Curried Beef — Beef, 2 oz. butter, 2 onions, a tablespoonful of curry powder, ¼ pint milk, lemon juice.

Slice the onions and fry in butter a light brown, mix well with the curry powder, adding the beef, cut into small pieces about an inch square, pour in milk and allow to simmer for thirty minutes, stirring frequently; when done add lemon juice. It greatly improves the dish to build a wall of mashed potatoes or boiled rice around it.

Potato Curry (1).—Cold potatoes, onion, salt and pepper, curry powder to taste, egg, bread crumbs, and gravy.

Mash cold potatoes with minced onion, salt, pepper, and curry powder to taste; form into small balls with egg and bread crumbs, fry crisp, serve with rich gravy flavored with curry powder.

Potato Curry (2).—Potatoes, onions, butter, curry powder, a little stock, cream, lemon juice.

Fry some sliced raw potatoes and onions slightly in butter with a little curry powder, then simmer until done in a very little stock; add some cream, butter and lemon juice before serving.

Potato Curry (3).—Curry powder, mashed potatoes, milk.

Put a good pinch of curry powder in mashed potatoes, allowing rather more butter and milk than usual. This last is a delicious accompaniment to cutlets.

Curry (Dry)—A few onions, $\frac{1}{4}$ lb. butter, $1\frac{1}{2}$ lbs. steak, a little flour and curry powder, salt to taste, juice of 1 lemon.

Slice up a good-sized onion, and fry it a golden color in $\frac{1}{4}$ lb. of butter; cut up $1\frac{1}{2}$ lbs. of fresh steak into pieces the size of dice. Dredge them well with flour and curry powder, add a little salt, and squeeze the juice of a lemon over them, then fry them lightly in the butter in which the onions have been previously cooked. Add all together, and stew gently in a saucepan for $\frac{1}{4}$ hour.

GRAVIES.

GRAVY may be made quite as good of the skirts of beef, and the kidney, as of any other meat, prepared in the same way.

An ox-kidney, or milt, makes good gravy, cut all to pieces, and prepared as other meat; and so will the shank end of mutton that has been dressed, if much be not wanted.

The shank-bones of mutton are a great improvement to the richness of gravy; but first soak them well, and scour them clean.

A Good Beef Gravy (for Poultry or Game) —½ lb. lean beef, ½ pint cold water, 1 small onion, a saltspoonful of salt, a little pepper, a tablespoonful of mushroom catsup or sauce, ½ teaspoonful of arrowroot.

Cut the beef into small pieces and put it and the water into a stewpan. Add the onion and seasoning, and simmer gently for three hours. A short time before it is required, mix the arrowroot with a little cold water, pour into the gravy while stirring, add the mushroom catsup and allow it just to come to a boil. Strain into a tureen and serve very hot.

Savory Gravy (Thick)—1 onion, butter, a tablespoonful of flour, ½ pint of broth or stock, pepper and salt, a small quantity of Worcestershire sauce.

Mince one onion fine, fry it in butter to a dark brown, and stir in a tablespoonful of flour. After one minute add ½ pint of broth or stock, pepper and salt, and a very small quantity of Worcester sauce.

Gravy for General Use —1 lb. of lean beef cut in small pieces and floured, put into a saucepan with 12 cloves, 24 peppercorns, 6 blades of mace, some nutmeg, pepper, salt, and 1½ pints of water.

Simmer gently for 2 hours, stirring frequently. Strain before using. Add a little of the browning for soups and gravies.

Plain Gravy—An onion, a little butter, ¾ pint of stock, pepper and salt, a small piece of lean ham or bacon, a dessertspoonful of Worcester sauce, a sprig of parsley and thyme.

Mince an onion finely, fry it in butter to a dark brown color, then add ¾ of a pint of stock, pepper and salt to taste, a small piece of lean ham or bacon minced small, a little Worcester sauce, a sprig of thyme and one of parsley. Let it boil five or ten minutes, put it by till wanted, and strain it before serving.

Gravy for Hashes—Remnants and bones of the joint intended for hashing, a pinch of salt and pepper, ¼ teaspoonful of whole allspice, a bunch of savory herbs, a saltspoonful of celery salt or ½ a head of celery, an onion, a small piece of butter, a little corn flour, and boiling water.

Put the bones (having previously chopped them), with the remnants of the meat, salt, pepper, spice, herbs and celery into a stewpan. Cover with boiling water and allow it to simmer for two hours. Cut up the onion in neat slices and fry in butter to a pale brown. Then mix slowly with the gravy from bones. Boil fifteen minutes, strain, then return to stewpan, flavor with catsup or any flavoring that may be preferred. Thicken with butter and flour and just allow it to come to the boil. Serve very hot.

Gravy for a Fowl (when there is no meat to make it from)—The feet, liver, gizzards and neck of the fowl, a little browned bread, a slice of onion, a sprig of parsley and thyme, some pepper and salt, 1 teaspoonful of mushroom catsup, a little flour and butter.

Wash the feet nicely, and cut them and the neck small; simmer them with a little bread browned, a slice of onion, a sprig of parsley and thyme, some pepper and salt, and the liver and gizzards, in $\frac{1}{4}$ pint water, till half wasted. Take out the liver, bruise it, and strain the liquor to it. Then thicken it with flour and butter, and add 1 teaspoonful of mushroom catsup.

Veal Gravy—Bones, any cold remnants of veal, $1\frac{1}{2}$ pints water, 1 onion, 1 saltspoonful minced lemon peel, a little salt, a blade of mace, a few drops of the juice of the lemon, butter and flour.

Place all the ingredients (excepting the lemon juice and flour) into a stewpan, and allow them to simmer for 1 hour. Strain into a basin. Add a thickening of butter and flour mixed with a little water, also the lemon juice. Give one boil and serve very hot. Flavor with tomato sauce or catsup.

Cheap Gravy for Fowls, Etc.—Boil the neck and feet of the fowl in $\frac{1}{2}$ pint water with any slight seasonings of spices or herbs, or salt and pepper only; stew very slowly for 1 hour. Just before serving, take the gravy from the dripping-pan, drain off the fat, and strain the liquor from the neck to it; pass the gravy again through a strainer, add salt and pepper, heat it, and serve very hot.

Gravy for a Goose or Duck—Prepare in same way as for general use, with the addition of an onion and some sage.

SAUCES.

THE appearance and preparation of sauces are of the highest importance. Brown sauces should not be as thick as white ones, and should possess a decided character, so that, both whether sweet or sharp, plain or savory, they would bear out their names. Care is also to be taken that they blend and harmonize with the various dishes they are to accompany.

White Sauce—One pint milk, 2 or 3 mushrooms, 1 onion, 1 carrot, 1 bundle sweet herbs, whole pepper and salt to taste, a few cloves, a little mace, 1 oz. butter, and 1 gill cream.

Put into 1 pint milk 2 or 3 mushrooms, 1 onion and a carrot cut into pieces, 1 bundle of sweet herbs, whole pepper and salt to taste, a few cloves and a little mace; let the whole gently simmer for about an hour; put 1 ounce of butter into a saucepan, and stir on the fire until it thickens. Finish by stirring in 1 gill cream.

Horseradish Sauce—Two oz. horseradish, 6 tablespoonfuls milk or cream, 3 dessertspoonfuls vinegar, 1 teaspoonful sugar, ½ do. pepper.

Grate the horseradish, mix it with salt, sugar and pepper. Add the cream or milk *very* gradually, and heat the whole over the fire, stirring well all the time. If allowed to boil it will spoil. Serve with hot roast beef.

Sauce for Wild Fowl—Half pint gravy, 1 small onion, 3 or 4 leaves basil, a piece of the thin rind of a lemon, 1 dessertspoonful lemon juice.

Boil the gravy, onion and basil together for a few minutes, strain, and add the lemon juice. Seville orange juice may be used instead of lemon.

Standard Sauce for Fish — Maitre d'hotel butter is prepared by mixing together, cold, 1 tablespoonful each of butter and finely chopped parsley; add 1 teaspoonful of lemon juice and a little pepper and salt. Work well together, and when ready to serve the fish, spread it generously with the butter and set the dish in the mouth of the oven for a minute or two. The parsley must be as fine as powder.

Egg Sauce for Fish—Boil 2 eggs for 10 minutes, and then lay them in cold water for 5 minutes. Remove the shells, and mince them very fine. Beat $\frac{1}{4}$ lb. butter, mix eggs and butter well together, make them hot, and serve with salt fish.

Egg Sauce for Puddings — Beat yolk of 1 egg with a little sugar and cream, stir till it boils, when add a few drops of flavoring to taste.

Liver Sauce—Livers of any kind of poultry, butter, flour, minced shallots, gravy stock, a small pinch of sweet herbs, pepper, spices and salt, and juice of $\frac{1}{2}$ lemon.

Scald the livers of the poultry, rabbits or hares and mince them finely. Melt a piece of butter in a saucepan, add a little flour to it and a small quantity of minced shallots. Let the whole fry for a minute or two, then add gravy stock in sufficient quantity to make a sauce, and a small pinch of powdered sweet herbs, and pepper, spices and salt to taste. Put in the minced livers and let the sauce boil 20 minutes, and at the time of serving add a small piece of fresh butter and the juice of $\frac{1}{2}$ lemon.

Fennel Sauce—Fennel, 3 oz. butter, flour, pepper and salt, yolks of 2 eggs, juice of 1 lemon.

Blanch a small quantity in boiling salted water, take it out, dry it in a cloth, and chop it finely; melt 3 oz. fresh butter, add rather more than a tablespoonful flour, mix well, and put in pepper and salt to taste, and about a pint hot water; stir on the fire till the sauce thickens, then stir in the yolks of 2 eggs beaten up with the juice of a lemon and strained. Add plenty of chopped fennel, and serve.

Shrimp Sauce—Half pint shrimps, juice of ½ lemon, butter, a dust of cayenne.

Take ½ pint shrimps, pick out all the meat from the tails, pound the rest in a mortar with the juice of ½ lemon and a piece of butter; pass the whole through a sieve. Make 1 pint melted butter, put the meat from the tails into it, add a dust of cayenne, and when the sauce boils stir into it the shrimp butter that has come through the sieve, with or without a tablespoonful of cream.

Mock Cream Sauce—Pour ½ pint boiling milk on 1 teaspoonful arrowroot, previously mixed in a small quantity of cold milk. Stir the mixture well, and, when moderately warm, add the white of 1 egg well beaten. Place the whole over the fire, and stir it till it nearly boils.

Fruit Sauce—Half pint sugar, cinnamon, bay leaf, cloves, and any kind of fruit.

Put ½ lb. sugar and ½ pint water over the fire to boil, skim and boil 5 minutes, add to this a piece of stick cinnamon about 2 inches long, 1 bay leaf and 4 cloves; at the end of 5 minutes add ½ pint any kind of mashed fruit; for instance, apricots, stewed apples; in fact, any fruit that will go nicely with the pudding with which you expect to serve the sauce. Strain the whole through a sieve, flavor, and it is ready to serve.

Cauliflower Sauce—Two small cauliflowers, 1½ oz. butter, 1 tablespoonful flour, pepper and salt, yolks of 2 eggs, juice of a lemon.

Boil 2 small cauliflowers; when done, pick them out into sprigs and arrange them, heads downward, in a pudding basin, which must have been made quite hot; press them in gently, then turn them out dexterously on a dish, and pour over them the following sauce, boiling hot: Melt $1\frac{1}{2}$ oz. butter in a saucepan, mix with it a tablespoonful of flour, and then add $\frac{1}{2}$ pint of boiling water; stir till it thickens; add salt and white pepper to taste; then take the saucepan off the fire, and stir in the yolks of 2 eggs beaten up with the juice of a lemon and strained.

Dutch Sauce — Three tablespoonfuls vinegar, 1 lb. butter, yolks of 2 eggs, pepper and salt.

Put 3 tablespoonfuls vinegar in a saucepan, and reduce it on the fire to a third; add $\frac{1}{4}$ lb. butter and the yolks of 2 eggs. Place the saucepan on a slow fire, stir the contents continuously, and as fast as the butter melts add more, until 1 lb. is used. If the sauce becomes too thick at any time during the process, add a tablespoonful of cold water and continue stirring. Then put in pepper and salt to taste, and take great care not to let the sauce boil. When it is made—that is, when all the butter is used and the sauce is of the proper thickness—put the saucepan containing it into another filled with warm (not boiling) water until the time of serving.

Sweet Sauce — One tablespoonful flour, sugar or molasses, 1 oz. butter, 1 tablespoonful lemon juice.

Mix a tablespoonful of flour quite smooth in 4 tablespoonfuls water, then stir into it $\frac{1}{2}$ pint boiling water, sugar or molasses to taste; stir over the fire until the sauce boils, when, if allowed, an ounce of butter may be added, with a tablespoonful of lemon juice. When sweetened with sugar, a little nutmeg or ground cinnamon may be used instead of lemon juice, if preferred. A tablespoonful of raspberry jam or any fruit syrup may be used to flavor the sauce, and is generally much liked.

Mayonnaise Dressing — Yolks of 2 hard-boiled eggs, mustard, vinegar, olive oil or butter.

Take the yolks of 2 hard-boiled eggs and mash smooth with ½ teaspoonful mustard and 2 tablespoonfuls olive oil; then add slowly ½ teacup vinegar; if olive oil is not liked, melted butter may be used instead.

Poor Man's Sauce — A good-sized onion, butter, ½ pint common stock or water, vinegar, parsley, pepper and salt, flour.

Mince a good-sized onion, not too finely, put it into a saucepan with a piece of butter equal to it in bulk. Fry till the onion assumes a light brown color, add ½ pint common stock or water and a small quantity of vinegar, pepper and salt to taste, and some minced parsley; then stir the sauce into another saucepan, in which a tablespoonful of flour and a small piece of butter have been mixed, over the fire. Let the sauce boil up, and it is ready.

A Cheap Brown Sauce — One pint brown stock, 1½ oz. flour, 2 oz. butter, 4 mushrooms, salt and pepper.

Put the butter into a stewpan and put it on the fire to melt; wash the mushrooms in cold water, cut off the stalks and peel them; when the butter is melted stir in the flour and mix to a smooth paste; then add the stock and mushrooms, and stir the sauce smoothly until it boils and thickens; then remove the stewpan to the back of the stove and let it simmer gently for 8 or 10 minutes; season with pepper and salt; be careful to skim off the butter as it rises to the top of the sauce. Should the sauce be not brown enough, a teaspoonful of caramel might be stirred into it; strain and serve.

Onion Sauce (Brown) — Two oz. butter, rather more than ½ pint of rich gravy, 6 large onions, pepper and salt.

Put into your stewpan the onions, sliced, fry them of a light brown color, with 2 oz. of butter; keep them stirred well to prevent them turning black; as soon as they are of a nice color, pour over the gravy, and simmer gently until tender; skim off all fat, add seasoning and rub the whole through a sieve; then put in a saucepan, and when it boils, serve.

Tomato Sauce — Ten lbs. ripe tomatoes, 1 pint best brown vinegar, 2 oz. salt, ½ oz. cloves, 1 oz. allspice, ½ lb. white sugar, 1 oz. garlic, ½ oz. black pepper, ½ oz. cayenne pepper.

Wipe the tomatoes clean, and boil or bake till soft; then strain and rub through a sieve that will retain the seeds and skins. Boil the juice for an hour, then add the above ingredients (all the spices must be ground). Boil all together for a sufficient time, which may be known by the absence of any watery particle, and by the whole becoming a smooth mass; 5 hours will generally suffice. Bottle without straining into perfectly dry bottles, and cork securely when cold. The garlic must be peeled. The proportions of spice may be varied according to taste.

Oyster Sauce — Oysters, butter, flour, milk, blade of mace, bay leaf, pepper and salt, cayenne, a few drops of lemon juice.

Parboil the oysters in their own liquor, beard them, and reserve all the liquor. Melt a piece of butter in a saucepan, add a little flour, the oyster liquor, and enough milk to make as much sauce as is wanted. Put in a blade of mace and a bay leaf tied together, pepper and salt to taste, and the least bit of cayenne. Let the sauce boil, add the oysters, and as soon as they are quite hot remove the mace and bay leaf, stir in a few drops of lemon juice, and serve.

Worcester Sauce—Two tablespoonfuls Indian soy, 2 ditto walnut catsup, 1 dessertspoonful of salt, 1 teaspoonful cayenne pepper, 1 nutmeg (sliced thin), 1 doz. cloves, ½ oz. root ginger pounded, a little lemon peel, a small head of garlic divided into cloves, 1 pint vinegar, 3 oz. lump sugar.

Dissolve the sugar in a little of the vinegar over the fire, add the other ingredients; put all into a wide-necked bottle. It should stand for a month before using, and is better if shaken every day. At the end of the month pour off clear into bottles.

Chestnut Sauce— Remove the outer shell from some fine chestnuts, scald them in boiling water, and remove the inner skin. Stew them in good white stock till quite tender, drain, and while hot press them through a sieve. Put the pulp into a saucepan, add a small piece of butter, a little sugar, pepper and salt. Stir over the fire till quite hot, but do not let it boil, and serve.

Mushroom Sauce— Remove the stalks and gritty part from ½ pint of mushrooms; wash, drain, and put them into ½ pint of well-flavored gravy, simmer them till quite tender, drain them, and keep them hot. Melt 1 oz. butter in a saucepan, add to it 1 oz. flour, stir over the fire till brown; pour in the gravy, stirring till it boils. Arrange the mushrooms in the center of the dish, the cutlets round them, and pour the sauce over.

Chile Sauce—One bu. ripe tomatoes, 2 doz. large onions; chop very fine and boil 1 hour; then add 1 pint salt, 2½ quarts vinegar, 5 red peppers chopped fine, 2 tablespoonfuls each of ground ginger and cinnamon, and 1 each of cloves and nutmeg. Boil steadily for about 2 hours; bottle and seal tightly.

Bread Sauce (for Poultry or Game)—Giblets, ¾ lb. stale bread, 1 onion, 10 whole peppers, 1 blade mace, salt, 2 tablespoonfuls cream.

Put the giblets into 1 pint water, add the onion, pepper, mace, salt. Allow it to simmer for 1 hour, then strain the liquor over the bread crumbs. Cover the stewpan and let it stand on the stove for 1 hour (do not allow it to boil), then beat the sauce up with a fork until it is nice and smooth. Allow it to boil 5 minutes, stirring well until it is thick, then add cream and serve hot.

Caper Sauce—Two oz. butter, 1 tablespoonful flour, 1 pint stock, pepper and salt, Worcester sauce, capers.

Put 2 oz. butter and 1 tablespoonful flour into a saucepan; stir the mixture on the fire until it acquires a brown color; add rather less than 1 pint boiling stock, free from fat; season with pepper, salt and a little Worcester sauce. When the sauce boils throw in plenty of capers; let it boil once more, and it is ready.

Sauce Hollandaise—Take a scant ½ cup good butter. Beat the butter to a cream and add the yolks of 3 eggs, beating them into the butter with the juice of ½ lemon. Add 1 sliced onion, 6 peppercorns and 1 bay leaf. Set the bowl containing the sauce in a basin of boiling water and stir it continually for a few moments. Then add a little boiling stock with a little grated nutmeg and 1 teaspoonful of salt. Continue stirring it for about 5 minutes longer, when it should be of the consistency of a custard and perfectly smooth. Strain it through a sieve, add 1 teaspoonful butter and serve.

Mint Sauce—Chop 1 bunch fresh mint fine, mix with 1 tablespoonful sugar, a pinch of salt and pepper, rub well together, and add ½ cup vinegar, with a squeeze of lemon juice.

STOCKS.

Common Stock—Take all the bones of joints, etc., that are available, carcasses and bones of poultry and game (not high), chop them all into convenient pieces and put them into a saucepan together with any scraps of meat, cooked or uncooked, resulting from remnants, the trimming of cutlets, etc. Add a couple of carrots, 1 onion, 1 bunch parsley, 1 bay leaf, a small sprig thyme, and 1 marjoram; salt to taste, a small quantity of white pepper and allspice mixed, and 2 or 3 cloves. Fill the saucepan with cold water until it covers the contents by 1 inch, and set it on the fire to boil slowly for about 4 hours; strain the liquor through a cloth into a basin and when cold, the cake of fat on the top being removed, the stock will be fit for use.

Gravy Stock—Place a layer of slices of onion in a saucepan holding 1 gal., over this a layer of fat bacon, and over all about 2 lbs. shin of beef chopped in small pieces; 1 pint common stock, or even water, being poured on the whole, set the saucepan on the fire for 1 hour, until the liquor is almost evaporated—what is called reduced to a "glaze"—then add sufficient cold common stock or cold water to cover contents of the saucepan, and 2 or 3 carrots cut in slices, 1 leek, 1 head celery (when in season), or some celery seed, 1 handful parsley, ½ clove garlic, 1 sprig marjoram and 1 of thyme, 1 bay leaf, 4 or 5 cloves, white pepper and salt to taste. After boiling for about 3 hours strain off the liquor, and, being absolutely freed from fat, it is ready for use.

Veal Stock—Toss a couple of onions, sliced, and 1 lb. lean veal cut in pieces in a saucepan with some butter until they assume a light color, then add ½ lb. ham chopped up small, and moisten with 1 pint common stock cold and perfectly free from fat. Let the liquor reduce almost to a "glaze"—then add 2 quarts cold common stock, 1 knuckle veal, or 2 calves' feet, a couple of carrots, head of celery, parsley, bay leaf, thyme, mace, pepper and salt, all in due proportion. After boiling 2 or 3 hours, strain free from fat.

VEGETABLES.

VEGETABLES should be carefully cleaned from insects, and nicely washed. Boil in plenty of water, and drain the moment they are done enough. If overboiled, they lose their beauty and crispness. To dress them with meat is wrong, except carrots with boiled beef.

To boil vegetables green, be sure the water boils when you put them in. Make them boil very fast. Don't cover, but watch them; and if the water has not slackened, you may be sure they are done when they begin to sink. Then take them out immediately. Hard water, especially if chalybeate, spoils the color. To boil green in hard water, put a teaspoonful of salt or wormwood into the water when it boils, before the vegetables are put in.

Vegetable Marrow (to Boil or Stew)—This excellent vegetable may be boiled as asparagus. When boiled, divide it lengthwise into two, and serve it on toast accompanied by melted butter; or when nearly boiled, divide it as above, and stew gently in gravy. Care should be taken to choose young ones not exceeding 6 in. in length.

Spinach—Wash and pick your spinach very carefully; drop into boiling water and cook 15 minutes. Drain thoroughly through a colander, then chop quite fine. Return to the stove, add 1 tablespoonful of butter, pepper and salt to taste; put in a vegetable dish and garnish with hard-boiled eggs.

To Stew Celery—Wash, cut into neat slices, removing the green parts. Plunge into sufficient boiling water to cover it, adding salt in the proportion of a dessertspoonful to 2 qts. of water.

Stew until tender, serve in a dish with white sauce over. The celery may be stewed in stock if preferred.

How to Serve Potatoes—A great deal of ignorance is often shown by excellent housekeepers in putting potatoes on the table. The usual practice of bringing them up in a porcelain or deep dish, with a close-fitting cover, would utterly destroy the best potatoes in ten minutes, however carefully cooked. They should be placed in a wooden dish, or served in a porcelain dish with towels above and below to absorb the moisture.

Potatoes (Stuffed)—Five medium-sized potatoes, ½ oz. butter, 1 tablespoonful grated cheese, pepper, salt, and yolk of 1 egg.

Bake the potatoes in their skins, and when done cut off a small slice from one end, scoop out the inside, and rub through a wire sieve. Add to it ½ an oz. butter, 1 tablespoonful grated cheese, pepper, salt, and the yolk of an egg. Mix well, refill the skins, fit on the slices which were cut off, and put into the oven again for 10 minutes before serving.

Lyonnaise Potatoes—Into a saucepan put a large lump of butter and a small onion finely chopped, and when the onion is fried to an amber color, throw in slices of cold boiled potatoes, which must be thoroughly stirred until they are turning brown; at this moment put in a spoonful of finely chopped parsley, and as soon as it is cooked, drain through a colander, so that the potatoes retain the moisture of the butter, and many particles of parsley.

Potatoes (Sautees au Beurre)—Cut with a vegetable cutter into small balls about the size of a marble; put them in a stewpan with plenty of butter and a good sprinkling of salt; keep the saucepan covered, and shake it occasionally until they are quite done, which will be in about an hour.

Savory Potatoes — Peel as many potatoes as you require. Put them in a pie-dish with a good-sized onion chopped fine, ½ teaspoonful of dried sage powdered, 2 oz. butter and 2 tablespoonfuls olive oil, and enough water to cover the bottom of the dish. Pepper and salt to taste, and bake in a slow oven.

Saratoga Potatoes—Saratoga chips are prepared in thin, paper-like slices (a slaw-cutter is required for this), and crisped, but not burned, in hot fat. The secret of preparing them properly lies in cutting them first in the thinnest slices possible, and soaking them for at least 1 hour in cold salt water. The last process draws the starch out of the potato, and is positively necessary to success. Before frying, each piece must be thoroughly dried on a towel. When taken out of the fat they may be drained on a sieve a moment in a very hot oven or over the stove, then cooled quickly in a draft.

Potatoes (Virginia Style)—Slice as for Saratoga potatoes, but thicker, soak in cold water, drain, and fry in covered pan with 2 or 3 spoonfuls of suet, turning brown before they are put in. Salt and pepper thickly while cooking at leisure.

Potato Pancakes—Grate 8 large potatoes in a porcelain bowl, add 4 eggs, not beaten, 1 teacup flour, ½ cup milk and 1 even teaspoonful baking-powder; stir all lightly together, taking care not to beat the eggs up too much. Fry the same as ordinary pancakes, but longer, to cook thoroughly.

Potatoes (a la Creme)—Slice the potatoes as for frying and soak in cold water ½ hour. Parboil in a frying-pan, pour the water off and let them stand on the fire uncovered till the steam is driven off; brown 1 spoonful of butter or fat and pour over them a minute after; then cover the potatoes with milk, in which they should boil till done. Salt and pepper while cooking and watch lest they burn. There should be just milk enough when done for a creamy gravy, thickened by the starch of the potatoes.

Fried Potatoes—American fried potatoes are boiled first and sliced cold to fry. They need a large frying-pan, or are best cooked on a griddle which has surface enough to let each piece lie next to the fire. Slice them ¼ inch thick so as not to break in turning. Salt and pepper, and when the large spoonful of fat is turning brown in the hot pan lay them in, brown quickly and turn with a broad griddle-cake turner.

Potatoes of secondary quality are best pared and sliced raw and fried. The heat of boiling fat, which is stronger than that of boiling water, drives the water out of them. Small, deep kettles are sold for frying, and the lard is kept in them and used many times over.

Potato Balls—Four large, mealy potatoes, cold; mash them in a pan with 2 tablespoonfuls of melted butter, a pinch of salt, a little pepper, 1 tablespoonful of cream and the beaten yolk of 1 egg; rub it together for about 5 minutes, or until very smooth; shape the mixture into balls about the size of a walnut or small rolls, dip them into an egg well beaten and then into the finest sifted bread crumbs; fry them in boiling lard.

Potato Croquettes—Boil 1 dozen potatoes, strain and mash well; add 2 yolks of eggs, beat well and season. When cold, mould in the shape of long corks and dip each piece into beaten eggs; then roll in crumbs and fry a golden brown.

Scalloped Potatoes — Cut 4 good-sized boiled or steamed potatoes into dice; put 2 tablespoonfuls of butter in a frying-pan, and, when melted, add 2 tablespoonfuls of flour; mix until smooth; then add 1 pint of milk, and stir continually until it boils; add a teaspoonful of salt and 3 dashes of black pepper; take from the fire. Put a layer of this sauce in the bottom of a baking-dish, then a layer of potatoes, then another layer of sauce, and so on until all is used, having the last layer sauce; sprinkle the top lightly with bread crumbs and put in the oven for 15 minutes to brown. Serve in the dish in which it was baked.

Cabbage (a la Cauliflower)—Cut the cabbage fine as for slaw; put it into a stewpan, cover with water and keep closely covered; when tender, drain off the water, put in a small piece of butter with a little salt, ½ cup cream, or 1 cup milk. Leave on the stove a few minutes before serving.

Farci (or Stuffed Cabbage)—Veal stuffing, slices of sausage meat, gravy.

Cook the cabbage in salt and water sufficiently to open the leaves, and insert between them layers of ordinary veal stuffing and slices of sausage meat; then tie it securely round with thread to prevent the meat falling out. Replace in the stewpan and cook briskly at first, then simmer till completely tender. Serve in the same manner as ragout — that is to say, with a little gravy poured over the whole.

Cabbage for Roast Meats—Take a medium-sized head of well-bleached cabbage and chop very fine. Put in a stew-kettle with just enough water to cook it tender, which will depend somewhat upon the strength of the fire. Add salt to taste, and when it is cooked, if any water remains in the kettle, drain it off; then add a lump of butter the size of a small egg, a little white pepper and enough milk to just about cover the cabbage. This is a very delicate way of preparing this vegetable, and it goes nicely with roast meats.

Stuffed Cucumbers—Boil large, firm cucumbers until tender, scoop out the seeds and in their place put a filling made of fine bread crumbs, well-seasoned, and a little minced ham or veal. Fasten the cucumbers together with tapes and put in a baking-pan with a large cupful of water and a good-sized piece of butter; baste frequently and bake ½ hour. A delicate and delicious dish.

Aux Pommes—One red cabbage, 3 or 4 moderate-sized apples, butter, salt, pepper, walnut, cloves, vinegar, red currant jelly, flour.

Put a red cabbage into a saucepan, having previously washed it well; just cover it with water; peel, halve and core 3 or 4 moderate-sized apples and add them to the cabbage with a piece of butter about the size of a walnut, salt, pepper and 3 or 4 cloves. Cook very gently over a slow fire for 3 hours. When ready to be served, add 1 dessertspoonful of vinegar, the same quantity of red currant jelly, and sufficient flour to thicken the sauce; pour over and send to table.

Tomatoes (Baked)—Half dozen tomatoes, bread crumbs, pepper, salt and butter.

Cut ½ dozen tomatoes in halves, remove the pips, and fill the insides with a mixture of bread crumbs, pepper and salt in due proportions; place a small piece of butter on each half tomato and lay them close together in a well-buttered tin; bake in a slow oven about ½ hour and serve. They may be eaten hot or cold.

Tomatoes (Stuffed)—Tomatoes, shallot, butter, bread crumbs, ham, parsley, sweet herbs, pepper, salt and toast.

Dip some tomatoes in hot water, peel them, cut them in halves and remove the pips; rub a baking-sheet with shallot, butter it well, and lay the tomatoes in it, filling each half with the following composition: Two parts bread crumbs, 1 part ham finely minced, and, according to taste, parsley and sweet herbs also finely minced, and pepper and salt. Put a small piece of butter on each half tomato, and bake them 15 minutes. Have ready some round pieces of buttered toast; on each of these put a half tomato, and serve.

Tomatoes with Macaroni—Tomatoes, butter, pepper, salt, bay leaf, thyme, stock or gravy, macaroni.

Cut up a quantity of tomatoes and remove from each the pips and watery substance; put them into a saucepan with a small piece of butter, pepper, salt, a bay leaf, and some thyme; add a few spoonfuls of either stock or gravy; keep stirring on the fire until they are reduced to a pulp, pass them through a hair sieve, and dress the macaroni with this sauce and plenty of Parmesan cheese freshly grated.

Tomato Fritters—One quart stewed tomatoes, 1 egg, soda, flour, lard.

Use 1 quart stewed tomatoes, 1 egg, 1 small teaspoonful of soda; stir in flour enough to make a batter like that for griddle cakes. Have some lard very hot on the stove, drop the batter in, a spoonful at a time, and fry.

Tomatoes (Broiled)—Large, fresh tomatoes, butter, pepper, salt, sugar, an eggspoonful of made mustard.

In buying tomatoes for broiling, be careful to select large and fresh ones. Do not pare them. Slice in pieces about ½ inch thick and broil them for a few minutes upon a gridiron; while they are broiling, prepare some hot butter in a cup, seasoning with pepper, salt, an eggspoonful of made mustard and a little sugar; when the tomatoes are finished, dip each piece into this, and then dish (the dish must be hot). If any of the seasoning remains, heat to the point of boiling and pour over the dish; serve immediately. This is a very nice dish if cooked well.

Onions (Boiled)—Skin them thoroughly. Put them to boil; when they have boiled a few minutes, pour off the water and add clean, cold water, and then set them to boil again. Pour this away and add more cold water, when they may boil till done. This will make them white and clear and very mild in flavor. After they are done, pour off all the water and dress with a little cream, salt and pepper to taste.

Spanish Onions (a la Grecque)—Peel off the very outer skins and cut off the pointed ends; put the onions in a deep dish, and put a piece of butter and a little salt and pepper on the place where the point has been cut off, cover with a plate or dish, and let them bake for not less than 3 hours. They will throw out a delicious gravy.

Peas and Carrots—Take 5 or 6 good-sized carrots, scrape, cut into small dice and soak for 1 hour in cold water, then boil for 1½ hours in three times enough water to cover them, with salt to season well. When thoroughly cooked, drain off the water and add 1 can of peas, well drained, and 1 cup of milk, and place on the stove again. Mix a heaping teaspoonful flour with a good heaping teaspoonful butter, and add when the milk boils up. Cook for a few moments, adding salt to taste, and a good shake of pepper.

Onions (Stuffed)—Very large Spanish onions, cold fat pork or bacon, bread crumbs, pepper, salt, mace, cream, 1 egg, butter, juice of $\frac{1}{2}$ lemon, browned flour, milk.

Wash and skin the onions. Lay in cold water 1 hour. Parboil in boiling water $\frac{1}{2}$ hour. Drain, and while hot extract their hearts, taking care not to break the outside layers. Chop the inside thus obtained very fine, with a little cold fat pork or bacon. Add bread crumbs, pepper, salt, mace, and wet with 1 or 2 spoonfuls cream or milk. Bind with a well-beaten egg, and work into a smooth paste. Stuff the onions with this; put into a dripping-pan with a very little hot water, and simmer in the oven for 1 hour, basting often with butter melted. When done, take the onions up carefully, and arrange the open ends upwards in a vegetable dish. Add to the gravy in the dripping-pan the juice of $\frac{1}{2}$ lemon, 4 tablespoonfuls cream or milk, and a little browned flour wet with cold milk. Boil up once, and pour over the onions.

Mushrooms—The cook should be well acquainted with the different sort of things called by this name by ignorant people, as the deaths of many persons have been caused by carelessly using the poisonous kinds. The eatable mushrooms first appear very small and of a round form on a very small stalk. They grow very fast, and the upper part and stalk are white. As the size increases the under part gradually opens and shows a fringy fur of a very fine salmon color which continues more or less till the mushroom has been picked, when it turns to a brown. The skin can be more easily peeled from the real mushroom than the poisonous kind. A good test is to sprinkle a little salt on the spongy part or gills of the sample to be tried; if they turn black they are wholesome, if yellow they are poisonous. Give the salt a little time to act before you decide as to their quality.

Mushrooms (Stewed)—Gather those that have red gills; cut off that part of the stem which grew in the earth; wash, and take the skin from the top; put them in a stewpan with some salt; stew them till tender; thicken with 1 spoonful butter and browned flour.

Mushrooms (Broiled)—Prepare them as directed for stewing. Broil them on a griddle; and when done, sprinkle salt and pepper on the gills, and put a little butter on them.

Mushrooms (Baked)—Pare the top and cut off part of the stalk, wipe them carefully with a piece of flannel or cloth and a little fine salt. Then put them into a baking-dish and put a piece of butter an each mushroom. Sprinkle with pepper to taste and bake for 20 minutes or ½ hour. When done serve on a hot dish with the gravy poured over the mushrooms.

Mushrooms (a la Creme)—Cut the mushrooms in pieces, and toss them over a brisk fire in butter seasoned with salt, a very little nutmeg, and 1 bunch herbs. When they are done enough, and the butter nearly all wasted away, take out the herbs, add the yolk of 1 egg beaten up in some good cream; make very hot and serve.

Parsnips—Boil, mash, season with butter, pepper and salt, make into little cakes: roll in flour and brown in hot lard.

Parsnips (American Fashion)—Scrape and boil some parsnips, then cut each lengthwise in four, and fry them very brown, and dish in pairs.

Parsnips (Buttered)—Boil the parsnips tender and scrape; slice lengthwise. Put 3 tablespoonfuls butter into a saucepan, with pepper, salt, and a little chopped parsley. When heated put in the parsnips. Shake and turn until mixture boils, then lay the parsnips in order upon a dish, and pour the butter over them and serve.

Parsnips (Fricasseed)—Scrape them, boil in milk till they are soft; then cut them lengthwise into pieces 2 or 3 inches long, and simmer in a white sauce, made of 2 spoonfuls broth, 1 piece mace, $\frac{1}{2}$ cupful cream, a piece of butter, and some flour, pepper and salt.

Cucumbers (to Dress)—Pare and cut the cucumbers into slices as thin as a wafer (it is better to commence at the thick end). Place in a glass dish; sprinkle with salt and pepper and pour over it $\frac{1}{2}$ teacupful vinegar and 3 tablespoonfuls salad oil. This is a nice accompaniment to boiled salmon, and is useful in concocting a salad. It is also an excellent garnish for lobster salad.

Cucumbers (Stewed)—Three large cucumbers, a little butter, $\frac{1}{2}$ pint brown gravy, a little flour.

Cut the cucumbers lengthwise, removing the seeds. Have the pieces a convenient size for the dish they are served in. Plunge them into boiling water with a little salt. Allow it to simmer for 5 minutes. Put the gravy into another saucepan, and when the cucumbers are done, remove from the water and place in the gravy, and allow to boil until they are tender. If there should be a bitter taste, add 1 teaspoonful granulated sugar. Dish carefully, skim the sauce, and pour over the cucumbers.

Cucumbers (Fried)—Pare cucumbers, cut in slices, press the slices upon a dry clean cloth; dredge with flour; have ready a pan of boiling oil or butter, put the slices into it, and keep turning them until they are brown; remove them from pan and lay upon a sieve to drain. Serve on a hot dish.

Lima Beans—One qt. of Lima beans, wash and soak them over night in cold water; simmer over a slow fire 4 hours; then add salt, pepper, butter (the size of an egg), and 1 qt. of sweet milk; boil for $\frac{1}{2}$ hour.

Lima and Butter Beans—Shell and place in cold water, allowing them to remain in the water $\frac{1}{2}$ hour; then put into boiling water with a little salt and cook until tender; drain, and butter and pepper.

French Beans—Top, tail and string the beans *carefully;* cut in pieces about an inch long; lay in cold salt water for a quarter of an hour; drain, plunge into saucepan of boiling water and boil until tender; drain in a colander; dish with lump of of butter stirred in.

Turnips (Boiled)—Pare and cut in pieces; put them into boiling water well salted, and boil until tender; drain thoroughly and then mash and add a piece of butter, pepper and salt to taste, and a small teaspoonful of sugar; stir till they are thoroughly mixed, and serve hot.

Turnips (German Recipe)—Six large turnips, 3 oz. butter, $\frac{1}{2}$ pint weak stock, 1 tablespoonful flour, pepper and salt.

Heat the butter in a stewpan, pare and cut the turnips into pieces the size of dice and season with pepper and salt; then place in the hot butter, toss over the fire for 5 minutes, add the stock and simmer gently until the turnips are tender. Brown the flour with a little butter; add this to the turnips and simmer 5 minutes. Boiled mutton may be served with this dish.

Turnips (a la Creme) — Small new turnips; peel and boil in salted water; drain thoroughly. Melt 1 oz. butter in a saucepan, add to it a dessertspoonful of flour, pepper, salt, grated nutmeg, and a small quantity of milk or cream; put in the turnips; simmer gently a few minutes, and serve.

Turnips (a la Maitre) — Boil some small new turnips as in the preceding recipe; drain them thoroughly, and melt some butter in the saucepan; put the turnips in, give them a toss or two, add a little chopped parsley, pepper and salt, a sqeeeze of lemon juice, and serve.

Carrots (to Boil) — Place upon the stove two quarts of warm water with a tablespoonful of salt; bring to a boil; wash and scrape six young carrots, remove any black specks, cut in halves, plunge into the boiling water, and boil until tender; drain, and serve upon a hot dish.

Carrots (Stewed) — Wash and scrape the carrots; split the largest. Then whiten them in hot water, and drain them on a sieve; then boil them in weak broth, with salt; then put some butter in a saucepan, with a dessertspoonful of flour; stir it and brown it. Add the carrots to it, broth and pepper. Stir, and let all simmer together.

Salsify (Boiled) — Scrape the roots, cut them in short lengths, and throw them into vinegar and water as they are being done. Boil them till tender in salted water, drain them, toss them into a saucepan with a piece of butter, a little lemon juice, and some minced parsley, add salt and serve.

Egg Plant (Baked) — Parboil 15 minutes. Then make a triangular cut in the top; remove the piece and take out the seeds. Let it lie for an hour in water, to which a tablespoonful of salt has been added. Make a stuffing of one cup of crumbs, two ounces of salt pork, and an onion chopped fine, 1 teaspoonful salt, $\frac{1}{2}$ teaspoonful pepper and nutmeg mixed; wet with half a cup of boiling water or stock, and fill the egg plant, tying a string around it to keep the piece in place. Bake an hour, basting often with a spoonful of butter in a cup of water.

Hotch-Potch — Put a pint of peas into a stewpan with a quart of water, and boil them until they will pulp through a sieve; then take the lean end of a loin of mutton, cut into small pieces and put it into a stewpan with a gallon of water, the carrots and turnips cut into small pieces, and a seasoning of pepper and salt; boil it until all the vegetables are quite tender, put in the pulped peas and a head of celery (or lettuce) and one onion, sliced; let it boil 15 minutes and serve.

Green Corn (Stewed) — Having cut the corn from the cob, put into boiling water and allow to stew $\frac{1}{4}$ hour; remove nearly all the water and cover with milk, and allow to stew until tender; before dishing, roll some pieces of butter in flour and mix with the corn, adding a little pepper and salt; give one boil and serve.

Green Corn (Boiled) — Strip off all the outer husks, allowing the innermost to remain; remove the silk and re-cover the ear with the remaining husk, secure with a piece of thread, plunge into boiling salted water, and boil ½ hour. Cut off stalks and dish upon a napkin.

Green Corn (Roasted) — Open the husks, remove the silk, close the husks closely, and roast in the ashes of a wood fire until tender; serve with butter, pepper and salt. This is frequently eaten in camp.

Summer Squash — Pare the outer rind, remove the seeds, quarter, and lay in ice water 10 minutes; put into boiling water, a little salt, and cook until tender; press all the water from them. Mash smooth, season with butter and pepper and serve not.

Winter Squash — Proceed as above, allowing more time to cook; before putting into the boiling water, allow it to soak in cold water 3 hours.

Cauliflower (Boiled) — Wash in 2 or 3 waters. Cut off the end of stalk and outer leaves, allow to lie in salt and water 5 minutes, plunge into boiling salted water, and boil 15 or 20 minutes; drain and serve hot.

Cauliflower (Fried) — Pick out all the green leaves from a cauliflower, and cut off the stalk close; put it head downward in a saucepan full of boiling salted water; do not overboil it; drain it on a sieve, pick it out into small sprigs, and place in a deep dish with plenty of vinegar, whole pepper, salt, and a few cloves. When it has lain about an hour in this drain it, dip in batter, and fry in hot lard to a golden color.

Cauliflower (Scalloped) — Choose a cauliflower of medium size, boil it 20 minutes; put into a saucepan 1 oz. butter, ½ gill milk, and 1 oz. bread crumbs; add cayenne and salt to taste, and stir till the bread has absorbed the milk and butter. Beat an egg and add this to the sauce, but be sure that it does not simmer after the egg has been added. Butter a flat tin dish, take off the fine leaves of the cauliflower and place them all round on it, break up the flower carefully and lay in the center, making it as high as possible; pour the sauce over this, sprinkle a few breadcrumbs on the top, and bake 10 minutes.

Green Peas (to Keep)—Shell, and put them into a kettle of water when it boils; give them 2 or 3 warmings only, and pour them in a colander; when the water drains off, turn them out on a table covered with cloth, and pour them on another cloth to dry perfectly; then bottle them in wide-mouthed bottles, leaving only room to pour clarified mutton-suet upon them an inch thick, and for the cork. Resin it down, and keep it in the cellar or in the earth. When they are to be used, boil them till tender, with a piece of butter, a spoonful of sugar, and a little mint.

Green Peas (Stewed)—Put a quart of peas, a lettuce and an onion, both sliced, a piece of butter, pepper, salt, and no more water than hangs round the lettuce from washing; stew them 2 hours very gently. When to be served, beat up an egg and stir it in, or a little flour and butter. Some think a teaspoonful of white powdered sugar is an improvement.

Green Peas (a la Francaise)—Put the required quantity of peas necessary for your dish into a perfectly clean and bright stewpan, with some water and butter in the following proportions: For every pint of peas 1 gill water and 1 oz. butter. When this is thoroughly amalgamated, add a little bouquet, tied together, of parsley, also salt, pepper, and another ½ oz. butter, then 8 or 9 small white onions, and a whole lettuce. Simmer the whole well for an hour, or more if the peas and other vegetables are not completely tender. The time, in fact, must be regulated according to the judgment of the cook. When done, take out the bunch of parsley, the lettuce, and the onions, which are very serviceable for hashes, stews or soups, even when used as above. The peas, when once cooking, must not be touched by a spoon or a fork, as it would bruise them and spoil the appearance of the entrée, but well tossed constantly to prevent them sticking to the stewpan, always kept briskly simmering, but never boiling; otherwise they will harden.

Baked Beans — Beans should be carefully looked over, thoroughly washed and put to soak over night in about twice their bulk of water. Put them in the kettle soon after breakfast the next morning, add about as much water as at first, place them where they will not burn, and let them cook slowly and without stirring until about ten o'clock. Then add half a pound of salt pork thoroughly washed and cut across the rind in small dice. Place the pork on the top of the beans and let it boil for an hour or more. Then lift the meat out, turn the beans and liquor into a baking-pan, press the water down until only the rind is out of the pork, and bake in a slow oven for several hours.

Asparagus — After scraping the stalks to cleanse them, place them in a vessel of cold water. Tie them up neatly into bundles of about 25 heads each, then place them in a saucepan of boiling water, sprinkling a handful of salt over it. When it is boiling remove any scum there may be; the stalks will be tender when they are done; they will take about twenty minutes or half an hour; be careful to take them up the minute they are done; have ready some toast, dip it in the liquor in which the asparagus was boiled; dish upon toast, and serve with a boat of melted butter.

Asparagus in Ambush — Two bunches of asparagus, 8 stale biscuits (or rolls may be used), 4 eggs, about ½ pint of milk, butter the size of an egg, flour, pepper and salt to taste.

Take the green tops of the two bunches of asparagus, boil them tender and mince finely. While they are boiling, take the biscuits or rolls, divide them, keeping the top half for a cover; place them all in the oven to crisp; make the milk hot, and then pour in the eggs, beaten; stir over the fire until it thickens, then add the butter rolled in flour, and lastly add the asparagus; spread the rolls with this mixture, put on the tops and serve hot.

Asparagus and Eggs — Twenty-five or 30 heads of asparagus, good rich butter, salt and pepper, 5 or 6 eggs.

Boil the asparagus (after cutting them into pieces of about ½ an inch) for 15 minutes; take a cup of rich butter and put it into a saucepan; drain the asparagus, and put it with the butter; heat them to a boil, seasoning with pepper and salt, and then pour into a buttered baking-tin or dish; break five or six eggs neatly over the surface of this, sprinkle with pepper and salt, and put it in the oven until the eggs are set nicely. Serve hot.

Asparagus Pudding — Green tops of 2 bunches of asparagus, 3 tablespoonfuls of prepared flour, 4 or 5 well-beaten eggs, 2 dessertspoonfuls of melted butter, 1 teacup of milk, 1 pinch of soda, pepper and salt to taste.

Boil the asparagus and when cool chop finely; take the eggs, butter, pepper and salt, and beat them up together, then put in the flour; stir the soda into the milk, and add gradually; lastly put in the asparagus. Put this into a buttered mould with a lid, or if it has no lid tie it down tightly with a floured cloth; boil for two hours. When done, turn out on a dish, and pour melted butter round it.

Artichokes, with White Sauce — Wash them well, peel and shape them to a uniform size; throw them into boiling salted water, and let them boil fifteen to twenty minutes; drain them at once thoroughly; put them on a dish and serve with the following sauce poured over them: Mix over the fire 1½ oz. butter with a tablespoonful of flour; add ½ pint of boiling water, white pepper and salt to taste; stir till the sauce thickens, then take the saucepan off the fire, and stir in the yolks of two eggs, beaten up with the juice of a lemon, and strained.

Artichokes, with Cream — Prepare and parboil them as in the preceding recipe; then put them into a saucepan with a due allowance of white sauce, and let them finish cooking in this, adding at the last a small quantity of cream and grated nutmeg.

Artichokes, with Gravy — Prepare them as above, cutting them to the size of pigeon's eggs. Parboil them for ten minutes, drain them and toss them in a saucepan with a piece of butter; then add a small quantity of good clear gravy and a dust of pepper. Let them simmer very gently till wanted.

Artichokes (Mashed) — Salted water, a piece of butter, a little cream, white pepper, nutmeg and salt.

Wash, peel and boil them in salted water; drain, and pass them through a hair sieve. Squeeze all the water out of the pulp; put it into a saucepan, and work it on the fire, with a piece of butter and a little cream, adding white pepper, nutmeg and salt if necessary. When quite hot and sufficiently dry, serve.

Artichokes (Fried) — Wash, peel and parboil them whole for ten minutes, then cut them in strips the size of a little finger. Flour them carefully, and fry in hot lard; or they may be dipped in batter and fried. Serve piled up on a napkin.

Artichokes (Stewed) — Mince a couple of shallots and fry them in plenty of butter; put in the artichokes parboiled and cut into pieces, moisten with a little stock, season with pepper, salt, and a little lemon juice; lastly add some finely-chopped parsley, and let the whole stew gently till quite done. A small quantity of Parmesan cheese may be added.

Artichokes, au Gratin — Wash, peel and boil them whole; cut them in slices the thickness of a cent. Butter a dish previously rubbed with a shallot; arrange the slices on it, strew over them some baked bread-crumbs, seasoned with pepper, salt and a little powdered thyme, add a squeeze of lemon, put a few pieces of butter on the top, and bake for ten or fifteen minutes.

Pumpkin (Stewed) — Halve, remove the seed, pare and slice neatly. Soak for an hour in cold water; then place in a saucepan of boiling water on the fire. Allow it to stew gently until it falls to pieces. Stir often. Then take it out, drain, squeeze, and rub through a colander, then put it back in the saucepan, adding two dessertspoonfuls of butter, pepper and salt to taste. Stir quickly, and when nearly boiling dish, adding more pepper if required.

Pumpkin (Baked) — Cut the pumpkin into quarters; remove seeds, cut into slices lengthwise about half an inch thick. Place in a baking-dish suitable for the purpose and arrange in layers about three slices deep. Put a very little water in the bottom of the dish and bake very slowly until done (the water must have evaporated). It takes a long time to bake. Butter the slices on both sides and dish.

SALADS.

ANY cold vegetable can be made into salad. I wonder that any one eats asparagus hot, it is so good cold. Scrape it thoroughly, boil till soft (about thirty-five minutes), lay away carefully till cold, then make French or mayonnaise dressing and pour over.

In making tomato salad scald the tomatoes first, then plunge in cold water, and the skins will come off easily. Set on the ice till cold, slice with a sharp knife, set the slices back upon each other so that each tomato shall retain its shape.

Avoid breaking the lettuce leaves, and see that they are perfectly drained. Arrange the lettuce prettily in a glass dish, and set the vegetable that accompanies it in the center. Never add the dressing till it comes to the table.

Sliced bananas or oranges with lettuce and mayonnaise dressing are delicious. The former are, however, a trifle rich for any one whose digestion is only moderately reliable.

In making cucumber salad, if the cucumbers are quite young, cut up one with the rind on. The peculiar slight bitter taste is very welcome to the palate of an epicure. Cucumbers should always lie in very salt ice water for a while to make them crisp and should not be seasoned until the last minute. Flabby cucumbers are as mean as cold batter-cakes.

Lettuce Salad (1)—Take 4 or 5 heads of cabbage lettuce, remove all outside leaves and cut off the stalks close; then cut each head apart into 4 or 5 "quarters," that is, cut through the stalk and then tear the rest. Put 4 tablespoonfuls olive oil into the salad bowl, with 2½ tablespoonfuls tarragon vinegar, pepper and salt according to taste, and beat the mixture with a fork some minutes; then put in the lettuce and keep it turning over swiftly for 5 minutes, adding a small pinch of mint, chopped as finely as possible.

Lettuce Salad (2)—Wash 2 heads lettuce, dry them thoroughly and break the leaves or cut them into convenient pieces. Put the yolks of 2 hard-boiled eggs into a basin with a teaspoonful of French mustard, pepper and salt to taste, and a tablespoonful of oil; work the mixture into a smooth paste, and add consecutively 3 tablespoonfuls of oil, 1 of tarragon and 1 of plain vinegar; then a little chervil, garden cress and tarragon finely chopped. Stir the mixture well, and lastly add the lettuce; turn it or work it well. Garnish the top with hard-boiled eggs.

Herring Salad—Heat through by turning on the stove 3 well-smoked herring, then tear off the heads and pull the skin away; split, take out the backbones, and cut up into small bits, or to shred them is better. Put in a salad bowl, add 1 small chopped onion, 2 hard-boiled chopped eggs, and 1 boiled potato; cut fine with a teaspoonful of chopped parsley; season with a teaspoonful of salt, 1 of pepper, 3 tablespoonfuls vinegar and 2 of oil. Mix well, and, if you have it, decorate with a boiled beet.

Potato Salad—Slice 8 cold boiled potatoes; dispose between the slices 1 silver-skinned onion cut quite fine; beat together 3 parts oil and 1 part, more or less, according to the strength of it, tarragon vinegar, with pepper and salt to taste. Pour this over the potatoes, and strew over all a small quantity of any of the following: Powdered sweet herbs, mint, parsley, chervil, tarragon or capers, or a combination of them all, finely minced.

Cold Slaw—To 1 quart cut cabbage, use ½ cupful cream (either sweet or sour), 2 tablespoonfuls vinegar, 2 eggs, 1 teaspoonful salt, 1 tablespoonful butter and a little pepper; put the vinegar on to boil, add the beaten eggs to the cream and butter, and stir these into the boiling vinegar till the butter is melted and the whole mass smooth and creamy; add the pepper and salt and pour, while hot, over the cabbage; when cold, it is ready for use.

Lobster Salad—Clean thoroughly some lettuce, endives and beetroots, cut them up and mix them with the following dressing: 4 tablespoonfuls oil, 2 tablespoonfuls vinegar, 1 teaspoonful made mustard, the yolks of 2 eggs, ½ teaspoonful anchovy sauce, and cayenne and salt. Pick out from the shells the flesh of 1 hen lobster, cut into well-shaped pieces, put ½ in the salad and garnish with the rest, also with the whites of 2 hard-boiled eggs chopped fine, and the yolks mixed with the coral and rubbed through a sieve.

Sardine Salad—Allow 3 sardines for each person; bone and fillet these, carefully removing all the skin, and set them aside until required. Boil 2 eggs for 3 minutes; shell them and break them up in your salad bowl with a spoon; mix with them a teaspoonful each French mustard and essence of anchovies, the strained oil from the tin of sardines with as much Lucca oil as will make 3 tablespoonfuls in all; add Chile, shallot, and good malt vinegar to taste (vinegar varies so much in acidity that it is difficult to specify the exact proportion). Cut up some nice crisp lettuce, and mix it well with the dressing, but only just before it is to be served. Put a little heap of mustard and cress in the center of the salad, with a whole red capsicum upon it. Arrange the sardines round, and outside these a border of mustard and cress, dotted here and there with thin slices of red capsicums.

Cabbage Salad—Chop fine 1 firm head cabbage, sprinkle lightly in a dish. Make the dressing as follows: Stir together 2 raw eggs, 1 teaspoonful white pepper, 1 teaspoonful mustard, a little salt, 2 teaspoonfuls melted butter and 1 cupful strong vinegar. Put this mixture in a small vessel set inside of another full of boiling water and stir 5 minutes; set aside to cool, then beat in ½ cup cream, pour over the cabbage and serve.

Tomato Salad—Peel some good-sized tomatoes, not over-ripe, cut them in slices and remove the pips, lay them in a dish with oil and vinegar in the proportion of 2 to 1, sprinkle pepper and salt over them according to taste, a few leaves basil finely minced, and some onions very finely sliced. They should lie in the sauce for a couple of hours before serving.

Egg Salad—Boil ½ dozen eggs until hard, shell them and cut them into slices and pour over them, while hot, the following dressing: Put in a soup plate ½ teaspoonful salt and ¼ teaspoonful black pepper, add 3 tablespoonfuls olive oil and stir until the salt is dissolved. Stir in 1 tablespoonful tarragon vinegar, 1 tablespoonful onion juice and 1 tablespoonful chopped parsley. Stand away in a cold place for 2 hours, and serve.

Chicken Salad — Draw, singe and boil the chicken. When done and perfectly cold remove the skin and cut the meat into dice. If you want it very nice, use only the white meat; save the dark for croquettes. After you have cut it set it away in a cold place until wanted. Wash and cut the white parts of celery into pieces about a half inch long, throw them into a bowl of cold water and also set them away until wanted. To every pint of chicken allow two-thirds of a pint of celery and a cup and a half of mayonnaise dressing. When ready to serve, dry the celery and mix with the chicken; dust lightly with salt, white pepper or cayenne, then mix with it the mayonnaise. Serve on a cold dish garnished with white celery tips. One cup of white cream may be added to every ½ pint of mayonnaise when ready to use it. It makes the dressing lighter, with less of the oily flavor.

Celery Salad — Two heads of celery, 1 tablespoonful salad oil, ½ teacup vinegar, a teaspoonful granulated sugar, pepper and salt to taste.

Well wash the celery, removing any unsightly parts, lay in iced water until wanted; then cut into pieces about an inch in length. Season with remaining ingredients, mix well and serve in salad bowl.

Red Cabbage Salad — One small red cabbage, 1 small dessertspoonful salt, ½ pint vinegar, 1½ dessertspoonfuls oil, a little cayenne pepper.

Secure a nice fresh cabbage, remove the outer leaves and cut the cabbage into nice thin slices, then mix in the above ingredients and allow to stand for two days, when it will be fit for use. This salad will keep good for several days.

Rev. Sidney Smith's Recipe for Salad Dressing.

" Two boiled potatoes, strained through a
    kitchen sieve,
Softness and smoothness to the salad give;
Of mordant mustard take a single spoon —

Distrust the condiment that bites too soon,
Yet deem it not, thou man of taste, a fault
To add a double quantity of salt;
Four times the spoon with oil of Lucca crown,
And twice with vinegar procured from town;
True taste requires it, and your poet begs
The pounded yellow of two well boiled eggs.
Let onions' atoms lurk within the bowl,
And, scarce suspected, animate the whole;
And, lastly, in the flavored compound toss
A magic spoonful of anchovy sauce.
Oh! great and glorious, and herbaceous treat,
'Twould tempt the dying anchorite to eat;
Back to the world he'd turn his weary soul,
And plunge his fingers in the salad bowl."

Boiled Salad Dressing — Put ½ pint of milk in a double boiler, and when it boils stir in 2 tablespoonfuls corn starch moistened with a little cold water. Stir until it boils and thickens, then add the yolks of 3 eggs, well beaten; stir a minute longer, take it from the fire and add a tablespoonful of butter, a teaspoonful of salt, and stir in by degrees 2 tablespoonfuls of vinegar. Stand it aside to get cold, and it is ready to use.

French Dressing — Half teaspoonful salt, the same of pepper, mixed with 1 tablespoonful vinegar or lemon juice; add 2 tablespoonfuls oil; heat together briskly and pour over the salad; before putting on the different plates toss and turn the salad so that it may mix well.

Mayonnaise Dressing — The yolks of 2 well-beaten eggs, 1 teaspoonful each of sugar and salt, ½ teaspoonful pepper and 1½ teaspoonfuls mustard; mix well. Heat to the boiling point 1 cupful vinegar and a lump of butter the size of a pigeon's egg; while this is heating beat to a stiff froth the whites of the 2 eggs and mix with the other ingredients, beating well; then add the boiling vinegar, a few drops at a time. Set on the fire 2 or 3 minutes, stirring constantly; beat a few minutes after removing it from the fire, and set away to cool.

PICKLES.

ENAMELED kettles should always be used in preference to those of brass or copper, as the verdigris produced by the vinegar on these metals is extremely poisonous. For some pickles use cold vinegar, as in boiling most of the strength is lost by evaporation. For French beans, broccoli, cauliflower, gherkins, etc., it is better to heat the vinegar, for which the following process is recommended: Put the vinegar and spice in a jar, cover it tightly, let it simmer on the back of the stove. Shake occasionally. Pickles should never be put into glazed jars, as salt and vinegar penetrate the glaze and produce a poison.

Glass or stone jars are preferable to any other; a small piece of alum in each jar will make the pickles firm and crisp. One tablespoonful of sugar to each quart of vinegar will be found a very great improvement to all pickles. Always use the very best cider vinegar.

Pickled Onions—In the month of September, choose the small, white, round onions, take off the brown skin, have ready a very nice tin stew-pan of boiling water, throw in as many onions as will cover the top; as soon as they look clear on the outside, take them up as quick as possible with a slice, and lay them on a clean cloth, cover them close with another, and scald some more, and so on. Let them lie to be cold, then put them in a jar, or glass, or wide-mouthed bottles, and pour over them the best vinegar, just hot but not boiling. To each gallon of vinegar add 1 oz. allspice and 1 oz. black pepper. When cold, cover them. Should the outer skin shrivel, peel it off. They must look quite clear.

Pickled Walnuts—Fifty walnuts (seasonable for pickling early in July). To each pint of vinegar allow 1 oz. black pepper, ½ oz. allspice, and ½ oz. bruised ginger.

Prick the walnuts with a fork, and put them in a brine (composed of 1 lb. salt to each quart of water). Let them remain in this 9 days, changing the brine three times. Put them in the sun until they turn black; put them into jars, allowing sufficient room to cover them with vinegar; boil (or scald) vinegar and spices in the above proportions. Cover closely and keep dry. They can be used in 6 weeks.

Jumbo Pickle—Chop fine a head of cabbage, sprinkle with salt; let it remain thus for 12 hours: then mix 1 onion finely minced with the cabbage; drain through a colander; add a good quantity of pepper and celery seed. Put it in a jar and cover with vinegar. Ready for use in 3 days.

Red Cabbage—Slice into a colander, and sprinkle each layer with salt; let it drain 2 days, then put it into a jar, and pour hot vinegar enough to cover, and put in a few slices of red beetroot. Observe to choose the purple red cabbage. Those who like the flavor of spice will boil it with the vinegar. Cauliflower cut in branches, and thrown in after being salted, will look a beautiful red.

Green Tomato Pickles—One peck green tomatoes; 1 dozen large white onions, sliced crosswise to fall into rings; 1 oz. whole pepper, 1 oz. white mustard seed, 1 oz. cloves, 1 oz. allspice. Put a layer of tomatoes and onions, then a good handful of salt, etc., till all are in a stone jar; then put a plate on top and weight down over night; in morning squeeze out with hand and put to boil in kettle, putting in layers with spice; add 1 gal. best malt vinegar, and boil 20 minutes. Put in stone jar to keep.

Damson and Cherry Pickles—To 5 pounds fruit put 3 pounds sugar, 1 qt. vinegar, 4 tablespoonfuls or $2'$ oz. cinnamon, 1 tablespoonful cloves, as much mace. Put the fruit in a jar. Boil the vinegar, sugar and spices, and pour them boiling hot on the fruit. Tie the spices loosely in muslin before boiling.

Ripe Peaches Pickle—Pare them and drop them in vinegar that has been boiled, with 1 teacup sugar to 1 qt. vinegar, and 12 cloves, a teaspoon of whole allspice and three large sticks of cinnamon. Always tie spice in cheese cloth or muslin loosely before boiling.

Picalilli—Small cucumbers, button onions, small bunches of cauliflower, carrots, ginger, grapes, strips of horse-radish, radishes, bean pods, cayenne pods, 4 qts. best vinegar, 4 tablespoonfuls salt, mustard and flour, 2 tablespoonfuls ground ginger, pepper, allspice and turmeric.

The brine for this pickle is made by putting a pint of rock salt into a pail of boiling water. Put the vegetables for pickling into the brine and cover tightly to prevent the steam escaping. Allow them to stand a night and a day. Change the brine a second time and allow them to remain the same length of time. The second brine may be used a second time if skimmed and scalded. Choose pickles from the brine of an equal size and of various colors. Great taste may be displayed in the arrangement of the pickles when putting them in bottles. To 4 qts. of best vinegar add the spices. Simmer these together (the mustard and turmeric must be blended together with a little vinegar before they are added to the liquor); when the liquor is on the point of boiling, pour into a vessel; cover tightly. When sufficiently cold pour into the bottles containing the pickle, and make air-tight. It will be ready for use in 5 or 6 months.

Beets — Vinegar, beets, 2 oz. whole pepper, 2 oz. allspice to every gallon of vinegar.

Carefully remove all dirt from the beets. Let them simmer in boiling water for 1½ hours, then take them out and leave to cool. Boil the remaining ingredients for 10 or 15 minutes and leave to cool. When cold pour it over the beets (which you have previously pared and cut into thin slices). Make air-tight and they will be ready for eating in a week or 10 days.

EGGS.

ABOUT one-third of the entire weight of an egg may be regarded as nitrogenous and nutritious matter; a greater proportion than that of meat, which is rated at only from 25 to 28 per cent. The lightest way of cooking eggs is by poaching. The yolk of an egg alone is better for invalids and will be frequently relished when the white would be rejected. When cream cannot be procured for coffee the yolk of a soft-boiled egg is a very good substitute. To prevent the juice of fruit pies from soaking into the bottom crust wash the crust over with beaten egg before putting in the fruit. When making frosting in warm weather, set the whites of the eggs on ice a short time before using. If the eggs you have to use for frosting are not quite as fresh as you could desire, a pinch of salt will make them beat stiffer. The white of an egg, an equal quantity of cold water and confectioners' sugar sufficient to make the required consistency, make a nice frosting which, as it requires no beating, is very easily made. When beaten eggs are to be mixed with hot milk, as in making gravies or custards, dip the hot milk into the beaten eggs a spoonful at a time, stirring well each time until the eggs are well thinned, then add both together. This will prevent the eggs from curdling.

The whites or yolks of eggs which are left after making cake, etc., will keep well for a day or two if set in a cool place—the yolks well beaten and the whites unbeaten. Whites or yolks of eggs may be used with whole eggs in any cake or other recipe calling for eggs, counting two yolks or two whites as one egg. When eggs are cheap and plentiful in summer, wash all those used in cooking before breaking, save the shells, and when a quantity are dry, crush them fine; beat half a dozen eggs well and stir them into the shells. Spread them where they will dry quickly, and when thoroughly dry, put in a thin cotton bag and hang in a dry place. In the winter, when eggs are dear, a tablespoonful of this mixture put in a cup, a little cold water poured over it and left to stand over night, or for half an hour or so in the morning before breakfast, will answer every purpose of a whole egg in settling coffee.

It is a good plan in testing eggs to apply the tongue to the large end of the egg, and if perfectly fresh the egg will feel warm, or they can be held to the light and if perfectly clear will be good; or try them in water—the freshest will sink first. Always keep them in a cool place.

Poached Eggs (on Toast)—If the eggs are not new-laid they will not poach well. Fill a shallow saucepan with water and salt, add a little vinegar, a few peppercorns, and some leaves of parsley. When the water is on the point of boiling (it should never be allowed to boil) break 2 or more eggs into it (according to the size of the pan); when done, take them out carefully, lay them on slices of hot buttered toast, and serve.

Poached Eggs (on Ham Toast)—Make some buttered toast, cut in pieces of uniform shape, spread over them a small quantity of grated ham, put a poached egg on each piece of toast, and serve hot.

Poached Eggs and Minced Chicken—Free some remnants of fowl from skin, etc., mince them with an equal quantity of ham or tongue, as well as a small quantity of truffles or mushrooms, all finely minced; toss the whole in a saucepan with a good-sized piece of butter mixed with a pinch of flour, add white pepper, salt and powdered spices to taste, and moisten with a little white stock; lastly, stir in, off the fire, the yolk of 1 egg beaten up with the juice of $\frac{1}{2}$ lemon, and strained; serve within a border of bread sippets fried in butter, and dispose the poached eggs on the top.

Stuffed Eggs—Cut some hard-boiled eggs in half, mince the yolks with a few olives and capers, some anchovies thoroughly washed, a few truffle trimmings, and a little tarragon, add some pepper, and fill each half egg with this mixture. Pour some liquefied butter over, and warm them in the oven. Then place each half-egg on a round sippet of bread fried in butter to a light yellow color, and serve.

Buttered Eggs—Break 4 eggs into a basin, and beat them well; put 2 oz. butter and 2 tablespoonfuls cream into a saucepan; add a little grated tongue, pepper and salt to taste; when quite hot, add the eggs, stir till nearly set, then spread the mixture on pieces of buttered toast and serve.

Fried Eggs—Melt a piece of butter in a small frying-pan, break 2 eggs in it carefully so as not to break the yolks; when nearly set, slip them out on a hot dish, pour the butter over them, sprinkle with salt and pepper, and serve.

Fried Eggs with Tomatoes — Melt a small piece of butter in a saucepan, put to it a small quantity of French tomato sauce, add pepper and salt to taste, and when quite hot turn it out on a dish, disposing on it the eggs fried in butter.

Scrambled Eggs — Beat up 4 eggs, with salt and pepper to taste; put 1 oz. butter into a saucepan; directly it is melted put in the eggs, and keep constantly stirring with a spoon until they are nearly set, adding at the last a little finely-minced parsley.

Scrambled Eggs with Asparagus — Parboil some asparagus points, cut the size of peas, in salted water, drain them and toss them in a little butter till quite hot. Scramble some eggs as in the preceding recipe, and, when nearly set, add the asparagus points instead of the parsley.

Scrambled Eggs with Tomatoes — Beat up 4 eggs with a tablespoonful of French tomato sauce, or one large tomato, peeled, freed from pips, and chopped small, and proceed as above.

Scrambled Eggs with Onions — Chop coarsely 2 slices of Spanish onion; put them into a saucepan with plenty of butter, and when they are thoroughly cooked, without having taken any color, throw in 4 eggs beaten together with pepper and salt to taste; keep on stirring till the eggs are nearly set, and then serve.

Scrambled Eggs with Fish — Pick out the meat of any remnants of fish, such as salmon, turbot, cod, haddock or whiting, and with a silver fork break it up small; take 2 tablespoonfuls of this and 4 eggs; beat the whole together with a little pepper and salt to taste, and a little parsley finely minced; then proceed as in first recipe.

Scrambled Eggs with Ham — Beat up a tablespoonful of grated ham with 4 eggs, and pepper to taste; put them into a saucepan with a piece of butter, and stir till nearly set.

Scrambled Eggs with Cheese — Put 4 eggs and 3 tablespoonfuls of Parmesan cheese into a basin with a sprinkling of pepper; beat all together, and proceed as in the first recipe, omitting the parsley.

Scrambled Eggs (on Toast) — Any of the foregoing may be served on slices of buttered toast, but if so served they must be even less set, at the time of serving, than when served plain; or neat bread sippets, fried in butter, may be served round them.

Sippets (Fried) — Cut out of a loaf slices from $\frac{1}{4}$ to $\frac{3}{8}$ in. thick, shape them into triangles or arrowheads, all of a size; put some butter in a frying-pan, and when quite hot lay the sippets in it; turn them frequently, adding more butter as it is wanted, and taking care that they are all fried to the same golden color. A readier way, but producing not so nice a sippet, is to lay the pieces of bread in the frying-basket, and dip it in a saucepan full of boiling fat. They must afterwards be laid in front of the fire to drain.

Omelet (Plain) — Beat up 3 or 4 eggs with 1 dessertspoonful of parsley very finely minced, and pepper and salt to taste; put a piece of butter, the size of an egg, into a frying-pan; as soon as it is melted pour in the omelet mixture, and, holding the handle of the pan with one hand, stir the omelet with the other by means of a spoon. The moment it begins to set cease stirring, but keep on shaking the pan for a minute or so; then with the spoon double up the omelet and keep shaking the pan until the under side of the omelet has become of a golden color. Turn it out on a hot dish and serve.

Omelet—One-half cupful sweet milk, 1 of fine bread crumbs, 2 eggs, whites and yolks beaten separately, ½ teaspoonful chopped sage or a whole one of parsley; pepper and salt to taste. Mix well, adding the white of egg last; melt a lump of butter in a large frying-pan, pour in your mixture, and, taking a silver knife, gently lift it away from the sides as the egg "sets." Then put in the oven until it browns on top, fold over and serve on a hot plate.

Omelet — The following makes a delicious omelet for four persons: Break 5 eggs, putting the whites in one dish and the yolks in another. Beat the yolks to a froth, then add a saltspoonful of salt, a little pepper, a heaping tablespoonful of finely chopped parsley, and 5 tablespoonfuls of cream. Beat all together for a moment and then add the whites, previously beaten to a stiff froth. Mix gently together and pour immediately into a hot spider containing a level tablespoonful of melted butter. Cook rather slowly in order not to burn the bottom before the omelet is cooked through, and when nicely browned fold half over. Place on a warm platter, and serve immediately.

Omelet (Savory) — Beat up 3 or 4 eggs with ½ shallot very finely minced, some parsley similarly treated, and a very small pinch of powdered sweet herbs; add pepper and salt to taste; then proceed as above.

Omelet (Cheese) — Beat up 3 eggs with 1 or 2 tablespoonfuls grated Parmesan cheese. Cook as above, and serve with some more grated cheese strewn over the omelet.

Omelet (Tomato) — Equal parts of sliced onions and tomatoes peeled and freed from pips;

chop them both coarsely. Fry the onions in butter. When cooked, without being colored, add the tomatoes, with pepper and salt, and keep stirring the mixture on the fire till it forms a sort of puree. Make a plain omelet, and insert this in the fold on dishing it.

Omelet (Mushroom)—Parboil a small quantity of button mushrooms, slice them small, and stew them just long enough to cook them in a small quantity of either white or brown sauce (see *Sauces*); then use as in preceding recipe.

Omelet (Fish)—Beat up 3 eggs with a quantity equal in bulk to 1 egg of the remnants of any cold fish (salmon or turbot) finely shredded with a fork, a pinch of minced parsley, pepper and salt to taste.

Omelet (Oysters)—See "Oysters."

CATSUPS, ETC.

Lemon Catsup — One doz. lemons, ½ breakfast cupful white mustard seed, 1 eggcupful turmeric and white pepper, ½ eggcupful cloves and mace, ½ a *small* teacupful white sugar, 1 saltspoonful cayenne, ½ a small teacupful horse-radish, ½ a small teacupful salt, 4 shallots.

Finely grate the rind of lemons, pound the spices in a mortar, grate the horse-radish. Thoroughly blend these ingredients, then sprinkle the salt over all, extract the juice from the lemons and add to the mixture. Allow to stand in a cool place for 3 or 4 hours. Boil in an enameled kettle 30 minutes, pour into a stone jar, cover tightly. Stir every day for 14 days, then strain, bottle and seal.

Tomato Catsup (1)—To 1 peck tomatoes allow 1 tablespoonful salt, mace, black pepper, cloves powdered, and 1 of celery seed; a teaspoonful cayenne, ½ lb. tin of mustard.

Make a small incision in each tomato, put into an enameled saucepan, and boil until perfectly soft, and the pulp dissolved; work through a colander, then through a hair sieve. Place upon the stove, adding the remaining ingredients (the celery seed must be confined in a muslin bag), and boil 6 hours. Stir occasionally for the first 5 hours, and all the last hour. Pour into a stone jar; allow to stand from 12 to 14 hours in a cold place. When perfectly cool add a pint of strong vinegar, remove the celery seed, bottle, cork, and seal. Keep in a dry, dark place.

Tomato Catsup (2)— Ripe tomatoes; to every lb. of juice add a pint of vinegar, a dessertspoonful sliced garlic, a small teaspoonful of salt and white pepper.

Place a number of ripe tomatoes in a jar; cover and bake till tender. Strain and work through a sieve, and add the above ingredients. Pour into a stewpan and boil until the ingredients are perfectly soft. Work through the sieve a second time, and to every pound squeeze the juice of three lemons. Boil again until of the thickness of cream. Set aside to get cold. Bottle, cork and seal, and keep in a dry, dark place.

Walnut Catsup — Wash the shells of walnuts, bruise them slightly, put them with salt in a stone jar for two or three weeks until they ferment, then boil them up, strain off the liquor, add to every 2 quarts 1 oz. each of allspice, ginger, black pepper, cloves and mace; boil the whole 1 hour; let it cool, bottle it, and tie a bladder over the corks.

French Mustard — One quart of brown mustard seed, 1 handful each of parsley, chervil, tarragon and burnet, 1 teaspoonful of celery seed, cloves, mace, garlic, salt to taste, enough vinegar to cover.

Put the whole into a basin with enough vinegar to cover the mixture. Let it steep 24 hours, then pound it in a marble mortar. When thoroughly pounded pass it through a fine sieve; add enough vinegar to make the mustard of the desired consistency, and put into jars for use.

Mint Vinegar — A wide-mouthed bottle or bottles. Fill them (loosely) with nice, fresh mint leaves, then add good vinegar to fill the bottle or bottles; cork well. Allow to stand for two or three weeks, and at the expiration of this time strain into fresh bottles and cork securely. Useful when mint is not in season.

Herbs (to Dry)—Gather the herbs for drying before they begin to flower. Free from dirt and dust and tie in bunches, having previously removed the roots. Dry in the oven or before the fire; in either case, dry *quickly*, as the flavor is better preserved by quick drying. Upon no consideration allow them to burn. Tie up in paper bags and hang in a dry place. N. B.—Take care to gather the herbs on a dry day.

Herb Powder (for winter use)—Take 2 oz. each of winter savory, sweet marjoram, lemon, thyme, lemon peel and 4 oz. of parsley.

Thoroughly dry the herbs and take off the leaves. Grind to a powder and pass through a sieve. Dry the lemon peel and pound as finely as possible, then mix all together thoroughly. Keep in glass bottles tightly corked.

Parsley (to keep for winter use)—Take fresh bunches of parsley; plunge into boiling water slightly salted, boiling for 3 or 4 minutes. Remove from the water, and drain dry very quickly before the fire, and put in bottles for use. Soak in tepid water 5 minutes when required for cooking.

Garlic Vinegar—Steep an ounce of garlic in 2 quarts of the best white vinegar; add a nutmeg scraped. This vinegar is much esteemed by the French.

A Useful Catsup—One and one-half pints mushroom catsup, ½ pint walnut pickle, 2 tablespoonfuls Chile vinegar, 2 shallots.

Take 1½ pints of freshly-made mushroom catsup, peel the shallots and add them to the catsup and allow it to simmer for 10 minutes, then add the pickle and vinegar and boil again for 10 minutes. Stand in a cool place, and when perfectly cold, bottle, and, having placed a small piece of shallot in each bottle, cork and set by for use.

FORCEMEATS.

WHETHER in the form of stuffing-balls or for patties, forcemeat makes a considerable part of good cooking, by the flavor it imparts to the dish it accompanies, and considerable care should be taken in preparing it. It is often the case, at many excellent tables where everything else is well done, to find very bad forcemeat or stuffing.

Forcemeat (for Fowls)—Quarter lb. suet, 2 oz. ham, the grated rind of ½ lemon, a dessertspoonful of minced parsley, 1 tablespoonful of minced sweet herbs, cayenne, salt, grounded mace to taste, 7 oz. bread-crumbs, 2 eggs.

Cut the ham into small, thin strips, chop the suet finely, also the lemon peel; add the seasoning, then the crumbs; thoroughly blend, and after the eggs have been well beaten add to the other ingredients, and it is ready for use. If wished, for balls, fry a golden brown in hot lard.

Forcemeat (Balls for Soup)—Eight oz. bread-crumbs, sweet herbs, salt and pepper to taste, 5 eggs.

Have the bread-crumbs finely grated, and the herbs pounded to a powder; sprinkle with pepper and salt; boil 2 eggs hard and mince finely. Mix all together and bind the whole with the remaining eggs. Form into little balls, and drop into the soup about 5 or 6 minutes before serving.

Oyster Forcemeat (for Roast or Boiled Turkey)—Two teacupfuls bread-crumbs, ½ oz. minced suet, 1 tablespoonful savory herbs a sprinkle of nutmeg, salt and pepper to taste, 2 eggs, 1½ doz. oysters.

Have the bread-crumbs and suet finely minced, add the herbs chopped as finely as possible; mix well. Having opened the oysters, beard and chop them (not very small) and add to the other ingredients; beat up the eggs, and with the hand work all together thoroughly; it is then ready for use.

Sage and Onion Stuffing (for Pork, Ducks, Geese) — Two teacups bread-crumbs, 4 large onions, 12 sage leaves, butter the size of an egg, pepper and salt to taste, 1 egg.

Peel and boil the onions for 5 or 6 minutes, dip the sage leaves in the same water (while boiling) for a minute or two, then chop finely; add seasoning, the bread-crumbs and butter; beat up the egg, and work all together. It is then ready for use

Quenelles—Moisten 1 cup of finely-crumbed bread with 3 tablespoonfuls of milk, add 2 tablespoonfuls of melted butter and as much finely-chopped meat (stewed veal or fowl, cold) as you wish, work in 1 well-beaten egg, and season all thoroughly with salt and pepper; flour your hands, and shape mass into round balls, rolling them into flour when shaped. Bring to a boiling heat in a saucepan 1 large cup well-seasoned gravy, drop in the balls, and boil fast for about 5 minutes. The gravy can be thickened and poured over them, or they can be rolled in flour or cracker crumbs, and fried in lard or butter.

BREAD AND CAKES.

OF all articles of food, *bread* is perhaps the most important; therefore it is necessary to be well acquainted with the quality of the ingredients and the art of making it. Flour ought to be a few weeks old before being used, and care must be taken to keep it perfectly dry. It is of the utmost importance to purchase only the best quality of flour, for it is the truest economy. Patent flour should be more scantily measured than winter wheat, as it contains more gluten. Do not place the sponge or dough too near the fire, as some cooks are liable to do in cold weather, or the quality of bread will be endangered. The proper heat should be gentle and equal for fermentation. Care must also be taken to mix and knead (brisk and long kneading will fully repay for the trouble) when it has reached the point for either. Bread requires a brisk oven, and should take about 1 to $1\frac{1}{2}$ hours to bake. The cook must be guided by experience as to the exact degree of heat.

The secret of biscuit-making is precision and dispatch. Laggards and lazy people are not successful biscuit-makers. The best cooks always say they simply throw their biscuits together, and certainly they are not long about it. The cause of success is that biscuits begin to bake before the effervescent qualities of the powder or soda are exhausted.

For good *cake* (as in bread) it is of great importance to use no ingredients but those of the finest quality. The flour must be dry and sifted. It will be found a good plan, after purchasing currants, to wash in three waters, pick and dry in a cloth. Then look them carefully over, discarding any stone, stalk or grit. Lay before the fire or in the sun to dry. Put by in a jar, and they will always be ready for use. Eggs should be well whisked, the whites and yolks beaten separately and strained. Butter must not be allowed to oil. Lemon peel should be cut thinly as possible. Sugar should be finely powdered. When soda is used it is a good plan to dissolve it in warm water. When all the ingredients are mixed, vigorous and patient beating will greatly add to the lightness of the cake. The heat of the oven is of great importance for cakes, especially those that are large. If the oven is not very quick, the batter will not rise. Should you fear scorching, put some paper over the cake. If the fire is not long enough lighted to have a body of heat, or if it has become slack, the cake will be heavy. To know when the cake is done, take a broom straw and pierce into the very center, draw it instantly out, and if the least stickiness adheres, put the cake back immediately and shut the oven.

Fine sugar should be used in cake-making to give good texture. Cake pans with movable bottoms are more easily managed, for they may be placed on a teacup and the rim will fall off. The milk in cake-making should be added slowly. Butter the tins, then flour them.

Yeast (1) —A double handful of hops, ½ doz. potatoes, ½ gal. water, 1 or ½ cupful ginger, small cup flour, a cup brown sugar, ½ cup salt, a cupful good yeast.

Allow the hops and potatoes to boil together in ½ gallon of water till done; strain and mash the ginger, then add remaining ingredients, excepting the yeast. Let stand until cool, then add the yeast. Next day cork up tight in a jug.

Yeast (2) — Two oz. hops, 1 gal. water, a handful salt, 1 lb. best flour, 3 lbs. potatoes.

Boil the hops in a gallon of water for ½ hour; strain it, and let it cool down to the heat of new milk; then put the salt and moist sugar; beat the flour with some of the liquor, and then mix all together. Two days after, add the potatoes, boiled and then mashed, to stand for 24 hours; then put into bottles, and it will be ready for use. Stir it frequently while making, and keep it warm. Before using, shake the bottle up well. It will keep in a cool place for two months.

To Make Baking-Powder — Take ½ lb. of ground rice, ¼ lb. carbonate of soda, 2 oz. tartaric acid. Mix them very thoroughly and smoothly. Allow 1 teaspoonful to 1 lb. of flour.

ANOTHER WAY—Mix well together 6 oz. carbonate of soda, 4 oz. tartaric acid, 1 teaspoonful salt, and 1 teaspoonful powdered sugar.

Home-Made Bread (1) — Four lbs. flour, 1 tablespoonful solid brewers' yeast, 1½ pints lukewarm milk and water, salt.

Put the flour into a deep pan, sprinkle a little salt into it, hollow out the middle with a wooden spoon (taking care to leave the bottom of the pan well covered with flour). Next take the yeast, which has been made solid by liberally mixing with cold water, and allowing it to settle 24 hours. Then proceed to pour the yeast into the hole in the flour, and mix with it as much flour as is round about it until it is of the consistency of thick batter; be careful there are no lumps. Sift plenty of flour over the top, cover with a clean cloth, and set it where the air is warm and equal. Allow to stand an hour or a little longer, and if the yeast has broken through it is then ready to be made into dough. Pour into the sponge the remaining milk and water. Mix into it as much of the flour as you can with the spoon. Now take plenty of the flour, sprinkle on the top of the leaven, and proceed to knead briskly, and when perfectly free from the lumps and it does not adhere to the hands, it may be covered with a cloth and left to rise a second time. When it begins to crack, which will be in about ¾ of an hour, it can be formed into loaves and baked. In forming the loaves divide in two and make up the shape and size required, and with a sharp knife make incisions in the top of each loaf. If baked in tins, take care to grease them before using. When baked stand on end to allow the steam to evaporate. The dough can be made without making a sponge (if desired) by mixing the yeast with the best part of the milk and water, and after a little salt has been added, proceed to work up the whole of the flour at once, and then act as above. The dough will soften in the rising, so it should be made firm at first.

Home-Made Bread (2) — Put the flour into a large pan; mix in a dessertspoonful of salt; make a hole in the middle, and pour in the yeast (half a teacup of yeast to two quarts of flour), with about a pint of water or milk (which use warm in winter, and cold in summer), not mixing in all the flour; then put a blanket, or towel, over the pan, and let it stand to rise near the fire, in winter. This is "putting bread in sponge." When it has risen, mix all the flour with the sponge; knead it well, and let it stand 2 hours till quite light. Then mold the dough on a board till elastic, and put the loaves into greased or floured baking-tins; prick them two or three times through with a fork; let them rise again for a quarter of an hour, and bake them in a quick oven.

White Bread — Sponge, a pan of buttermilk, or sour milk, flour, 1 teacupful of yeast.

For the sponge take a pan of buttermilk or sour milk which has just turned thick. Put it on the stove and scald. When the curd is well separated from the whey strain or skim it out. Let the whey cool until it will not scald, then stir in the flour, beating thoroughly. It should be about as thick as batter for griddle cake. Sweet milk, or even water, may be used as a wetting for the sponge, if good sour milk or buttermilk cannot be had. But fresh buttermilk is, perhaps, the best of all. When the sponge is about milkwarm, beat in a teacupful of yeast. One teacupful of the yeast is enough for three ordinary white loaves, one loaf of brown bread and a tin of rolls. The sponge should be made at night. Let it stand until morning. Unless the weather is very cold, it is not necessary to put it near the fire. In the morning, when the sponge is light, take out enough for your loaf of brown bread. Mix the remainder with flour, taking care not to put in too much, as that will make the bread dry and hard. Knead ½ an hour. The whiteness and delicacy of the bread will be much increased by thorough kneading. Put the dough away to rise again. When it is light, if you wish to make rolls, save enough of the dough for that purpose. Make the remainder into loaves. Set them away to rise. When light, bake.

Fine Wheat Bread—For 4 loaves: 1 pint water, 1 cake compressed yeast, 1 tablespoonful salt, 1 tablespoonful sugar.

Mix hard or sitff, as for baking, at first. Set it to rise; when it has risen, knead it again; let rise again. If mixed in the morning — which is the best when using compressed yeast — after the second rising, put it in the pans, and it will be ready to bake in the afternoon. Be sure and knead it when it first rises, and then let it rise again.

Plain Bread — Half lb. white flour, 1 teaspoonful baking-powder, a pinch of salt, ¼ pint milk and water.

The simplest way of making bread in small quantities is as follows: Take ½ lb. of white flour, and, while in a dry state, mix in thoroughly a small teaspoonful baking-powder and a pinch of salt. Then add about a quarter of a pint of milk and water, or water alone; knead it as quickly as possible, and put immediately into a very hot oven; the whole secret of making light bread after this fashion lies in attention to these last rules. If the oven is well heated, it will rise almost directly, and it should be baked until the outside is quite crisp and hard. I generally knead mine into the desired shape, but they can be baked in tins if preferred. For brown bread, I use three parts of brown and one of white flour, and a little extra baking-powder; also adding a little more water, if necessary, to mix it.

Rice and Wheat Bread—One lb. rice, 2 quarts water, 4 lbs. flour, 4 large spoonfuls yeast, salt.

Simmer 1 lb. rice in 2 quarts water till it becomes perfectly soft; when it is of a proper warmth, mix it extremely well with 4 lbs. flour, and yeast and salt as for other bread; of yeast about 4 large spoonfuls; knead it extremely well; then set it to rise before the fire. Some of the flour should be reserved to make up the loaves. If the rice should require more water, it must be added, as some rice swells more than others.

French Bread — One-fourth pk. fine flour, yolks of 3 and whites of 2 eggs, salt, ½ pt. good yeast, ½ pt. milk.

With ¼ pk. fine flour mix the yolks of 3 and whites of 2 eggs, beaten and strained, a little salt, ½ pt. of good yeast, that is not bitter, and as much milk, made a little warm, as will work into a thin, light dough; stir it about, but don't knead it; have ready 3 wooden quart dishes, divide the dough among them, set to rise, then turn them out into the oven, which must be quick. Rasp when done.

Sago Scones — Take a teacupful of sago and soak in cold water, put it on with 1 qt. sweet milk, let it boil till quite dissolved, stirring occasionally; add a little salt, then pour out on the baking-board and let it lie till cold. Mix up with flour, taking care not to make it too stiff; roll out quite thin, cut to the size wanted, and bake.

Brown Bread — One pt. corn meal, 1 pt. rye flour, 1 tablespoonful brown sugar, 1 teaspoonful salt, 2 of baking-powder, 1 tablespoonful lard, ¾ pt. milk.

Sift together the above ingredients, excepting the lard and milk; rub into the mixture the lard and add the milk. Mix into a batter-like cake and bake 1 hour. Protect it with brown paper if it should brown too fast at first.

Boston Brown Bread — One and one-half cups yellow cornmeal, 1 cup rye flour, 1 cup Graham flour, 1 cup New Orleans molasses, 2 full teaspoonfuls baking-powder and a little salt.

Mix all to a consistency of a thick batter with either milk or water, pour into a buttered mold or tin pail, and steam in boiling water 4 hours.

Rye Bread—Two cups Indian meal, scalding water, a small cup of white bread sponge, sugar, salt, a teaspoonful of soda, rye.

Make the Indian meal into a thick batter with scalding water; when cool add the white bread sponge, a little sugar and salt, and the soda, dissolved. In this stir as much rye as is possible with a spoon; let it rise until it is very light; then work in with your hand as much rye as you can, but do not knead it, as that will make it hard; put it in buttered bread tins, and let it rise for about 15 minutes; then bake it for $1\frac{1}{2}$ hours, cooling the oven gradually for the last 20 minutes.

Corn Bread—Take 2 cups flour, 1 cup cornmeal, $\frac{1}{2}$ cup sugar, 1 egg, 2 tablespoons butter, $1\frac{1}{2}$ cups sweet milk, 3 teaspoons baking-powder; quick oven.

Corn Bread Steamed—Three cups cornmeal, boiling water, 1 cup flour, 2 cups sour milk, 1 cup molasses, 1 teaspoonful soda, a little salt.

Scald 2 cups cornmeal with boiling water, add another cup of meal and remaining ingredients. Mix thoroughly, and steam 3 hours.

Bread Omelet—A teacupful bread-crumbs, 1 teacupful sweet milk, 6 eggs, pepper, salt, a small lump of butter.

Let the milk come to the boiling point, pour it over the crumbs and let it stand a few minutes; take the eggs, beat them well and pour into the bread mixture; season with salt and pepper and a small lump of butter; when thoroughly mixed, butter a hot skillet and pour the mixture in, letting it fry slowly; when one side is browned nicely, cut it in squares and turn. Serve at once.

Barley Scones—Take 1 quart sweet milk and put it on in a pan with a little salt. When it boils, stir in barley-meal until it is as thick as porridge, pour out on the baking-board and let it stand till cold. Knead up with barley-meal to a nice soft dough, roll out and cut to the size wanted, and bake.

Rusks—One pint new milk, 2 tablespoonfuls yeast, flour, 2 tablespoonfuls butter, 1 cupful sugar, 2 eggs, 2 saltspoonfuls salt.

Rusks require a longer time for rising than ordinary rolls or biscuits. Prepare a sponge of the yeast, milk and flour (sufficient to make a thin batter) and allow it to rise all night. Next morning add eggs, butter and sugar (which must have been mixed well together), salt and flour enough to produce a soft dough. Shape into neat balls of equal size, place in a pan and allow to rise until very light. Flavor according to taste. Bake in a quick, steady oven till of a pretty brown color, glaze with the yolk of an egg and sprinkle with powdered white sugar.

Butter Rolls—One quart flour, $\frac{1}{2}$ teaspoonful salt, 2 teaspoonfuls baking-powder, 1 egg, 1 pint milk, 1 tablespoonful lard.

Sift the flour, salt and baking powder together, rub in the lard cold, then add the egg and milk; mix as soft as possible. Roll it out $\frac{1}{2}$ inch in thickness and cut with a plain, round biscuit cutter. Dip them in melted butter, fold $\frac{1}{3}$ of each piece over the remainder and bake in a quick oven for 15 minutes.

Vienna Rolls—One quart milk, $\frac{1}{2}$ teaspoonful salt, 3 teaspoonfuls baking-powder, 1 tablespoonful lard, 1 pint milk.

Mix into a dough easily to be handled without sticking to the hands; turn on the board and roll out to the thickness of $\frac{1}{2}$ inch, cut it out with a large cake cutter, spread very lightly with butter, fold one-half over the other and lay them in a greased pan without touching. Wash them over with a little milk, and bake in a hot oven.

French Rolls—Two eggs, ½ pint milk, 1 tablespoonful yeast, 1 oz. butter.

Beat 2 eggs and mix with them ½ pint milk and a tablespoonful yeast; knead well and let stand till morning; then work in 1 oz. butter; mold into small rolls, and bake at once.

Cinnamon Rolls—Save a piece of dough, about enough to make a loaf, out of your bread before you make it out for baking. To this dough add 1 egg, 1 tablespoonful butter, ½ cupful milk, 1 cupful sugar and 1 tablespoonful cinnamon. Work thoroughly, make into rolls and set to rise. When almost done draw to the oven-door, spread lightly with butter and cover with a mixture made of 3 tablespoonfuls butter and 1 tablespoonful cinnamon. Good hot or cold.

Parkin—One and three-fourths lbs. flour, ½ lb. oatmeal, 4 oz. butter, 2 lbs. molasses, a teacupful milk, 6 teaspoonfuls baking-powder, 1 dessertspoonful ground ginger.

Mix the dry ingredients well together, warm the molasses with milk (do not make it *hot*) and mix the whole. Bake in a well-buttered tin for 1 hour. Cut into squares before taking out of the tin. It should be 1½ inches thick.

Breakfast Rolls—Two quarts flour, 1 tablespoonful sugar, 1 tablespoonful butter, ½ cupful yeast, 1 pint scalded milk, or water if milk is scarce, and a little salt.

Set to rise until light; then knead until hard and set to rise, and when wanted make in rolls; place a piece of butter between the folds, and bake in a slow oven.

Graham Biscuits—One quart water or milk, butter the size of an egg, 3 tablespoonfuls sugar, 2 tablespoonfuls baker's yeast, and a pinch of salt; enough white flour to use up the water, making it the consistency of batter cakes, and as much Graham flour as can be stirred in with a spoon.

Set it away till morning; in the morning grease pan, flour hands; take a lump of dough the size of a large egg; roll lightly between the palms; let them rise 20 minutes and bake in a tolerably hot oven.

Sally Lunn—Two lbs. flour, ½ lb. butter, 3 eggs, 1 pint milk, ½ gill yeast, salt according to taste.

Cut up the butter in the flour, and with your hands rub it well together; beat the eggs; add them gradually to the flour alternately with the milk; stir in the yeast and salt. Bake it in an earthen mold, or iron pan, 1 hour.

Breakfast Muffins—Three eggs, 1 breakfast-cupful milk, 1 tablespoonful butter melted, 1 tablespoonful sugar, a pinch of salt, 2 heaped teaspoonfuls baking-powder.

Whisk the eggs and mix with the milk; put the melted butter into a basin with the above ingredients, mixing in flour enough to make a batter. Bake in round tins, and when almost done wash the top of each with a feather dipped in milk.

Graham Muffins—One quart Graham flour, 2 teaspoonfuls baking-powder, a piece of butter the size of a walnut, 1 egg, 1 tablespoonful sugar, ½ teaspoonful salt, milk enough to make a batter as thick as for griddle cakes.

Bake in muffin-rings, about 20 minutes, in a quick oven.

Rice Muffins—Two cups cold boiled rice, 1 pint flour, 1 teaspoonful salt, 1 tablespoonful sugar, 2 teaspoonfuls baking-powder, ½ pint milk, 3 eggs.

Mix into a smooth and rather firm batter, and bake as above.

Oatmeal Muffins — One cup oatmeal, 1½ pints flour, 1 teaspoonful salt, 2 teaspoonfuls baking-powder, 1 pint milk, 1 tablespoonful lard, 2 eggs.

Mix smoothly into a batter rather thinner than for cup cakes. Fill the muffin-rings ⅔ full and bake in a hot oven.

Crumpets—Two eggs, 1 teaspoonful each of salt and sugar, 4 teaspoonfuls baking-powder, 1 qt. milk, 3 pts. flour.

Mix into a stiff batter and bake in greased muffin rings on a hot greased griddle.

Waffles—Two eggs, 1 pt. milk, ½ oz. butter, ½ gill yeast, salt to taste, and flour enough to form a thick batter.

Warm the milk and butter together; beat the eggs, and add them by turns with the flour; stir in the yeast and salt. When they are light, heat your waffle-irons and butter them, pour in some of the batter, and brown them on both sides; butter them, and serve them with or without sugar and cinnamon.

Waffles (without Yeast)—Three eggs, 1 pt. milk, 1 teaspoonful butter, as much flour as will make a batter.

Beat the yolks and whites separately; melt the butter, and while lukewarm stir it into the milk; whisk the yolks very light, add to them the milk and flour alternately; beat it well; lastly stir in the whites, which should be whisked very dry. The batter should not be beaten after the whites are in. Grease your waffle-irons after having heated them; fill them nearly full of the batter, close them, and place them over the fire; turn the irons so as to bake the waffle on both sides. When done, take it out and butter it. These must be baked the moment they are mixed.

Rice Waffles —One gill rice, 3 gills flour, salt to taste, 1 oz. butter, 3 eggs, as much milk as will make it a thick batter.

Boil the rice in very little water until it is soft; drain it and mash it fine. Then add the butter to the rice whilst it is warm; whisk the eggs very light, the yolks and whites separately. Add the yolks to the rice, and as much milk as will form a batter. Beat the whole very hard, then stir the whites of the eggs gently into the mixture. Grease your waffle-irons, and bake them. If the batter should be too thin, add a little more flour.

Italian Bread—Mix 1 pt. each of milk and water and bring to a boil, add 1 teaspoon salt, and sprinkle in gradually 1 pt. meal and 2 tablespoonfuls of flour. Cook 2 hours. Pour to the depths of ½ inch in shallow pans to cool; when cold cut in round cakes; put in overlapping rows in pan; pour melted butter over, then grated cheese; brown in oven.

Crackers —One pt. flour, 1 dessertspoon butter, a pinch of salt and milk enough to make a stiff dough. Beat well, stick and bake.

Beaten Biscuit— One qt. flour, 2½ oz. lard, 1 teacup milk, 1 teaspoon salt. Mix the greater part of the flour with the other ingredients and beat 15 minutes, adding the rest of the flour by degrees. They require a steady heat, but not too hot an oven. They should bake ½ hour, otherwise they will be heavy and dark in the middle.

Puff Biscuit—One and one-half pts. flour, 3 teaspoonfuls baking-powder and 1 teaspoonful salt, 1 tablespoonful lard, 1½ cups milk. Chop the lard through the flour; sift in salt and add the milk. Roll out quickly, touching as ittle as possible. Cut in rather large circles; spread one-half of the circle with butter, then fold the other over it; bake 15 minutes. If you choose, you can sprinkle sugar on the top.

Pop-Overs—Make of equal proportions (say 2 cups) milk and flour, 2 eggs, a little salt butter the size of an egg.

Mix the salt in the flour; mix well, melt the butter and add to other ingredients; the last thing, grease and half fill the tins; bake quickly.

Crullers—Take 2 cups sugar, 1 cup sweet milk, 3 eggs and 1 tablespoonful butter; beat all together, then add a good pinch of salt, 1 teaspoon level full of grated nutmeg, 1 heaping full of cinnamon and the grated rind of a lemon. Now mix thoroughly together 3 cupfuls flour and 2 heaping teaspoonfuls baking-powder; sift into the bowl containing the other ingredients and mix them. Add enough more flour to give them the proper consistency for rolling out. Fry in hot lard, which must be exactly hot enough to insure success. If too hot they are burned; if not hot enough, as is so often the case, your crullers slowly take up the lard and come out greasy and indigestible.

Musk Cakes—One qt. milk, ¼ pound butter, flour enough to make a dough, salt according to taste, Indian meal sufficient to thicken the milk, ½ pint of yeast.

Boil the milk, and stir into it as much Indian meal, mixed with cold milk, as will make a mush as thick as batter; add the butter and salt while the mush is hot; as soon as it becomes lukewarm stir in the yeast and as much flour as will form a dough; cover it and stand it to rise. When light, make it out into biscuits, put them in buttered pans, and as soon as they rise again, bake them in a hot oven.

Buckwheat Cakes—One pint buckwheat flour, 1 qt. water, salt according to taste, 1 gill home-made yeast.

Mix the water (which should be lukewarm if the weather is cold) with the meal; add the salt and yeast; beat it well; when light, bake them on a griddle. Grease the griddle; pour on a little of the batter; spread it so as to form a cake about the size of a breakfast-plate; the cakes should be very smooth at the edges. When they are done on one side, turn them; when brown on both sides, put some butter on the plate, put the cake on it, butter the top, bake another and put on it, butter hot, and send them to the table. Buckwheat cakes are much better if they are sent to the table with only 1 or 2 on the plate.

Rye Batter Cakes—One pint of rye meal, milk, salt according to taste, 1 gill home-made yeast.

Add enough lukewarm milk to the rye to make a thin batter, with salt; beat it well, then add the yeast; when they are light, bake them on a griddle, as buckwheat cakes.

Plain Currant Cake—Take $\frac{1}{2}$ lb. flour, 2 teaspoonfuls baking-powder, $\frac{1}{4}$ lb. butter, $\frac{1}{4}$ lb. sugar, 6 oz. currants, milk.

Rub the butter into the flour, add the other ingredients, and mix with milk into a moist dough. Bake in a well greased tin for about 40 minutes.

Icing for Cakes—Beat up the whites of 3 eggs with $\frac{3}{4}$ lb. of powdered white sugar till light; pour it over the cake, smoothing it with a knife.

Set the cake in a warm place till the sugar becomes hard.

Sponge Jelly Cake—Three eggs, 4 oz. sugar, 1 cup flour, 1 dessertspoonful baking-powder, 3 tablespoonfuls boiling water.

Mix the baking-powder with the flour, and beat each of the eggs separately. Then mix all the ingredients together, and bake in jelly tins in a brisk oven. When cool, chocolate frosting put between the cakes makes them very delicious, or jelly if preferred.

Jelly Rolls—Three eggs, ½ cupful butter, 1½ teaspoonfuls baking-powder, ⅔ of a cup of pulverized sugar, 1 cupful flour, a little salt.

Bake in shallow pans—a dripping-pan well buttered is good for this purpose; put in the dough till it is about ½ inch thick; take it carefully from the tins when baked and lay on a cloth; spread jelly over it evenly with a knife; roll while hot; if this is not done the cake will crumble.

Sponge Jelly Cake (Rolled)—Five eggs, 1 cup sugar, 1 cup flour, 1 teaspoonful baking-powder.

Beat the yolks and sugar to a cream, add the whites, beaten to a stiff froth; then the flour, in which the baking-powder has been mixed. Bake in a dripping-pan. When done, turn out on a cloth, spread jelly on the bottom of the cake, and roll from the side.

Johnny Cake—One pt. corn meal, 1 teacupful sugar, 1 pt. milk, 2 eggs, 1 teaspoonful butter, salt to taste, 1 teaspoonful dissolved saleratus.

Mix the butter and sugar with the meal; boil half the milk. Add the dissolved saleratus and the eggs, after they have been well beaten, to the remaining half of the cold milk. Pour the boiling milk over the meal and let it cool. Then add the cold milk and saleratus. Bake in a shallow pan.

Icing for Cakes (1) — Four eggs, 1 lb. finely powdered white sugar, vanilla, strawberry, lemon, or any other flavoring.

Beat well the whites of the eggs, adding the sugar to stiffen in small quantities; continue until you have beaten the eggs to a stiff froth; it will take about ½ an hour if well beaten all the time; if not stiff enough then, add more sugar; spread carefully on the cake with a broad-bladed knife; to color icing yellow put the grated peel of a lemon (or orange) into a piece of muslin, strain a little juice through it and press hard into the other ingredients. Strawberry juice or cranberry syrup colors a pretty pink color.

Icing for Cakes (2) — The whites of 2 eggs, ½ lb. castor sugar, and the juice of a lemon or a few drops of orange-flower water.

Beat the mixture until it hangs upon the fork in flakes, then spread over the cake, dipping the knife in cold water occasionally; stand it before the fire, and keep turning the cake constantly, or the sugar will catch and turn brown. As soon as it begins to harden it may be removed. The icing must not be put on until the cake itself is cold; otherwise it will not set. A few drops of cochineal will color it if desired.

Lemon Icing—Squeeze the juice of 2 lemons into a basin with ½ lb. of powdered white sugar, and beat it for a short time. If wanted pink, add cochineal.

Eggless Icing—Take 1 cupful confectioner's sugar and 2 tablespoonfuls water; beat thoroughly and spread on your cake, which should be ice-cold. The icing will whiten when it has stood a little while. You may color it with pink sugar or chocolate if you like.

Excellent Frosting—Boil together 1 cup granulated sugar and 4 tablespoonfuls hot water until it threads from the spoon, stirring often. Beat the white of 1 egg until firm; when the sugar is ready set it from the stove long enough to stop boiling, then pour onto the egg slowly, but continually, beating rapidly; continue to beat until of the right consistency to spread on the cake, and flavor while beating. It hardens very quickly after it is ready to put on the cake, so it is best to have the white of another egg ready to add a little if it gets too hard to spread smoothly. Boil the sugar the same as for candy; when right for candy it is right for frosting; if at last it hardens very rapidly it has been boiled too hard, but a little white of egg will rectify it. Or if not boiled enough (that is, if it remains too thin after beaten until cold) put in pulverized sugar, adding a little and beating hard; then, if not just right, a little more, and beat again until thick enough.

The one thing is to have the sugar boiled just right; if you hit that point you will not have a bit of trouble; if not, it will require "doctoring." A good deal depends upon stirring the sugar into the white of the egg at first; if too fast or too slow it will cook the egg in lumps. If you should not get it just right at first do not be discouraged; when once you get it perfect you will never make it any other way. This quantity is for one cake.

Almond Icing—Put in a brass or copper pan 4 lbs. moist sugar, with 1 pint of water. Boil 8 minutes, draw off the fire, and mix 2 lbs. ground sweet almonds, stirring till thick, then pour over the cake and dry slowly.

Chocolate Icing—One-quarter cake chocolate, ½ cup sweet milk, 2 dessertspoonfuls corn starch, 1 teaspoonful vanilla.

Mix together the chocolate, milk and starch; boil for 2 minutes, flavor with the vanilla, and sweeten with powdered white sugar to taste.

Plain Fruit Cake—One lb. flour, ¼ lb. dripping, 2 teaspoonfuls baking-powder, a little allspice and salt, ¼ lb. currants, ¼ lb. white sugar, and ½ pt. milk.

Mix into the flour the baking powder and salt, then with the hands rub the dripping in the flour until it resembles bread-crumbs. Add the currants, allspice and sugar. Take care that the ingredients are well mixed; pour in the milk and mix with a wooden spoon. Grease a quartern tin and pour the mixture into it; bake 1 hour. To insure the cake being done stick a piece of broom straw into it. This answers the same purpose as a knife and is better, as the knife is apt to make the cake heavy. Turn the cake on end to allow the steam to evaporate.

Plain Fruit Cake (2)—One lb. flour, ½ lb. raisins, 4 oz. dripping, 4 oz. white sugar, 1 teacup milk, 1 egg, 2 teaspoonfuls baking-powder, a little salt, 1 oz. lemon peel.

Add to the flour the baking-powder and salt; rub the dripping into the flour with your hands. Take care it is well incorporated. Stone the raisins, grate the lemon rind, and with the sugar add to the other ingredients. Well whisk the egg, and mix in the milk, adding to the mixture; thoroughly mix. Grease a cake tin and bake 1 hour. Proceed to test as above.

Economical Fruit Cake—Five oz. butter, 2 lbs. flour, ½ lb. sugar, 1 lb. currants, 1 gill yeast, enough milk to make a thick batter, 1 tablespoonful of powdered cinnamon.

Mix the flour, leaving out ¼ lb., with the butter cut in small pieces, the sugar, cinnamon and fruit; add milk enough to form a thick batter, and lastly stir in the yeast. Mix it over night, and set it away to rise; in the morning stir in the remainder of the flour, and let it rise; when light, mould it out very lightly; butter your pan, and bake it in an oven about as hot as for bread.

Plum Cake—One lb. each of butter, sugar and flour, 10 eggs, 1 lb. raisins, ½ lb. each of currants and sliced citron, 1 teaspoonful of ground cloves, 1 of mace, 1 nutmeg, the juice and grated peel of 1 lemon, ½ coffeecup of molasses.

Beat the butter till it is soft and creamy, then add the sugar. Beat the whites and the yolks of the eggs separately; stir the yolks in with the butter and sugar; stir the flour in gradually (having first mixed 1 heaping teaspoonful of cream of tartar with it). When the flour is about half worked in, put in ½ teaspoonful soda dissolved in as little water as is possible to use; then add the whites of the eggs, and lastly the fruit, which is well covered with the rest of the flour. Bake in a large tin, with a buttered paper on the sides as well as on the bottom; it will need to bake slowly for 5 hours. Then do not attempt to lift it from the tin until it is perfectly cold. This cake should be made several days before it is used.

Delicious Coffee Cake — Sift 1½ pints of flour with 2 teaspoonfuls of baking-powder. Cut in bits a heaping tablespoonful of butter and mix it through the flour. Stir in a cupful of syrup, and mix it with cold coffee to the consistency of soft dough. Work into the dough a teaspoonful of ground cloves, one of cinnamon and one of allspice, also half a pound of seeded raisins, and half a pound of currants well floured. Bake in oblong pans in moderate oven for an hour. This cake should stand about two days before cutting.

Johnny Cake — One pint of flour, 1 pint of corn meal (yellow is best), 1 pint of sweet milk, 2 large tablespoonfuls of molasses, a teaspoonful of salt, 2 well-beaten eggs, and 2 tablespoonfuls of melted butter. Beat thoroughly, and when ready to bake add two heaping teaspoonfuls of baking-powder. Have your pans well greased and warm, and bake in quick oven about twenty-five minutes.

Cheese Sticks — Mix well $\frac{1}{2}$ cup of butter into 1 cup of flour, add 1 teaspoonful each of salt and sugar; mix with enough water to make a soft dough and roll out very thin. Have ready $\frac{1}{2}$ cup of grated cheese, sprinkle a little on the dough with a very little cayenne pepper and roll out again; do this until the cheese is all used up, then cut it into strips, lay in greased pans and bake in quick oven.

Aunt Patty's Egg Bread — Two cups white Indian meal, 1 cup cold boiled rice, 3 eggs well beaten, 1 tablespoonful melted butter, 3 cups sweet milk, 1 teaspoonful salt, and pinch of soda. Stir the beaten eggs into the milk, add meal, salt, butter, last of all the rice. Beat well a few minutes, and bake in shallow pan.

Seed Cake—Ten oz. flour, 2 oz. sugar, 2 teaspoonfuls baking-powder, and 1 teaspoonful caraway seeds, 1 egg, 3 oz. butter, a little salt, and $\frac{1}{2}$ glass milk.

Mix the baking-powder and salt in the flour, rub in the butter also (with the hands). Add the sugar and caraway seeds, taking care to thoroughly blend them. Well whisk the egg and add the milk to it; add to the other ingredients and beat well for about 10 minutes. Grease a baking-tin and pour the mixture in. It will take about 1 hour to bake.

Cookies—Take 4 cupfuls flour, 2 cupfuls sugar, ½ cupful butter, ½ nutmeg, 3 eggs, 1 teaspoonful soda, 2 teaspoonfuls cream of tartar, sufficient milk to make dough soft enough to drop on a tin.

Mix the flour, butter, sugar and spices together, add the eggs, dissolve the soda and tartar in the milk, and mix the whole well together. Drop dessertspoonfuls on a greased baking-sheet and bake in a good oven.

Rice Cake—Two handfuls rice, a little less than a quart of milk, sugar to taste, rind of lemon cut in 1 piece, a small stick of cinnamon, 4 eggs, a small quantity of candied citron.

Pick and wash in 2 or 3 waters the rice and put it to cook in the milk, sweeten to taste, add the lemon rind and cinnamon. Let the rice simmer gently until it is tender and has absorbed all the milk. Turn it into a basin to cool, and remove the lemon rind and cinnamon. Then stir into it the yolks of 4 and the white of 1 egg. Add a little candied citron cut in small pieces. Butter and bread-crumb a plain cake-mould, put the mixture into it and bake in a quick oven ½ hour.

Rice Cakes—Eight oz. rice flour, 4 oz. white sugar, 4 oz. butter, 3 eggs.

Work the butter to a creamy substance, add the sugar and flour, and mix in the well-whisked eggs. Roll upon pastry-board and shape into cakes with a cake-cutter. Bake in a slow oven.

Indian Loaf Cake—One lb. Indian meal, ¼ lb. butter, 2 eggs, ½ lb. sugar, ¼ lb. raisins, ¼ lb. currants.

Cut up the butter in the Indian meal; pour over it as much boiling milk as will make a thick batter; beat the eggs very light; when the batter is cool pour them into it. Seed the raisins; wash, pick and dry the currants; mix them with the raisins, and dredge as much wheat flour on them as will adhere to them. Stir the fruit into the batter, and add the sugar. Bake it in a moderate oven 2 hours.

Queen Cakes—One lb. dried flour, 1 lb. sifted sugar, 1 lb. washed currants, 1 lb. butter, 8 eggs.

Mix the flour, sugar and currants; wash the butter in rosewater, beat it well, then mix with it the eggs, yolks and whites beaten separately, and put in the dry ingredients by degrees; beat the whole for 1 hour; butter little tins and put the mixture in, only filling half full, and bake; sift a little fine sugar over just as you put into the oven.

Ginger Cup Cake — Two cupfuls butter, 2 cupfuls sugar, 1 cupful molasses, 1 cupful cream, 3 eggs, 1 tablespoonful *dissolved* saleratus, 4 heaping cupfuls flour, ½ cupful ginger.

Beat the butter and sugar to a cream; whisk the eggs light, and add to it; then stir in the other ingredients. Butter a pan or earthen mould, and pour in the mixture. Bake in a moderate oven, or it may be baked in queen-cake pans.

Ginger Nuts—Half lb. butter, ½ lb. sugar, 1 pint molasses, 2 oz. ginger, 2 tablespoonfuls cinnamon, as much flour as will form a dough, ½ oz. ground cloves and allspice mixed.

Stir the butter and sugar together; add the spice, ginger, molasses, and flour enough to form a dough. Knead it well, make it out in small cakes, bake them on tins in a very moderate oven. Wash them over with molasses and water before they are put in to bake.

Ginger Bread—Half lb. moist sugar, 2 oz. ground ginger, 1 lb. flour, ½ lb. butter, ½ lb. molasses.

Put the butter and molasses into a jar near the fire; when the butter is melted mix it with the flour while warm, and spread the mixture thinly on buttered tins, mark it in squares before baking, and as soon as baked enough separate it at the marks before it has time to harden. Time to bake, 15 minutes.

Honeycomb Ginger Bread—Half lb. flour, ½ lb. coarsest brown sugar, ¼ lb. butter, 1 dessertspoonful allspice, 2 dessertspoonfuls ground ginger, the peel of ½ lemon, grated, and the whole of the juice; mix all these ingredients together, adding about ½ lb. molasses so as to make a paste sufficiently thin to spread upon sheet tins.

Beat well, butter the tins, and spread the paste very thinly over them, bake it in a rather slow oven, and watch it till it is done; withdraw the tins, cut it in squares with a knife to the usual size of wafer biscuits (about 4 inches square), and roll each piece round the fingers as it is raised from the tin.

Drop Ginger Cakes—Put in a bowl 1 cupful brown sugar, 1 cupful molasses, 1 cupful butter, then pour over them 1 cupful boiling water, stir well; add 1 egg, well beaten, 2 teaspoonfuls soda, 2 tablespoonfuls each of ginger and cinnamon, ½ teaspoonful ground cloves, 5 cupfuls flour. Stir all together and drop with a spoon on buttered tins; bake in a quick oven, taking care not to burn them.

Yorkshire Tea Cakes — Six handfuls flour, 1 egg, 1 oz. yeast, a piece of lard about the size of 2 eggs, a little salt, and about a pint of new milk.

Mix the yeast with a little sugar, flour and water. Rub the lard into the flour, and when the yeast has risen stir it in with a little warm milk. Leave it to rise before the fire, then stir it all together with the rest of the milk warmed, and add to the egg beaten up. Knead it well together and leave it to rise before the fire, but not too near; cover it with a cloth. When risen enough, knead it into cakes, let them stand before the fire until they rise, and bake in a moderate oven.

Currant tea cakes are made by adding currants and a little brown sugar to the dough.

Metropolitan Cake—Light part: 2 cups sugar, ¾ cup butter, 1 cup sweet milk, 2½ cups flour, whites of 5 eggs, 3 teaspoonfuls baking-powder. Dark part: ½ cup molasses, ½ cup flour, 1 cup raisins, 1 teaspoonful cinnamon, ½ teaspoonful cloves, 2 large spoonfuls of the light part.

Bake the light part in 2 cakes. Bake the dark part in 1 cake and place between the 2 light cakes with jelly or frosting.

Almond Biscuits—One-quarter lb. almonds, ½ lb. flour, ½ lb. sugar, ¼ lb. butter, a very small egg.

Blanch and mince the almonds, add them to the flour and sugar, moisten with the egg, and mix with the butter, previously melted. Roll out rather thin, cut with a biscuit cutter, and bake for ¼ hour.

Virginia Silver Cake — Three-fourths lb. butter; 1 lb. white sugar (loaf sugar pounded and sifted is the best here), ¾ lb. flour, ¼ lb. corn starch, whites of 18 eggs, 1 teaspoonful cream tartar. Cream the butter, then sift the flour, corn starch and cream tartar gradually into the butter; add last of all the beaten whites;

flavor with almond. This cake requires much watching in baking, and a slow oven.

Sponge Cake—Five eggs, ½ lb. loaf sugar, the grated rind and juice of one lemon, ¼ lb. flour.

Separate the yolks from the whites. Beat the yolks and sugar together until they are very light; then add the whites, after they have been whisked to a dry froth; alternately with the flour stir in the lemon, put the mixture in small pans, sift sugar over them and bake.

Hickory Nut Cake—One and one-half cupfuls sugar, ½ cupful butter, a scant ½ cupful sweet milk, 2 cupfuls flour, 3 eggs, 2 teaspoonfuls cream tartar, 1 of soda or 3 teaspoonfuls baking-powder.

Bake in layers. Filling for same: 1 cupful sweet cream or milk; let it come to a boil; then stir in 1 tablespoonful of corn starch which has previously been wet with cold milk; sweeten to taste; let it just boil up; remove from the fire, and stir in 1 pint of pulverized hickory nut meats. Flavor to taste, and when partially cool spread between each 2 layers.

Strawberry Shortcake — Butter, flour, strawberries, sugar, whipped cream.

Make a rich, short crust with butter and flour, allowing 1 ounce more of flour than butter; bake in flat tins of equal size (the pastry when baked should be about an inch thick); open the shortcake, butter it well, and cover ½ with a layer of strawberries previously mixed with sugar; have alternate layers of berries and pastry, finishing with the former, over which place a layer of whipped cream.

Shortcake (Spanish)—Three eggs, ½ cup butter, 1 cup sugar, ⅔ cup sweet milk, a little cinnamon, 2 cups flour and 1 teaspoonful baking-powder.

Stir the flour in, do not knead it; the eggs, butter and sugar should be beaten together till very light; bake in a shallow tin; when it is done spread a thin frosting over the top; make this of the white of 1 egg, a little pulverized sugar and a teaspoonful of cinnamon; set it in the oven to brown.

Blackberry Shortcake — Two qts. flour, 3 tablespoonfuls butter, 2 of lard, 2½ cups buttermilk or thick sour milk, yolks of 2 eggs, a teaspoonful of soda and salt.

Mix the salt in the flour, then work in the shortening; beat the yolks of the eggs; dissolve the soda in a little hot water and add to the above proportion of milk; add these to the first mixture; quickly make into a paste, roll out half an inch thick, having upper and under crust. Lay the paste in a well greased baking-tin, cover thickly with berries, sprinkle with sugar, cover with the top crust. Bake about half an hour; cut into squares and eat (splitting these open) with sugar and butter.

Short-Cake (Scotch) — Four oz. white sugar, ½ lb. slightly salted butter, 1 lb. flour.

Mix the flour and butter with the hands; then add the sugar, and work all into a smooth ball; then roll out until it is an inch thick; prick over with a fork and pinch round the edges, and bake for ½ hour in an oven with a moderate fire, in a round or square pan, according to taste.

Chocolate Cake — Half lb. butter, yolks of 12 eggs, ½ lb. white sugar, same of ground almonds, ¼ lb. chocolate, 2 tablespoonfuls cinnamon, ½ teaspoonful pounded cloves.

Melt the butter and stir it until it froths, beat the yolks of the eggs and stir into the butter; add the sugar and pounded almonds, grated chocolate, cinnamon and pounded cloves, beat well for 15 minutes; then beat the whites of the eggs to a froth, and add these to the above mixture; butter the mould, and bake the above in a moderate oven for $1\frac{1}{4}$ hours.

Almond Macaroons — Blanch and skin 8 oz. of Jordan almonds and 1 oz. of bitter ones; dry them on a sieve, and pound them in a smooth paste in a mortar, adding occasionally a very little water, to prevent them from getting oily; add to them 5 oz. pulverized sugar, 1 teaspoonful rice flour, and the whites of 3 eggs beaten in a stiff froth; put this on paper in drops the size of walnuts, bake in a slow oven until they are of a light color and firmly set; take them from the paper by wetting the under side of it.

Cocoanut Macaroons — Stir together the whites of 2 eggs beaten to 1 lb. of desiccated cocoanut and 1 cupful powdered sugar. Work till it becomes a soft paste and drop in spoonfuls on a buttered tin. Bake in a slow oven.

Silver Cake — Three-fourths lb. sugar, $\frac{1}{2}$ lb. flour, $\frac{1}{4}$ lb. butter, whites of 8 eggs, 1 heaped teaspoonful essence of bitter almonds.

Cream the butter and sugar; whisk the eggs to a stiff froth and add; lastly the flour and flavoring. Flavor icing of this cake with rose-water.

Cocoanut Cake — Six oz. butter, 1 lb. sugar, 1 lb. flour, 1 large cupful milk, 1 teaspoonful soda, 2 of cream-of-tartar.

Rub the butter into the flour; add the sugar and cream-of-tartar; well whisk the eggs; dissolve the soda in a little warm water, adding these to other ingredients. Bake in layers as for jelly cake. Icing to place between the layers: 8 oz. white sugar, whites of two eggs. Well whisk the eggs and sugar, add the grated cocoanut and place between the layers.

Scotch Snow Cake—Seven oz. white sugar, 1 lb. arrowroot, ½ lb. butter, whites of 7 eggs, any flavoring that is preferred.

Beat the butter until like cream, and while beating add gradually the arrowroot and sugar. When the whites of the eggs are beaten to a stiff froth, mix with the other ingredients and beat for a quarter of an hour. Flavor to taste, pour into buttered mould and bake for $1\frac{1}{4}$ hours.

White Bride Cake—Put 1 lb. of butter into a basin and beat it with your hand till it comes to a fine cream; add $1\frac{1}{4}$ lbs. pulverized sugar, and beat together until it is fine and white: then add 1 lb. sifted flour, give it a stir, and then add the whites of 14 eggs; continue to beat it and add another pound of flour and 14 more whites; beat well; mix all together, paper your dish around the sides and bottom, put in your batter and bake in a moderate oven.

Shrewsbury Cake—One lb. sugar, pounded cinnamon, a little grated nutmeg, 3 lbs. flour, a little rosewater, 3 eggs, melted butter.

Sift the sugar, cinnamon and nutmeg into the flour (which must be of the finest kind); add the rosewater to the eggs and mix with the flour, etc.; then pour in enough melted butter to make it a good thickness and roll out. Mould well, roll thinly, and cut into such shapes as you like.

Marble Spice Cake—Three-quarters of a pound of flour, well dried; 1 lb. white sugar, ½ butter, whites of 14 eggs, 1 tablespoonful cream tartar mixed with flour.

When the cake is mixed, take out about a teacupful of batter and stir into it 1 teaspoonful of cinnamon, 1 of mace, 1 of cloves, 2 of spice and 1 of nutmeg. Fill your mould about an inch deep with the white batter, and drop into this, in several places, a spoonful of the dark mixture; then put in another layer of white, and add the dark as before; repeat this until your batter is used up. This makes one large cake.

Corn-Starch Cake — Four eggs, whites only; 1 cup butter, ⅔ cup corn-starch, ½ cup sweet milk, 1 cup flour, 2 teaspoonfuls baking-powder, lemon or rosewater flavoring.

Cream the butter and sugar thoroughly either with the hand or a silver spoon; mix the corn-starch with the milk and add; then add the eggs, beaten stiff, next the sifted flour, into which the baking-powder has been stirred. Put into well greased mould and bake.

Cracknels — One qt. flour, ½ nutmeg, 4 eggs, 4 spoonfuls rosewater, 1 lb. butter.

Mix the flour, the nutmeg, grated, the yolks of the eggs, beaten, and the rosewater, into a stiff paste with cold water; then roll in the butter and make into cracknel shape; put them into a kettle of boiling water, and boil them till they swim; then take them out, and put them into cold water; when hardened, lay them out to dry and bake on tin plates.

Lemon Biscuits — One lb. flour, ½ lb. white sugar, ¼ lb. fresh butter, 1 oz. lemon peel, 1 tablespoonful lemon juice, 3 eggs.

Add the butter to the flour and rub finely with the hands; mince the lemon peel and stir it and the sugar into the former mixture; well whisk the eggs and lemon juice, and thoroughly mix the whole. Drop from a spoon to a greased baking-tin about 2 inches apart. Bake for 20 minutes.

Cocoanut Biscuits—Six oz. cocoanut grated, 9 oz. white sugar, 3 eggs.

Whisk the eggs for about 12 minutes, then sprinkle in the sugar gradually, lastly the cocoanut; form with your hands into little pyramids; place upon white paper, and the paper on tins. Bake in a cool oven until slightly brown.

Rice Biscuits—One-half lb. ground rice, 5 oz. white sugar, 4 oz. butter, 2 eggs.

Well beat the butter; stir in gradually the ground rice and sugar; well whisk the eggs and add to the other ingredients. Roll out on the paste board and cut into shapes with paste cutter. Place upon greased tin and bake a quarter of an hour in a slow oven.

Delicious Rolls—One and one-half pints new milk, 1 cupful hop yeast, $\frac{1}{2}$ teaspoonful salt, and flour for forming dough, which must be covered and left to rise over night. In the morning add the whites of 2 well-beaten eggs, $\frac{1}{2}$ cupful butter and flour, and knead the dough briskly for 10 minutes; roll to the thickness of $\frac{1}{2}$ an inch, cut in 4-inch squares, brush the tops with sweet milk and fold them over cornerwise; place them close together in buttered pans. Set in a warm place until light, when bake in a quick oven.

Graham Gems—Two tablespoonfuls sugar, 1 tablespoonful butter, well-stirred together; add 1 coffeecupful sweet milk, graham to make a stiff batter, then 1 well-beaten egg, saltspoonful of salt and 2 teaspoonfuls good baking-powder. This makes a dozen gems. Bake 15 or 20 minutes.

PASTRY

A GOOD hand at pastry will use less butter and produce lighter crust than others. Salt butter is very good, and if well washed makes a good, flaky crust. If the weather is warm the butter should be placed in ice water to keep it as firm as possible; when lard is used take care that it is perfectly sweet.

In making pastry, as in other arts, "practice will make perfect;" it should be touched as lightly as possible, made in a cool place, and with hands perfectly cool; if possible, use a marble slab instead of pastry board; if the latter is used, it is better to procure it made of hard wood.

It is important to use great expedition in the preparation of pastry, and care must be taken not to allow it to stand long before baking, or it will become flat and heavy. A brisk oven will be required for puff pastry; a good plan to test the proper heat is to put a small piece of the paste in before baking the whole. Be sure that the oven is as near perfection as possible; for an oven in which the heat is not evenly distributed can never produce a well-baked pie or tart; where there is an unequal degree of heat the pastry rises on the hottest side in the shape of a large bubble and sinks into a heavy, indigestible lump on the coolest. Raised pie crust should have a good soaking heat, and glazed pastry rather a slack heat. When suet is used it must be perfectly free from skin and minced as finely as possible: beef suet is considered the best.

All moulds, pie-dishes, patty-pans, and vessels of all descriptions used for baking or boiling must be well buttered.

The outside of a boiled pudding often tastes disagreeably, which arises from the cloth not being nicely washed and kept in a dry place. It should be dipped in boiling water, squeezed dry, and floured when to be used. If bread, it should be tied loosely; if batter, tightly over. The water should be boiling briskly when the pudding is put in. Batter pudding should be strained through a coarse sieve when all is mixed. In others the eggs separately. A pan of cold water should be ready, and the pudding dipped in as soon as it comes out of the pot, and then it will not adhere to the cloth.

Snow is an excellent substitute for eggs either in puddings or pancakes. Two large spoonfuls will supply the place of one egg, and the article it is used in will be equally good. This is a useful piece of information, especially as snow often falls at the season when eggs are the dearest.

Apple Pudding (Boiled)—Suet or butter crust, apples, sugar to taste, a little minced lemon peel, 2 tablespoonfuls lemon juice.

Butter a pudding mould, line with the paste, pare, core and cut the apples into small pieces. Fill the basin and add the sugar, finely minced lemon peel and juice. Cover with the crust, press the edges firmly, cover with a floured cloth. Tie securely and plunge into boiling water. Allow to boil 2 hours. Remove from basin and send to table quickly.

Apple Charlotte — Soak ½ box gelatine 2 hours in 2 small cups of cold water. Pare and steam 8 medium-sized apples; when they are tender press through the colander and add 3 cups of sugar and the juice of 1 large lemon. Mix the gelatine with the hot apples and stir until they are cold, then set on ice to harden. Serve very cold with whipped cream. This is an old English dainty.

Currant Dumpling — One lb. flour, 5 oz. beef suet, 7 oz. currants, 1 glass of water.

Mince the suet finely, mix with the flour and currants, which of course have been washed, picked and dried; mix with the above proportion of water or milk, divide into dumplings about the size of an orange; tie in cloths, plunge into boiling water, and boil from 1 to 1¼ hours. Serve with butter and white sugar.

Lemon Dumplings — Ten oz. fine breadcrumbs, 1 large tablespoonful flour, ½ lb. finely chopped beef suet, the grated rinds of 2 small lemons, 4 oz. powdered sugar, 3 large eggs beaten and strained, and last of all the juice of the 2 lemons also strained.

Mix the ingredients well, divide into four dumplings, tie them in well-floured cloths, and let them boil an hour.

Apple Pudding (Baked) — Ten apples, 4 oz. brown sugar, 3 oz. butter, 4 eggs, 2½ breakfast cups of bread-crumbs.

Pare and cut into quarters the apples, removing the cores. Boil them to a pulp. Well whisk the eggs and put them and the butter into the apple pulp. Stir the mixture for 5 minutes. Grease a pie dish and place a sprinkling of bread-crumbs, then of apple, and proceed in this manner until all are used. Bake for ¾ of an hour. The top layer must be of bread-crumbs.

Batter Pudding — One and one-half cupfuls flour, 1 teaspoonful baking-powder, $\frac{1}{2}$ teaspoon salt, 1 tablespoon butter, 2 eggs, 1 pint milk.

Steam 1 hour and serve with sauce. Adding a cupful of raisins, or any other desirable fruit, either fresh or dried, to the above pudding, makes a most delicious dish.

Bread Pudding — Bread and boiling milk, allowing $\frac{1}{2}$ a pint to 1 lb. soaked bread, 2 beaten eggs, a little nutmeg, sugar.

Soak the bread in cold water, then squeeze it very dry, take out any lumps, and add the milk, beat up the eggs, sweeten to taste, add nutmeg, and bake the pudding slowly until firm. If desired, a few sultanas may be added to the pudding; or, if the bread is light, such as the crusts of French rolls, it may be soaked in as much cold milk as it will absorb, and when it is perfectly soft have sugar, eggs and flavoring added to it.

Caramel Pudding — A handful of white sugar, $\frac{1}{4}$ pint water, yolks of 8 eggs, 1 pint milk.

Boil the sugar and water until of a deep brown color, warm a small basin, pour the syrup in and keep turning the basin in your hand until the inside is completely coated with the syrup, which, by that time, will have set. Take the yolks of the eggs and mix gradually and effectually with the milk. Pour this mixture into the prepared mold. Lay a piece of paper on the top. Set it in a saucepan full of cold water, taking care that the water does not come over the top of the mould, put on the cover, and let it boil gently by the side of the fire for 1 hour. Remove the saucepan to a cool place, and when the water is quite cold take out the mould, and turn out the pudding very carefully.

Creamed Sponge Cake—Cut the top from a stale sponge cake loaf in 1 piece, ½ an inch thick. Dig and scrape the crumbs from inside of loaf and upper slice, leaving enough to keep the outside firm. Spread a thick layer of fruit jelly on the inside. Heat a cup of milk to a boil, stir in a tablespoonful of cornstarch wet with cold milk, and the cake crumbs rubbed fine. Stir until thick, take from the fire, beat in 2 whipped eggs and 2 tablespoonfuls of sugar. Make all into smooth batter; set in boiling water on the range and stir for 5 minutes after the mixture is really hot enough. Turn into a bowl, flavor with almond or vanilla, and let it get cold. Fill the cake with it, fit on the top, wash all over with whipped white of egg; sift powdered sugar evenly over it until no more will adhere to the surface, and let it harden.

Martha's Pudding—One-half pint milk, 1 laurel leaf, a piece of cinnamon, 1 cupful bread-crumbs, 3 eggs, nutmeg and lemon-peel, 1 teaspoonful orange-flower water.

Put the laurel leaf and cinnamon into the milk and boil, then pour over the bread-crumbs, add the eggs well beaten, the nutmeg, lemon-peel and flower-water. Sweeten to taste, butter a basin, stick currants or split raisins in rows upon it. Stir all the ingredients well together and pour into the basin. Cover with a cloth and boil 1½ hours.

Chocolate Pudding—One quart milk, 14 even tablespoonfuls grated bread-crumbs, 12 tablespoonfuls grated chocolate, 6 eggs, 1 tablespoonful vanilla, sugar to make very sweet.

Separate the yolks and whites of 4 eggs; beat up the 4 yolks and 2 whole eggs together very light with sugar. Put the milk on the range, and when it comes to a perfect boil pour it over the bread and chocolate; add the beaten eggs, sugar and vanilla; be sure it is sweet enough; pour into a buttered dish; bake 1 hour in a moderate oven. When cold, and just before it is served, have the 4 whites beaten with a little powdered sugar, and flavor with vanilla and use as a meringue.

Currant Pudding (Boiled) — Fourteen oz. flour, 7 oz. suet, 7 oz. currants, a little milk.

Have the currants washed and dried, mixed with the finely minced suet and flour. Moisten the whole with sufficient milk to form a stiff batter. Place in a floured cloth and plunge into boiling water. Boil 4 hours and serve with butter and sugar.

Gingerbread Pudding — Two oz. lard or butter, 2 tablespoonfuls brown sugar, 2 ditto golden syrup, 1 egg, 1 teacupful milk, 1 teaspoonful ground ginger, 8 oz. flour 1 teaspoonful baking-powder.

Work the butter and sugar together, then add the egg beaten well, the ginger, syrup and milk, and then the flour and baking-powder. Steam 4 hours.

Ginger Pudding — Nine oz. flour, 5 oz. suet, 5 oz. sugar, 1 large tablespoonful grated ginger.

Chop the suet finely, add to the flour, sugar and vinegar; mix well. Butter a mould and put the ingredients in perfectly dry. Cover securely with a cloth and boil 3 hours. To be eaten with sweet sauce.

Cherry Pudding — One pint flour, 1 cup milk, butter the size of an egg, 2 eggs, ½ cup sugar, 2 teaspoonfuls baking-powder, a little salt and a pint of cherries which have been stoned. Boil 1 hour. If one has not a regular boiler, the batter may be turned into a 5-pound lard pail, or any tin pail holding about 2 quarts. Cover tightly, and place in a large kettle of boiling water, which should also be covered. Never let the pudding stop boiling for a second until it is removed.

Orange Pudding—The rind of 1 Seville orange, 6 oz. fresh butter, 6 oz. white sugar, 6 eggs, 1 apple, puff paste.

Grate the rind and mix with the butter and sugar, adding by degrees the eggs well beaten; scrape a raw apple and mix with the rest; line the bottom and sides of a dish with paste, pour in the orange mixture, and lay it over crossbars of paste. It will take half an hour to bake.

Lemon Pudding—Two eggs, 2 cupfuls sugar, 4 tablespoonfuls corn-starch, 2 lemons, butter.

Beat the yolks of the eggs light, add the sugar; dissolve the corn-starch in a little cold water, stir into it 2 teacupfuls of boiling water; put in the juice of the lemons, with some of the grated peel. Mix all together with a teaspoonful of butter. Bake about 15 minutes. When done spread over the top the beaten whites of the eggs, and brown.

Fairy Pudding—Over ½ box gelatine pour 1 cup of cold water and let it soak 1 hour. Let 1 pint of rich milk come to a boil and add to it 3 well-beaten eggs and ½ cup of sugar; when it thickens, stir in the gelatine and in 2 minutes take from the fire and flavor with almond extract. Line a mould with stale cake, pour in the mixture and set away on ice. Whip 1 pint of cream and pile on the top; serve very cold.

Marmalade Pudding—Two oz. lard or butter, 2 tablespoonfuls brown sugar, 4 oz. marmalade, 1 egg, 1 teacup milk, 8 oz. flour, 1 teaspoonful baking-powder.

Well mix the butter and sugar, then add the eggs well beaten, the marmalade and milk, then the flour and baking-powder. Steam 4 hours.

Boiled Batter Pudding — Three-fourths lb. flour, 3 eggs, a pinch of salt, a pint of milk.

Put the flour and salt in a basin and break the eggs in it and mix well. Then add the milk gradually, stirring well to make the batter smooth. Beat it with a wooden spoon for a few minutes, put it into a well-buttered basin, tie over with a well-floured cloth and boil for $1\frac{1}{4}$ hours.

Holiday Pudding — A plain sponge cake, strawberry jam, icing, a rich custard, some preserved ginger.

Make the sponge cake in a round mold; take out the inside of the cake with a cutter, not too near the edge; put in a layer of strawberry jam, not too thickly spread. Cut the inside of the cake you have taken out in slices, spread some jam between each slice (different sorts of jam may be used, but strawberry does very nicely), and replace the cake. Ice it nicely over; put it into a very slow oven to try the icing. Then make the custard and pour into it small pieces of preserved ginger. Pour into the cake and serve hot.

Cabinet Pudding — One and one-half pints new milk, white sugar, 1 lemon, cinnamon, mace, cloves, 5 eggs and the yolks of 4, butter, 4 or 5 sponge cakes.

Boil the milk with enough white sugar to sweeten it, the peel of a fresh lemon cut thinly, the cinnamon, mace and cloves. Boil these ingredients as for a custard. Beat up the eggs. Pour the boiling milk, etc., on to these, stirring continually, then strain the whole through a hair sieve and leave to cool. Take a good-sized pudding mould, butter it well and line it with sponge cake cut into thin slices. Pour the custard into the mould and tie it close. It will take $1\frac{1}{2}$ hours to boil. It is an improvement, after buttering the mould and before placing the sponge cakes, to arrange some stoned raisins, slices of candied peel and nutmeg. Serve hot with sauce.

Fig Pudding—One lb. flour, 2 oz. bread crumbs, 2 oz. finely-chopped suet, 2 oz. sugar, 1 egg, $\frac{1}{4}$ lb. figs cut in slices.

Flavor with nutmeg; mix all with milk and boil 2 hours.

Steamed Pudding—One cupful suet chopped fine, 1 cupful molasses, 1 cupful currants washed and dried, 1 cupful sour milk, 1 teaspoonful soda, a little salt, flour.

Mix well, using flour enough to make a stiff dough; pour into a mold and steam 4 hours.

Oxford Dumplings—Two oz. grated bread, 4 oz. currants, 4 oz. suet chopped fine, 1 large spoonful flour, 1 oz. pounded sugar, 3 eggs, grated lemon peel and a little spice.

Mix with the yolks of the eggs well beaten and a little milk. Divide into 5 dumplings $\frac{1}{2}$ inch thick, and fry a nice brown in plenty of lard. Serve with white sauce and sifted sugar on them.

Fruit Pudding—Crust: One-fourth oz. suet to 6 oz. flour; pinch of salt, and water enough to make a thick paste; fruit and sugar.

Make the crust of suet, flour, salt and water; roll it out thin before putting into a buttered basin, then add the fruit mixed with the sugar. except in the case of apples, which are sometimes hardened by boiling with sugar; put on a lid of paste, and boil the pudding $1\frac{1}{2}$ hours. Care should be taken to roll the crust thin, in order to get as much fruit as possible into the pudding. It is a good plan to stew a little fruit, and serve it with the pudding, as it should be given to children in large proportion to the crust.

Strawberry Saracen—Toast very thin slices of stale bread and line the bottom and sides of a China dish with them, after buttering generously. Trim the bread to fit the dish neatly. Fill the space with strawberries packed and heaped as full as the dish will hold; sift plenty of sugar all through and over them, and set the dish in a moderate oven for about half an hour. It will be found that the berries melt a great deal, so they must be plentiful. Serve very cold with rich, thick cream. This is one of the most delicious desserts imaginable, notwithstanding that there are people who consider it almost a crime to cook strawberries in any way.

Mince Pies—The sooner the Christmas mince meat is prepared and set away to ripen so much better will the pies made of it be. Take 3 lbs. lean beef from the round and boil it in enough water to cover it. When very tender, set it away till cold, and then chop very fine, carefully removing any piece of gristle or fat. Next weigh out 5 lbs. Greening apples; after peeling and coring them, chop fine and add to the meat. Chop fine 1 lb. kidney suet and 2 lbs. seeded raisins and add to the above with 2 lbs. clean currants, ¾ lb. citrons, finely shredded, and 4 oz. each of candied orange and lemon peel (or the grated rind of 2 oranges and 2 lemons), and the pulp of 2 oranges and 2 lemons chopped and freed from seeds and tough bits. To these ingredients add enough sugar to sweeten to taste, also 2 even tablespoonfuls cinnamon, 1 tablespoonful mace, 1 tablespoonful alspice and 1 tablespoonful cloves, together with a grated nutmeg and a good teaspoonful salt. Now add enough sweet cider to secure the right consistency—3 pints or two quarts. Any fruit juice is an improvement, especially the juice from spiced pears or peaches. Some liberally disposed housewives contribute a jar of preserved strawberries, or raspberries, or cherries, to their pot of mince, which is a rare improvement. When all has been thoroughly mixed, place the stone pot containing the mince meat on the back of the range to warm slowly through, gradually moving it forward till it boils; then push it back to simmer for a few moments, after which it should be set away to cool. Keep in a cool place till wanted, and in making the pies sprinkle in about a dozen seeded raisins to each one.

Plum Pudding—Two lbs. beef suet, 1½ lbs. bread crumbs, 1½ lbs. flour, 2 lbs. raisins, 2½ lbs. currants, ½ lb. mixed peel, 1½ lbs. foots sugar, 14 eggs, a little nutmeg, ginger, allspice (powdered), a large pinch of salt, ½ pint milk.

Chop the suet as finely as possible, and any stale piece of bread can be used for grating, allowing the above quantity; mix with the suet and flour. Stone the raisins, and have the currants perfectly washed and dried, the peel cut into thin slices and added to the suet, bread and flour, mixing well for some minutes; then add the sugar and continue working with the hands for 5 minutes. Put the eggs into a bowl (breaking each into a cup first to ascertain that it is fresh and to remove the speck), add to them grated nutmeg, powdered ginger and powdered allspice, according to taste, and a large pinch of salt; then stir in ½ pint milk; beat all up together, and pour it gradually into another bowl, working the whole mixture with the hand for some time. If the mixture be too stiff, add more milk, and continue to work it with a wooden spoon for at least ½ hour. Scald 2 pudding cloths, spread each in a bowl and dredge them well with flour. Divide the composition in 2 equal parts, put each in its cloth and tie it up tightly. To boil the pudding, place 2 inverted plates in saucepans filled with water, and when the water boils fast put each puddings into its saucepan. Let them boil 6 hours, keeping the saucepan full by adding more water as it is required, and taking care that it never ceases boiling. Then take the pudding out and hang them up till the next day, when the cloth of each pudding should be tightened and tied afresh, and 3 hours' boiling, as in the first instance, will make them ready for table.

Baked Custard—Five eggs, 5 tablespoonfuls sugar, 1 quart milk, 2 teaspoonfuls almond or other flavoring extract. Beat the whites and yolks of the eggs separately, to the yolks add the sugar, then, a little at a time, the milk, next the flavoring, and lastly the whites of the eggs, stir well together and bake in thick cups set in a pan of water in rather quick oven until firm—this usually takes about 30 minutes.

A Teetotaler's Christmas Pudding — Pick and stone 2 lbs. good Valentias; pick, wash and dry 1 lb. currants; chop 2 lbs. beef suet; have ready ½ lb. brown sugar, 6 oz. candied peel, cut thin, 2½ lbs. flour, 6 eggs, a quart or more of milk, 1 oz. mixed spice, and a tablespoonful salt.

Put the flour into a large pan, add the plums, currants, suet, sugar, peel, spice and salt, and mix them well together *while dry*. Beat the eggs well in a large basin, and add a portion of the milk, stirring it at the same time. Make a well in the middle of the flour and pour in the milk and eggs. Keep stirring till all the ingredients are thoroughly mixed. Add more milk, if necessary, and stir up again; the batter should be rather stiff. Have a good stout cloth ready; wet and flour it well, lay it over a pan, pour in the batter, and tie it firmly up. When the water in the copper or large kettle *boils*, put the pudding in and let it boil gently for 5 or 6 hours. Turn it carefully out of the cloth. Serve with or without sauce.

Dutch Boiled Pudding—Mix well together 1 cupful suet, 1 cupful milk, 1 cupful molasses, 1 tablespoonful ginger, 1 teaspoonful ground cloves, $\frac{1}{4}$ nutmeg; add flour to make a stiff batter, and 1 teaspoonful baking-powder, and last of all mix in the batter $1\frac{1}{2}$ cupfuls of any kind of fruit well floured. Wet a cloth-bag—an old napkin makes a good bag—and sprinkle conscientiously with flour; then pour in the batter and tie up the neck of the bag very tightly, leaving a generous room for the pudding to swell, for it is as expansive as gossip. Have a kettle of boiling water and dump in the bag. You must turn the bag every 10 minutes for the first hour, then boil it for two hours longer, and if you have not let the supply of water run too low, or forgot to turn it, or scalded yourself in the manipulations and thus left too much of the pudding above water in your haste, or pricked the bag with your turning fork, or done anything else ruinous, you will have a pudding not nearly so indigestible as you might suppose.

Puff Puddings — One pint flour, 2 teaspoonfuls baking-powder and a teaspoonful salt, enough milk to make a soft batter, and 1 pint of any kind of ripe berries. Make your batter, grease cups thoroughly, and into each one put a tablespoonful of the batter and one of the berries, covering them with more batter. Set the cups in a steamer and steam 20 minutes. Make the sauce as follows: Mix 1 cup sugar and ½ cup butter; to this add 2 eggs; beat well and add 1 cup milk and one of the berries. Set inside of a vessel of boiling water until ready to use, stirring often.

Roly Poly Jam Pudding—Suet crust and 10 oz. of any kind of jam.

Having made a nice suet crust, roll to the thickness of about ½ inch. Place the jam in the center and spread equally over the paste, allowing a margin of about ½ inch for the pudding to join. Roll up lightly, join the ends securely, place upon a floured cloth, and secure with tape, allowing a little for the pudding to swell. Plunge into boiling water and boil 2 hours.

Red Currant Pudding—Some red currants and raspberries, sugar, slices of bread.

Stew the red currants and raspberries with sugar till thoroughly done, pour off all the juice, and put the fruit while hot into a pudding basin lined with bread made to fit exactly; fill the basin up with fruit, and cover it with a slice of bread made to fit exactly; let it stand till quite cold with a plate on it. Boil up the juice which was poured off with a little more sugar, and let that get cold. When served the pudding must be turned out on a dish and the juice poured all over it so as to color the bread thoroughly. It can be served with custard or cream.

Raspberry Pudding—One pint bread-crumbs, 1 quart milk, 2 cupfuls sugar, 1 lemon, butter, a cupful of preserved raspberries, 4 eggs.

Mix the bread-crumbs, milk, 2 cupfuls sugar, the peel of the lemon grated, the yolks of the eggs, and a small piece of butter, and bake. When done spread over the top a cupful of preserved raspberries; put over that a meringue made with the whites of the eggs, a cupful of sugar and the juice of the lemon. Return it to the oven to color; let it partly cool and serve it with rich cream.

Sweet Potato Pudding — Two cups mashed sweet potato (the potato must first be boiled), a cup of sugar, a small cup of butter, 3 eggs, ¼ teaspoonful soda dissolved in a little hot water, a teaspoonful lemon extract, and ½ teaspoonful grated nutmeg.

Beat the eggs until they are very light, rub the butter and sugar to a cream, and mix all with the potato; cover a deep plate or shallow pudding dish with a thick crust; then put in the mixture and bake slowly for ¾ of an hour.

Rice and Raisin Pudding — Five eggs, 1 cup rice, 1 cup sugar, butter the size of an egg, 2 handfuls of raisins.

Simmer the rice in a quart of milk until tender; remove from the stove to cool. Well whisk the yolks of the eggs and add to the rice, also the rest of the milk, sugar, and butter; then well beat the whites of the eggs, stone the raisins, and add to the other ingredients. Grate nutmeg on the top and bake 1 hour.

Raspberry Bavarian Cream — Cover ½ box gelatine with ½ cupful cold water and let soak ½ hour; set over boiling water and stir until dissolved; add 6 tablespoonfuls sugar and a pint of raspberry juice; strain into a tin pan. Set on ice and stir until thick; add a pint of whipped cream. Mix thoroughly, pour in a mold, and stand aside to harden.

Arrowroot Blanc Mange — Moisten 2 dessertspoonfuls of best arrowroot with water, rub to a smooth paste and throw it into 1 cupful of boiling milk; stir steadily and boil until it thickens. Serve cold, sweetened and flavored to taste.

Baked Lemon Pudding — Three oz. crumbs, 3 oz. sugar, 3 oz. butter, the grated rind and juice of a lemon, ¾ pint milk, 3 eggs, some good paste.

Mix the dry ingredients, pour over them the milk, made hot. When cold, add the eggs and lemon juice. Line a greased dish with thin paste, putting a double strip round the edge; pour the mixture into it, and bake in a moderate oven.

Rice and Apple Pudding — A cupful of rice, 6 apples, a little chopped lemon peel, 2 cloves, sugar.

Boil the rice for 10 minutes; drain it through a hair sieve until quite dry. Put a cloth into a pudding basin and lay the rice round it like a crust. Cut the apples into quarters, and lay them in the middle of the rice with a little chopped lemon peel, cloves and some sugar. Cover the fruit with rice, tie up tight, and boil for an hour. Serve with melted butter, sweetened and poured over it.

Cream Tapioca Pudding — Three tablespoonfuls tapioca, 4 eggs, 3 tablespoonfuls sugar, 3 tablespoonfuls prepared cocoanut, 1 quart milk.

Soak the tapioca in water over night, put it in the milk and boil ¾ of an hour. Beat the yolks of the eggs into a cup of sugar, add the cocoanut, stir in and boil 10 minutes longer; pour into a pudding dish; beat the whites of the eggs to a stiff froth, stir in 3 tablespoonfuls of sugar; put this over the top and sprinkle with cocoanut, and brown 5 minutes.

French Tapioca — Two oz. fine tapioca, ½ pint milk, 1 well-beaten egg, sugar and flavoring.

Take the tapioca de la couronne, and boil it in ½ pint water until it begins to melt, then add the milk by degrees, and boil until the tapioca becomes very thick; add the egg, sugar and flavoring to taste, and bake gently for ¾ of an hour. This preparation of tapioca is superior to any other, is nourishing, and suitable for delicate children.

Velvet Pudding—Five eggs, 1½ cupfuls sugar, 4 tablespoonfuls corn starch, 3 pints milk.

Dissolve the corn starch in a little cold milk, and add 1 cupful of sugar and the yolks of the eggs beaten. Boil 3 pints of milk and add the other ingredients while boiling; remove from the fire when it becomes quite thick; flavor with vanilla and pour into a baking-dish; beat the whites of the eggs to a stiff froth, add ½ cup sugar, turn over the pudding, and place it in the oven and let brown slightly.

Sauce for Velvet Pudding— Yolks of 2 eggs, 1 cupful sugar, 1 tablespoonful butter, 1 cup milk.

Well beat the yolks, sugar and butter; add to the milk (boiling), and set on the stove till it comes to boiling heat; flavor with vanilla.

Florentine Pudding—1 quart milk, 3 tablespoonfuls corn starch dissolved in a little cold milk, 3 eggs, ½ teacupful sugar; flavoring, lemon or vanilla, or, according to taste, white sugar.

Put the milk in a saucepan and allow it to boil. Add to the corn starch (mixed in the milk) the yolks of the 3 eggs beaten, the sugar and flavoring; stir in the scalding milk, continue stirring until the mixture is of the consistency of custard. Pour into baking-tin; beat the whites of the eggs in a teacup of pulverized sugar and when the pudding is cooked spread on the top; place in the oven to brown. Can be eaten with cream, but is very nice without.

Sweet Macaroni— One-quarter lb. best macaroni, 2 quarts water, a pinch of salt, 1 teacupful milk, ¼ lb. white sugar, flavoring.

Break up the macaroni into small lengths, and boil in the water (adding the salt) until perfectly tender; drain away the water, add to the macaroni, in a stewpan, the milk and sugar, and keep shaking over the fire until the milk is absorbed. Add any flavoring and serve with or without stewed fruit.

Gingerbread Pudding—One-quarter lb. suet, 2 oz. ground ginger, ½ lb. sugar, 2 tablespoonfuls molasses, 1 teaspoonful baking-powder, 1 lb. flour, about ½ pint milk.

Mix the dry ingredients, dissolve the molasses in the milk, beat all well together, and boil in a well-floured cloth for 3 hours.

Oatmeal Pudding—Two oz. fine Scotch oatmeal, ¼ pint cold milk, 1 pint boiling milk, sugar to taste, 2 oz. bread crumbs, 1 oz. shred suet, 1 or 2 beaten eggs, lemon flavoring or grated nutmeg.

Mix with the oatmeal, first, the cold milk, and then add the boiling milk; sweeten and stir over the fire for 10 minutes, then add the bread crumbs; stir until the mixture is stiff, then add the suet and eggs; add flavoring. Put the pudding in a buttered dish and bake slowly for an hour.

Apple Snowballs—One-half lb. rice, 5 or 6 large apples, a little butter and sugar.

Wash the rice, put it into plenty of water, and boil quickly for 10 minutes, drain it and let it cool. Pare the apples, take out the core with a vegetable cutter, and fill the hole with a small piece of butter and some sugar. Enclose each apple in rice, tie in separate cloths, and boil for 1 hour. Serve with sweet sauce.

Sunday Pudding—One-quarter lb. breadcrumbs, ½ pint milk, sugar and flavoring to taste, 2 eggs, strawberry jam.

Boil the bread-crumbs in the milk, sweeten and flavor, and when the bread is thick stir in the yolks of the eggs. Put the pudding into a buttered tart dish, bake slowly for ¾ of an hour. Then spread over the top a layer of strawberry jam, and on this the whites of the eggs beaten with a teaspoonful of sifted sugar to a strong froth. Dip a knife in boiling water, and with it smooth over the whites; put the pudding again into a moderate oven until the top is a light golden brown. Serve immediately.

Yorkshire Pudding — One egg, a pinch of salt, milk, 4 tablespoonfuls flour.

Beat the egg and salt with a fork for a few minutes. Add to this 4 tablespoonfuls of milk and the flour; beat (with a spoon) very well, while in a batter, for 10 minutes. Then add the milk till it attains almost the consistency of cream. Take care to have the dripping hot in the pudding tin. Pour the batter into the tin to the thickness of about a quarter of an inch, then bake under the roasting joint. The above will make a pudding of moderate size, perhaps one dozen squares. The great secret of a pudding being light is to mix it 2 hours before cooking it.

Malvern Pudding—Some thin slices of dry bread, fresh fruit, sugar, custard.

Line a basin with the slices of bread. Boil some fresh, juicy fruit with sugar, in the proportion of ½ lb. to 1 lb. of fruit. Pour into the lined basin, and cover with slices of bread. Put a saucer on the top with a heavy weight on it. Turn out next day and pour custard round it.

Orange Custard — The juice of 12 oranges, the yolks of 12 eggs, 1 pint of cream, sugar to taste.

Sweeten the juice, and stir it over a slow fire until the sugar dissolves, taking off the scum as it rises. When nearly cold stir in the yolks, well beaten, and the cream. Stir again over the fire until it thickens. Be careful *not* to boil it, or it will curdle.

Apple Solid — Take 3 lbs. sliced apples, 1½ lbs. lump sugar, the juice and grated rind of 2 lemons.

Dip the lumps of sugar in water, and boil with the apples and lemon until stiff. Put into a mould, and, when cold, turn out. May be served with custard poured round.

Apple Snow — Take 4 apples, 3 dessert-spoonfuls of sugar, the grated rind of a lemon, the whites of 3 eggs.

Peel, core and stew the apples, mix with them the sugar and lemon rind. Beat the whites of eggs to a stiff froth, mix with the apples, and beat the whole until quite white. Pile on a glass dish.

Preserve Sandwiches — One-half lb. sifted sugar, ½ lb. butter, 2 eggs, 2 oz. ground rice; work them well together, then add 7 oz. flour.

Spread half this mixture upon buttered paper in a shallow tin, then a layer of preserve, and cover with the other half of the paste. Bake in a quick oven, and when cold and ready for use cut it into pieces like sandwiches, and sprinkle sugar over.

Graham Pudding — Two cups Graham flour, 2 eggs, 1 quart milk, butter the size of an egg, salt to taste.

Put a pint of milk into a buttered stewpan, and allow to heat slowly. Mix the rest of the milk in the flour, and beat lightly with the butter, eggs and salt. Then pour the hot milk upon it, mix well, return to the fire surrounded by *boiling* water, and stir constantly for ¼ hour; grate nutmeg upon it. Serve in uncovered dish, and eat with butter and sugar.

Cottage Pie.— Two lbs. potatoes, scraps of cold meat, 1 onion, 1½ oz. butter, pepper and salt to taste, ½ glass milk.

Boil and mash potatoes (or if there are any cold ones at hand, they will do as well); put the milk and butter on the fire to boil, and when boiling pour upon the mashed potatoes and mix to a paste; place the meat in a pie dish with a little fat in layers, mince the onion and sprinkle each layer with it, also pepper and salt; half fill the dish with water or gravy and cover with the potatoes, smoothing neatly and marking with a fork into a pattern; bake ½ hour.

Boiled Bread Pudding.— One-half lb. bread-crumbs, 2 oz. powdered loaf sugar, 1 pint milk, 2 oz. currants, 1 oz. candied peel cut very small, 3 eggs.

Mix the crumbs and sugar; make the milk hot, and pour it over them. When nearly cold add the other ingredients, and boil in a mould for 2 hours, or steam 3 hours. Serve with lemon sauce.

Eel Pie.— Eels, salt, pepper and nutmeg, puff paste, 1 onion, a few cloves, a little stock, 1 egg, butter, flour and lemon juice.

Skin and wash some eels, remove the heads and tails; cut up the fish into pieces about three inches long, season them with salt, pepper and nutmeg. Border a pie dish with puff paste, put in the eels with a chopped onion, and a few cloves; add a little clear stock; cover with puff paste, brush over the crust with the yolk of an egg, and bake. Make a sauce with the trimmings of the eels, some white stock seasoned with salt and pepper; thicken it with butter and flour, add some lemon juice, strain, and pour it quite hot through a funnel into the pie.

Pigeon Pie—Pigeons, pepper and salt, a piece of butter, a bunch of parsley, a beefsteak, 2 hard-boiled eggs, 1 cup water, a few pieces of ham, crust.

Rub the pigeons with pepper and salt, inside and out; in the former put a piece of butter, and, if approved, some parsley chopped with the livers, and a little of the seasoning; lay the steak at the bottom of the dish, and the birds on it; between every two a hard egg. Put the water in the dish, and if you have any ham in the house, lay a piece on each pigeon; it is a great improvement to the flavor. Observe, when the ham is cut for gravy or pies, to take the under part rather than the prime. Season the gizzards, and the two joints of the wings, and put them in the center of the pie, and over them, in a hole made in the crust, three feet nicely cleaned, to show what pie it is.

Chicken Pie — Two young fowls; seasoning: white pepper, salt, a little mace and nutmeg, all of the finest powder, and cayenne. Some fresh ham cut in slices, or gammon of bacon, some forcemeat balls, and hard eggs. Gravy from knuckle of veal or a piece of scrag, shank bone of mutton, herbs, onion, mace, and white pepper.

Cut up the fowls; add the seasoning. Put the chicken, slices of ham, or gammon of bacon, forcemeat balls and hard eggs by turn in layers. If it be baked in a dish put a little water, but none if in a raised crust. By the time it returns from the oven have ready a gravy made of the veal or scrag, shank bones of mutton and seasoning. If to be eaten hot you may add truffles, morels, mushrooms, etc., but not if to be eaten cold. If it is made in a dish put as much gravy as will fill it; but in raised crust the gravy must be nicely strained, and then put in cold as jelly. To make the jelly clear, you may give it a boil with the whites of two eggs, after taking away the meat, and then run it through a fine lawn sieve.

Giblet Pie—Some goose or duck giblets, water, onion, black pepper, a bunch of sweet herbs, a large teacupful of cream, sliced potatoes, plain crust, salt.

Line the edge of a pie dish with a plain crust. Stew the giblets in a small quantity of water with the seasoning till nearly done. Let them grow cold, and, if not enough to fill the dish, lay a beef, veal or two or three mutton steaks at the bottom. Add the giblets that the liquor was boiled in. Lay slices of cold potatoes on the top and cover with the crust; bake for $1\frac{1}{2}$ hours in a brisk oven.

Lemon Pie (1)—Crust, 1 lemon, $1\frac{1}{4}$ cups white sugar, 1 cup water, a piece of butter the size of an egg, 1 tablespoonful flour, 1 egg.

Make your crust as usual; cover your pie-tins (I use my jelly-cake tins) and bake exactly as for tart crusts. If you make more than you need, never mind, they will keep. While they are baking, if they rise in the center, take a fork and open the crust to let the air out. Now make the filling as follows: For one pie take a nice lemon and grate off the outside, taking care to get only the yellow; the white is bitter. Squeeze out all the juice; add white sugar, water and butter. Put in a basin on the stove. When it boils stir in the flour, and the yolk of one egg, beaten smooth with a little water. When it boils thick take off the stove and let it cool. Fill your pie crust with this. Beat the white of an egg stiff, add a heaping tablespoonful of sugar; pour over the top of the pie. Brown carefully in the oven.

Lemon Pie (2) — One cup sugar, 1 tablespoonful butter, 1 egg, 1 lemon, juice and rind, 1 teacupful boiling water and 1 tablespoonful corn-starch.

Dissolve the corn-starch in a little cold water, then stir it into the boiling water; cream the butter and sugar, then pour over them the hot mixture; cool, add the lemon juice, rind and beaten egg; bake with or without upper crust.

Peach Pie — Puff or short crust, peaches, sugar.

Line a dish with a nice crust, skin the peaches, remove the stones, and put the fruit into the dish, with a little sugar and water. Cover with crust and bake a golden brown.

Rhubarb Pie — Rhubarb, a little lemon peel, sugar, water, short crust.

Use a deep pie dish, wipe the stalks with a clean, damp cloth, cut into pieces about an inch in length, mince the lemon peel, line the edge of the dish with the crust, then fill the dish with rhubarb, sugar and lemon, adding a cup of water. Cover with crust, making a hole in the middle. Bake about ¾ of an hour.

Gooseberry Pie — Top and tail the berries, line the edge of a deep dish with short crust. Put the berries into it with at least 6 ounces of moist sugar and a little water. Cover with upper crust and bake from ½ to ¾ of an hour.

Damson Pie — Damsons, ¼ lb. moist sugar, crust.

Line the edge of a deep dish with crust, place a small cup in the middle, fill the dish with the fruit, sprinkling the sugar over; cover with crust and bake about ¾ of an hour. If puff paste is used, just before it is done remove from the oven and brush over with the white of an egg, beaten to a froth. Sift a little white sugar over and return to the oven till finished.

Cocoanut Pie— One cup grated cocoanut, ½ pint milk, 2 crackers, 3 eggs, butter, salt, rind of ½ lemon, sugar if desired, puff crust.

Make a nice puff crust, line a dish and bake; when done, set aside to cool; soak the cocoanut in the milk, pound the crackers well, whisk the eggs, and grate the rind of the half lemon. Mix all together, adding a little salt, sugar and butter. When well mixed place in the pie-dish, and put in the oven to slightly brown.

Pumpkin Pie (1)— One pint well-stewed and strained pumpkin, 1 quart scalding hot rich milk, 1½ cups sugar, 4 eggs, 1 teaspoonful salt, 1 tablespoonful ginger and 1 of ground cinnamon.

Bake in pie-plate lined with good paste; do not let mixture stand after it is put together, but bake at once.

Pumpkin Pie (2)— One quart stewed pumpkin pressed through a sieve, 9 eggs, whites and yolks beaten separately, 2 quarts milk, 1 teaspoonful mace, 1 of cinnamon and 1 of nutmeg, 1½ cups sugar.

Beat all together and bake with one crust.

Pumpkin Pie (3)—A pumpkin, 1 good cupful molasses; to a whole pumpkin allow 3 pints rich milk, 4 eggs, some salt, a little cinnamon, brown sugar to taste, crust.

Prepare the pumpkin by cutting into small pieces; stew rapidly until it is soft and the water is stewed out, then let it remain on the stove to simmer all day. When well cooked, add the molasses, and cook all down until dry; then sift through a colander; it will nearly all go through if properly cooked; then add the milk, spices and eggs. Too much spice destroys the flavor of the pumpkin. Sweeten to taste, then bake in a crust the same as for custard. Let it cook until of a dark brown color. This is a very wholesome dish.

French Pancakes — Five eggs, nearly a pint of cream, 1 oz. butter.

Beat the cream till it is stiff, and the yolks and whites separately and add to the cream, and beat the mixture for 5 minutes; butter the pan and fry quickly; sugar and roll, and place on a hot dish in the oven. Serve very hot.

Rice Pancakes — One-half lb. rice, 1 pint cream, 8 eggs, a little salt and nutmeg, ½ lb. butter, flour.

Boil the rice to a jelly in a small quantity of water; when cold, mix it with the cream, well-whisk the eggs and add also with a little salt and nutmeg. Then stir in the butter, just warmed, and add, slowly stirring all the time, as much flour as will make the batter thick enough. Fry in as little lard as possible.

Irish Pancakes — Eight eggs, 1 pint cream, nutmeg and sugar to taste, 3 oz. butter, ½ pint flour.

Beat 8 yolks and 4 whites of eggs, strain them into the cream, put in grated nutmeg and sugar to taste; set 3 oz. fresh butter on the fire, stir it, and as it warms pour it to the cream, which should be warm when the eggs are put to it; then mix smooth almost ½ pint flour. Fry the pancakes very thin, the first with a piece of butter, but not the others. Serve several on one another.

Apple Pie — Puff paste, apples, sugar (brown will do), a small quantity of finely minced lemon peel, and lemon juice.

Prepare the paste (see recipe *Puff Paste*), spread a narrow strip round the edge of your baking-dish, and put in the fruit, which you have previously peeled, cored and cut into convenient slices. Sweeten according to taste and add the flavoring; cover with a pie crust, making a small hole in the middle, and place in the oven to bake. When nearly done, ice the crust with the white of an egg beaten to a froth and spread lightly over it. Sprinkle with white sugar and replace in the oven until done.

Orange and Apple Pie — Puff paste, oranges, apples, sugar.

Cover a tin pie-plate with puff pastry and place a layer of sliced oranges, with the pips removed, on it, and scatter sugar over them; then put a layer of sliced apples, with sugar, and cover with slices of oranges and sugar. Put an upper crust of nice pastry over the pie, and bake it for ½ hour, or until the apples are perfectly soft. Take the pie from the tin plate while it is warm, put into a china plate and scatter sugar over the top.

To Ice or Glaze Pastry—The whites of 3 eggs, 4 oz. sugar.

Place the whites upon a plate (beaten with a knife to a stiff froth); just before the pastry is done, remove from the oven; brush with the beaten egg and sprinkle the white sugar upon it. Return to the oven to set.

Glaze —The yolks of 3 eggs, a small piece of warm butter, white sugar.

Beat the yolks and butter together, and, with a pastry brush, brush the pastry just before it is finished baking; sift white sugar upon it and return to the oven to dry.

Light Paste for Tarts — One egg, ¾ lb. flour, ½ lb. butter.

Beat the white of an egg to a strong froth, then mix it with as much water as will make the flour into a very stiff paste; roll it very thin, then lay the third part of half a pound of butter upon it in little pieces; dredge with some flour left out at first and roll up tight. Roll it out again, and put the same proportion of butter, and so proceed till all be worked up.

Strawberry Tart—One lb. sifted flour, yolks of 2 eggs, 1 gill ice water, ¾ lb. fresh butter, 1 tablespoonful sifted sugar, strawberries.

Rub the butter into the flour and sugar, add the yolks of eggs, and mix well with a knife; then add just enough ice water to make a paste that will roll out. It must be a firm paste, rather dry. Be careful that the flour is dry and the butter cold. Roll out the paste about one-third of an inch thick; line with it a pie-dish at least 1 inch deep with straight sides; trim the edges neatly, and bake the empty crust in a quick oven for 10 to 12 minutes. When the tart is to be served fill it neatly with strawberries, pour some of the syrup over and serve with a pitcher of cream. The strawberries should not be allowed to stand long in the crust, or its crispness will be destroyed. The crust should be firm, brittle and crisp, not flaky.

Sponge Cake—Three cups granulated sugar, 7 eggs beaten separately, 1 cup lukewarm water, 1 lemon, juice and grated rind, 3 cups flour and 2 teaspoonfuls baking-powder.

Put the yolks of the eggs in your cake bowl and beat them very light with a silver fork; then add your sugar a little at a time, beating thoroughly; next add the lemon, then alternately the water and the flour, into which the baking-powder has been sifted; lastly add the whites of the eggs beaten very stiff and merely stirred in lightly, not beaten. Bake in a moderate oven, and do not move the pan once put in.

Pastry.

Puff Paste — One lb. flour, ¾ lb. butter, 1 egg, with water.

Mix the flour with a lump of butter the size of an egg to a very stiff paste with cold water; divide the butter into six equal parts, roll the paste and spread on one part of the butter, dredging it with flour; repeat until all the butter is rolled in.

Short Crust — Half lb. flour, 3 oz. butter, 2 oz. white sugar, a pinch of salt, yolks of 3 eggs.

Rub into the butter the flour and the powdered loaf sugar; beat up the yolks of the eggs, the salt, and enough milk or water to make the flour into a paste; work the paste lightly, and roll it out thin. If not wanted sweet, the sugar may be left out.

Suet Crust for Meat Puddings—Eight oz. flour, 5 oz. beef suet, a little salt.

Remove all skin from the suet, chop finely, and mix with the flour, adding a little salt mix; well, add by degrees a little cold water and make into a paste; flour the paste board and place the paste upon it, roll out to the thickness of ¼ inch. It is then ready for use.

Potato Paste — Pound boiled potatoes very fine, and add, while warm, a sufficiency of butter to make the mash hold together, or you may mix it with an egg; then, before it gets cold, flour the board pretty well to prevent it from sticking, and roll it to the thickness wanted. If it has become quite cold before it be put on the dish, it will be apt to crack.

Cocoanut Potato Pie—Three eggs, one large potato, ½ cup cocoanut, 1 pint milk, 1 tablespoonful butter, sugar to taste, and a little salt.

Boil and mash the potato and add the sugar, butter and salt, then the beaten eggs, and lastly the milk, in which part of the cocoanut has been soaked. Reserve the white of an egg for frosting; add to it the rest of the cocoanut and spread a little red sugar over the top.

Cream Fritters — Three tablespoonfuls potato flour, 1 pint new milk, 2 whole eggs, yolks of 4 eggs, a pat of very fresh butter, powdered white sugar to taste, a few drops essence of almonds, bread-crumbs.

Make a smooth paste with the flour and a part of the milk; then gradually add the remainder of the milk, the eggs and yolks, the butter, white sugar to taste, and essence of almonds. Put the mixture into a saucepan on the fire, stirring all the while till it is quite thick. Spread out on a slab until of thickness of ½ an inch. When quite cold cut into lozenges; egg and bread-crumb them, or dip in the butter; fry a nice color in lard and serve sprinkled with white sugar.

Cheese Fritters — About a pint of water, a piece of butter the size of an egg, the least piece of cayenne, plenty of black pepper, ¼ lb. ground Parmesan cheese, yolks of 2 or 3 eggs, and whites of 2 beaten to a froth, salt, flour.

Put the water into a saucepan with the butter, cayenne and black pepper. When the water boils throw gradually into it sufficient flour to form a thick paste; then take it off the fire and work into it the Parmesan cheese, and then the yolks and whites of the eggs. Let the paste rest for a couple of hours, and proceed to fry by dropping pieces of it the size of a walnut into plenty of hot lard. Serve sprinkled with very fine salt.

Puffs for Dessert — One pint milk and cream, the whites of 4 eggs beaten to a stiff froth, 1 heaping cup sifted flour, 1 scant cup powdered sugar; add a little grated lemon peel and a little salt.

Beat these all together till very light, bake in gem pans, sift pulverized sugar over them and eat with sauce flavored with lemon.

Plain Puffs — Yolks of 6 eggs, 1 pint sweet milk, a large pinch of salt, whites of 6 eggs, flour.

Beat the yolks of the eggs till very light, stir in the milk, salt, and the whites beaten to a stiff froth, and flour enough to make a batter about as thick as a boiled custard. Bake in small tins in a quick oven.

Banana Fritters — Sift 3 cups flour and $1\frac{1}{2}$ teaspoonfuls baking-powder; to this add the yolks of 2 eggs, a little salt, $\frac{1}{2}$ cup sugar and enough milk to make a moderate batter; whip the whites of the eggs and then add a tablespoonful of melted butter. Slice $\frac{1}{2}$ dozen bananas and stir into the batter; fry at once in plenty of boiling lard, and drain on coarse brown paper before serving.

Spanish Puffs — A teacupful water, a tablespoonful white sugar, a pinch of salt, 2 oz. butter, flour, yolks of 4 eggs.

Put the water into a saucepan with the sugar, salt and butter; while it is boiling add sufficient flour for it to leave the saucepan; stir one by one the yolks of the four eggs; drop in a teaspoonful at a time into boiling lard; fry them a light brown.

Cream Puffs — One pint water, $\frac{1}{2}$ lb. butter, $\frac{3}{4}$ lb. sifted flour, 10 eggs, 1 small teaspoon soda. Mock cream: 1 cup sugar, 4 eggs, 1 cup flour, 1 quart milk, flavoring.

Boil the water, rub the flour with the butter; stir into the water while boiling. When it thickens like starch remove from the fire. When cool stir into it the well-beaten eggs and the soda. Drop the mixture onto the buttered tins with a large spoon. Bake till a light brown, in a quick oven. When done, open one side and fill with mock cream made as follows in the above proportions: Beat eggs to a froth; stir in the sugar, then flour; stir them into the milk while boiling; stir till it thickens, then remove from the fire and flavor with lemon or vanilla. It should not be put into the puffs until cold.

Orange Puffs—Rind and juice of 4 oranges, 2 lbs. sifted sugar, butter.

Grate the rind of the oranges, add the sugar, pound together and make into a stiff paste with the butter and juice of the fruit; roll it, cut into shapes and bake in a cool oven. Served piled up on a dish with sifted sugar over.

Orange Fritters — Six large oranges peeled and sliced, two well-beaten eggs, 2 tablespoonfuls of sugar, and enough flour to make a batter about as stiff as if for flannel cakes; dip the oranges into the batter, being sure that they are well covered by it, then fry in plenty of boiling lard; drain on coarse brown paper, sift powdered sugar over the fritters and serve.

Apple Fritters — Sift together 1 cupful flour, 2 tablespoonfuls sugar, 1 teaspoonful bakingpowder and 1 saltspoonful salt. Beat 1 egg very light, and add $\frac{1}{3}$ cupful milk; pour this gradually into the dry mixture, beating well; add 2 apples cut fine. Drop by spoonfuls into hot fat and fry; drain and sprinkle with powdered sugar. Pastry flour should be used for fritters, as bread flour contains too much gluten. Bread flour should be used only when yeast is added. The apples should be cut fine or chopped; the fritters are also very good if the apples are cut in thick slices, dipped in the batter, and then fried.

Charlotte Russe — Soak ¼ box gelatine in ½ cup cold milk 1 hour; when dissolved, set up in hot water, using gelatine lukewarm; into 1 pint whipped cream add ½ cup pulverized sugar, a little salt and the beaten whites of 2 eggs, and flavor with vanilla; then add gelatine and strain while pouring in; stir until gelatine is well mixed with the cream, and, when nearly stiff enough to drop, turn into mould lined with lady fingers or narrow slices of sponge cake, first dipping the cake into white of egg.

Apple Jelly — One lb. apples, 1 lemon, ¼ lb. lump sugar, 1 oz. gelatine, ½ pint water and a little cochineal.

Peel and core the apples, put them in a stewpan with the sugar, water, grated rind and juice of the lemon; stew till tender, rub through a sieve, then stir in the gelatine, previously melted in a gill of boiling water. Color part of the apples with cochineal, and pour into a mould with alternate layers of colored and plain apple. May be served with or without whipped cream.

Apple Turnovers — One lb. flour, 5 oz. dripping or butter, small teaspoonful baking-powder, 4 apples (allowing 1 for each turnover), 4 teaspoonfuls brown sugar.

Pare, core and slice the apples. Mix the baking-powder into the flour, then add the dripping or butter, mixing well together. Moisten with cold water and stir to a paste. Roll out; cut into circles about 7 inches in diameter. Put the apple on one of the rounds and sprinkle with sugar. Moisten the edges of the paste and shape in the form of a turnover.

Snow Cream — One-half oz. gelatine, 1 tumbler water, the juice of 1 lemon, ¼ lb. loaf sugar, and 2 eggs.

Soak the gelatine in half the water for 1 hour, and fill up with the other half *boiling*; add to it the lemon juice and sugar. Whisk the whites of the eggs well; put them to the other ingredients, and whisk the whole for ¼ of an hour. Put into a mould to set. With the yolks of the eggs and nearly ½ pint of milk, make a custard, sweetened and flavored with lemon. Pour it round the cream when turned out.

Lemon Sponge — One oz. gelatine, 1 pint water, the juice of 3 lemons, the thin rind of 2, ¾ lb. lump sugar, and whites of 2 eggs.

Boil all, except the eggs, together for 10 minutes, and let it stand until cold and beginning to set. Beat the whites well, add them to it, and whisk the whole until it becomes a stiff froth. May be put into a mould or piled in glass dishes.

Chocolate Blanc Mange — One qt. of rich fresh milk or cream, 3 oz. chocolate, ¼ lb. white sugar, 1 2-oz. box of gelatine dissolved in ½ pint water.

Boil milk, chocolate and sugar together a few minutes, after first dissolving the chocolate and rubbing it smooth in a little of the milk. Then add the gelatine and 10 drops of vanilla. Stir well and remove from the fire in about 5 minutes. When lukewarm pour through a strainer into moulds that have been previously dipped into a bath of cold water.

Russian Cream — Jelly. — To 1 package Cox's gelatine add 1 pint cold water. When dissolved add 1 pint hot water, 2 cups sugar, juice of 6 lemons. Stir slowly until well dissolved, then strain into moulds.

Cream. — Cover 1 package gelatine with cold water. When dissolved add 1 cup new milk, 1 cup sugar; heat to boiling point, stirring frequently, then set away to cool. Whip 1 quart of thick cream until light, beat the whites of 6 eggs, and add both to the mixture; when cool flavor with vanilla. Place the jelly in the bottom of the moulds, and when stiff and cold add the cream; turn out of mould and serve in slices.

Flummery — Three large handfuls of small white oatmeal, 1 large spoonful of white sugar, 2 large spoonfuls of orange-flower water.

Put 3 large handfuls of very small white oatmeal to steep a day and night in cold water; then pour it off clear, and add as much more water, and let it stand the same time. Strain it through a fine hair-sieve, and boil it till it be as thick as hasty-pudding, stirring it well all the time. When first strained, put to it the white sugar and flower water. Pour it into shallow dishes, and serve to eat with milk or cream and sugar.

Isinglass Blanc Mange — One oz. isinglass, 1 qt. water, whites of 4 eggs, 2 spoonfuls rice water, sugar to taste, 2 oz. sweet and 1 oz. bitter almonds.

Boil the isinglass in the water till it is reduced to a pint; then add the whites of the eggs with the rice water to prevent the eggs poaching, and sugar to taste; run through the jelly-bag; then add the almonds; give them a scald in the jelly, and pour them through a hair-sieve; put in a china bowl; the next day turn it out, and stick it all over with almonds, blanched and cut lengthwise. Garnish with green leaves or flowers.

Orange Fool — Juice of 3 Seville oranges, 9 well-beaten eggs, ½ pint cream, a little nutmeg and cinnamon, white sugar to taste.

Mix the orange juice with the eggs, cream and spices. Sweeten to taste. The orange juice must be carefully strained. Set the whole over a slow fire, and stir it until it becomes about the thickness of melted butter; it must on no account be allowed to boil; then pour into a dish for eating cold.

Gooseberry Fool — One quart gooseberries, water, sugar, 1 quart cream.

Pick 1 quart of quite young gooseberries, and put them into a jar with a very little water and plenty of sugar; put the jar in a saucepan of boiling water till the fruit be quite tender, then beat it through a colander, and add gradually 1 quart of cream with sufficient sugar to sweeten.

Stewed Apples and Rice — Some good baking apples, syrup, 1 lb. sugar to 1 pint water, lemon peel, jam, some well-boiled rice.

Peel the apples, take out the cores with a scoop so as not to injure the shape of the apples, put them in a deep baking-dish, and pour over them a syrup made by boiling sugar in the above proportion; put a little piece of shred lemon peel inside each apple, and let them bake very slowly until soft, but not in the least broken. If the syrup is thin, boil it until it is thick enough; take out the lemon peel, and put a little jam inside each apple, and between each a little heap of well-boiled rice; pour the syrup gently over the apples, and let it cover the rice. This dish may be served either hot or cold.

Spiced Apples — Four lbs. apples (weigh them after they are peeled), 2 lbs. sugar, $\frac{1}{2}$ oz. cinnamon in the stick, $\frac{1}{4}$ oz. cloves, and 1 pt. vinegar.

Let the vinegar, spices and sugar come to a boil; then put in the whole apples, and cook them until they are so tender that a broom-splint will pierce them easily. These will keep for a long time in a jar. Put a clean cloth over the top of the jar before putting the cover on.

Apple Charlotte—Some good cooking apples, sugar (1 lb. apple pulp to ½ lb. sugar), lemon flavoring, fried bread.

Bake good cooking apples slowly until done; scrape out all the pulp with a teaspoon, put it in a stewpan in the above proportion; stir it until the sugar is dissolved and the pulp stiff. Take care it does not burn. Add a little lemon flavoring, and place the apple in the center of a dish, arranging thickly and tastefully around it neatly cut pieces of the carefully fried bread. If it is desired to make this dish very nice, each piece of fried bread may be dipped in apricot jam. Rhubarb charlotte may be made in the same manner. The rhubarb must be boiled and stirred until a good deal of the watery portion has evaporated, and then sugar, ½ lb. to 1 lb. of fruit, being added, it should be allowed to boil until it is thick.

DESSERT.

Oranges—Oranges may be prepared for table in the following manner: Cut gently through the peel only, from the point of the orange at the top to dent made at the bottom, dividing the outside of orange into cloves or sections, seven or eight in number. Loosen the peel carefully, and take each section off, leaving it attached only at the bottom. Scrape the white off the orange itself, and turn in each section double to the bottom of the orange, so that the whole looks like a dahlia or some other flower.

Almonds and Raisins—Serve on a glass dish, the raisins piled high in the center. Blanch the almonds and strew over them.

Frosted Currants — Froth the white of an egg or eggs, dipping the bunches into the mixture. Drain until nearly dry, then roll in white sugar. Lay upon white paper to dry.

Impromptu Dessert — Cover the bottom of a large glass dish with sliced orange; strew over it powdered sugar, then a thick layer of cocoanut. Alternate orange and cocoanut till the dish is full, heaping the cocoanut on the top.

Dessert of Apples—One lb. sugar, 1 lb. finely flavored ripe sour apples, 1 pint rich cream, 2 eggs, ½ cup sugar.

Make a rich syrup of the sugar; add the apples nicely pared and cored. Stew till soft, then mix smoothly with the syrup and pour all into a mould. Stir into the cream (or if there is none at hand, new milk must answer) the eggs well beaten; also the sugar, and let it just boil up in a farina kettle; then set aside to cool. When cold take the apples from the mould and pour this cream custard around it and serve. If spice or flavoring is agreeable, nutmeg, vanilla or rose water can be used.

Dish of Figs—One cup sugar, ⅓ cup water, ¼ teaspoonful cream of tartar.

Let the sugar and water boil until it is a pale brown color; shake gently the basin in which it is boiling, to prevent it burning, but do not stir it at all until just before you take it from the fire; then stir in the cream of tartar. Wash and cut open some figs; spread them on a platter, then pour the sugar over them. Take care to have each fig covered; set them in a cool place till the sugar has time to harden.

A Dish of Nuts—Arrange them piled high in the center of a dish; a few leaves around the edge of the dish will greatly improve the appearance. In dishing filberts serve them with the outer skin on. If walnuts, wipe with a damp cloth before serving.

HOME-MADE CANDIES.

MEN, women and children—not to mention dogs and horses—like sugar, and the taste is entirely defensible. These white crystals, this frost of honey, feed the ever-burning flame of the body, supplying animal heat, which is life, and rousing the nervous energies like phosphates, or better than phosphates in some cases. I have had brain-fag so entire that it seemed as if I never could write or had written a line, relieved by taking a syrupy small glass of *eau sucrée*, when shortly ideas gathered and took shape and the blank brain resumed its work. I can't help fancying that the sweets craved so ardently by children have much to do with furnishing nerve aliment to their fast-growing systems. Sugar contributes both animal heat and nervous force, and seems to be a transformation of the elements of heat, as the diamond is transformed carbon.

In the terrible retreat from Moscow, the few of Napoleon's army who secreted a few pounds of sugar to eat were enabled to support the intense cold. In tropic countries Europeans learned to drink *eau sucrée* before long walks as a preventive of sunstroke and paralysis, and the French Algerian troops carry sugar on their marches to enable them to withstand the desert heat. Persons with spinal inflammation and paralytic tendencies often have a craving for sweets, which is nature reaching instinctively for help, and indulgence in such cases is followed by improvement.

As much pure sugar or sweets as can be eaten without producing acidity is not only safe but beneficial for any one who craves it. Disturbance seldom follows in any ordinary case when the sweets are perfectly pure and are taken at proper times, not nibbled constantly between meals.

Confectionery is one of the perquisites of childhood, and as choice French candies are beyond the capacity of many a mother's purse, and cheap ones are often made unwholesome, if not positively dangerous, by adulteration, home-made candies have become very popular, many delicious and attractive varieties being as easily made as any other toothsome dainties. As a preventive of "graining," glucose (grape sugar or syrup) is much used in the manufacture of candy. But as it is not always convenient to procure, and often imparts a bitter flavor, the recipes here given are for the use of cream of tartar instead.

A preparation called "fondant"—made by removing boiled syrup from the fire just before it will harden—is the foundation of nearly all French candies, and when once the art of making this is mastered a large variety of candies are easily made.

Fondant—To 1 lb. sugar add ½ pint cold water and ¼ teaspoonful cream of tartar, and boil rapidly for 10 minutes without stirring. Dip the fingers into ice water, drop a little of the syrup into cold water, then roll it between the fingers, and if it forms a soft, creamy ball that doesn't adhere it is done. If not hard enough boil a little longer, and if too hard add a little water, boil up and test again. Set aside in the kettle to become lukewarm, then stir the mass with a ladle until it is white and dry at the edge. It should then be taken out and kneaded, exactly as one would knead bread dough, until it is creamy and soft. By covering with a damp cloth and keeping in a cool place it will keep well for several days, and several times this amount may be made at one time. In making several pounds it is better to divide the mass before kneading, and each part may be flavored differently.

Chocolate Creams—Dust the moulding-board with as little flour as possible and roll a piece of fondant into a cylindrical shape. Cut it into regular-shaped pieces, roll between the palms of the hands until round, lay on paraffine paper and let harden until the next day. Melt a cake of chocolate in a rather deep vessel that has been set in a pan of hot water; add a piece of paraffine half as large as a walnut, the same amount of butter, and $\frac{1}{4}$ teaspoonful vanilla. Roll the cream in this, by using a steel fork or crochet needle, and place again on paraffine paper.

Nut Rolls—Take equal parts of walnut, butternut, or whatever variety of nut meats you prefer, and fondant, mix well, and form into a roll. Cover this with plain fondant, roll in granulated sugar and let harden until next day, then slice crosswise.

Molasses Nut Balls and Bars—Boil 2 cupfuls brown sugar, 1 of New Orleans molasses, and $\frac{1}{2}$ cup water until it will snap when tested in cold water. Take from the stove, add 2 cupfuls chopped walnut meats, stir until nearly cold, and then roll into balls between the palms of the hand; wrap in paraffine paper.

For walnut or peanut bars boil together a cupful of New Orleans molasses, 1 of brown sugar, and half a cup of water. When it stands the test of water add a tablespoonful each of butter and vinegar. When it boils up remove from the fire, add 3 teacupfuls peanut or walnut meats, pour into buttered shallow pans, smooth the top, and when nearly cold cut in bars or squares with a buttered knife.

Cocoanut bars are made in the same way, using fresh cocoanut that has been dried out 2 hours after being grated, or shredded cocoanut.

Crystallizing Syrup — Any variety of bon-bons made with fondant may be crystallized to make another attractive variety by the following process: Boil $1\frac{1}{2}$ lbs. sugar and $\frac{1}{2}$ pint water until it forms a thread that will snap easily. Remove from the fire, and when nearly cold sprinkle a tablespoonful of water on the top to dissolve the film. Have the candies in a shallow pan, pour the syrup carefully over, touching each part; cover with a dainty cloth, resting on the syrup to prevent the formation of a crust. After standing 6 hours, with a hat pin remove the candies, place on paraffine paper, spread a damp cloth over, and leave until dry.

Jelly Rolls — Roll out evenly a piece of plain fondant, spread with any variety of fruit jelly or marmalade preferred, and when hard cut into slices and crystallize as above.

Chocolate Caramels — Half lb. Baker's chocolate, 3 lbs. sugar, half granulated and half brown, the latter not too moist, $\frac{1}{2}$ lb. butter, 1 small cup milk.

Mix the ingredients and boil until it hardens in cold water, which should be about 20 minutes. Stir all the time if you wish the caramels to be "crumbly."

Cocoanut Bon-bons — To the white of one egg and an equal quantity of water add enough pulverized sugar and grated cocoanut to enable you to make into balls; lay the balls on greased plates. Take two cups of sugar and one of water and boil until it creams, then add one teaspoonful of vanilla or rose water; set the dish containing this mixture on another containing boiling water, so it will not get too hard; then roll the balls in it as you would chocolate creams, and lay on greased plates to harden.

Almond Taffy — Boil together ½ pint water and 1 lb. brown sugar for 10 minutes. Blanch and slice through the middle 1½ oz. almonds; stir them in the syrup with 2 oz. of butter. Let the mixture boil hard for 10 minutes. Pour on a well-buttered dish to the thickness of ½ inch.

Everton Taffy—Put a pound of brown sugar in a buttered pan, together with 3 tablespoonfuls of water. Let it boil until it becomes a smooth, thick syrup. Add ½ pound of butter, stirring well. Let this boil ½ hour; add lemon flavoring.

Butterscotch —Use 3 cupfuls of New Orleans molasses, 2 cupfuls granulated sugar, ¾ cupful butter, and a very little water. Cook quickly about 20 minutes. Try a little in cold water, to see when it becomes crisp. Just before taking up add ⅛ teaspoonful baking-soda well mashed and smooth. Pour into buttered tins and cut as soon as it becomes perfectly cool.

Sugar Candy—Put in a shallow pan 3 cupfuls granulated sugar, ½ cupful water, ½ cupful vinegar, and at the last, ½ tablespoonful butter, with ½ teaspoonful cooking-soda, dissolved in hot water. Cook quickly, without stirring, for 1 hour, or until it crisps in cold water. Pull while quite hot with buttered finger tips, and continue pulling until the candy is white. Chop into small pieces.

Candied Fruit — Boil 1 cupful granulated sugar, 4 tablespoonfuls water, 2 tablespoonfuls vinegar and $\frac{1}{4}$ spoonful soda. Avoid stirring. When the mixture is boiled to a syrup, dip into it cherries, grapes, pine-apple, oranges, pears, etc. When well dipped place the fruit on paraffine paper and put in a warm place to dry. Chestnuts and filberts thus candied are delicious.

Hoarhound Candy — Hoarhound candy is a favorite cough remedy. To 1 quart of water add a small handful of hoarhound herb, and boil $\frac{1}{2}$ hour. Strain, pressing all the liquid from the herbs. Add 3 lbs. of brown sugar, and boil to the "hard crack." Put in a piece of butter as large as a walnut. When the butter is dissolved, pour the mass on a greased platter or marble slab. When almost cold, square off with a knife.

Molasses Taffy — Boil together 2 cupfuls of brown sugar, 1 of New Orleans molasses, $\frac{1}{2}$ cupful of water, and 2 tablespoonfuls of vinegar; when crisp, add a tablespoonful of butter, stir 1 minute, then remove from the fire, add $\frac{1}{2}$ teaspoonful soda; when nearly cold pull until a beautiful golden color.

French Almond Rock — Put 1 lb. of loaf-sugar and a teacupful of water into a saucepan, stir it until the sugar is melted, take off the scum that comes to the top, and when boiled for $\frac{1}{4}$ hour add 1 tablespoonful vinegar or lemon juice. Stir in sliced almonds to taste, pour out on a well-buttered tin and cut into slices.

Lemon Candy — Into a bright tinned kettle put $3\frac{1}{2}$ lbs. of sugar, $1\frac{1}{2}$ pints of water, and a full tablespoonful of cream of tartar. Place over a hot fire and stir until the lumps disappear. Boil briskly until the candy is hard and brittle when a little is thrown into cold water. Take the candy from the fire and pour it on a large platter, greased with a little butter. When cooled sufficiently to be handled, add a teaspoonful of finely powdered tartaric acid, and the same quantity of extract of lemon, and work them into the mass. The acid should be fine and free from lumps. The mass must be worked enough to distribute the acid and lemon extract evenly, but no more, as too much handling destroys its transparency. It may now be formed into sticks or drops, or spread out flat on tins in thin sheets.

Molasses Candy — Dissolve 1 cupful of sugar in $\frac{1}{2}$ cupful of vinegar, mix with 1 quart of molasses, and boil, stirring often, until it hardens when dropped from a spoon into cold water; then stir in a piece of butter the size of an egg and 1 teaspoonful of saleratus, the latter dissolved in hot water. Flavor to your taste, give a hard final stir, and pour into buttered dishes. As it cools, cut into squares for "taffy," or, while soft enough to handle, pull white into sticks, using only the buttered tips of your fingers for that purpose.

"Old-Fashioned" Molasses Candy — Into a kettle holding 4 times the amount of molasses to be used, pour a convenient quantity of good New Orleans molasses. Boil over a slow fire half an hour, stirring all the time, and taking off the kettle if there is any danger of the contents running over. Do not let the candy burn. When a little dropped in cold water becomes quickly hard and brittle, add a teaspoonful of carbonate of soda, free from lumps, to every 2 quarts, stir quickly to mix, and pour on greased platters to cool. When sufficiently cool, pull back and forth, the hands being rubbed with butter to prevent the candy from sticking to them, until the candy is of a bright yellowish brown color. If you wish, flavor with vanilla or lemon.

Cocoanut Kisses — Beat together the whites of 2 eggs with as much granulated sugar as they will take up, making a rather stiff batter. Add a piece of butter the size of an English walnut and half a teaspoonful of vanilla or lemon extract. When beaten perfectly smooth, add grated cocoanut, which should be fresh and carefully prepared. Stir in the cocoanut, beating for some minutes. Then drop the prepared confection upon buttered tins and place them in a current of air to dry. Many confectioners put them at once in the oven; but they sometimes spread out if the heat is applied too soon. They may remain in the oven until slightly brown, or may merely be allowed to heat through and dry.

Mrs. Senator Cullom's Candy — Mix together the whites of 2 eggs, an equal quantity of cold water, and enough confectioners' sugar to make a stiff dough. It will require about 2 lbs. To prepare fruits and nuts, take seeds out of dates and fill with the cream; blanch almonds and cover with cream. Candied cherries are nice, taking little balls of the cream and putting a cherry on each. English walnuts are used in the same way as cherries.

Marshmallows — Dissolve 1 lb. clear white gum-arabic in 1 quart water; strain, add 1 lb. refined sugar, place on fire. Stir continually until sugar is dissolved and the mixture becomes of the consistency of honey. Next add gradually the beaten whites of 8 eggs; stir the mixture all the time until it thickens and does not adhere to the finger, pour into a tin slightly dusted with starch, and when cool divide with a sharp knife.

Peppermint Drops—The peppermint and wintergreen drops which follow the ice cream course to prevent possible disturbance from chilling with the frozen dainties are made of pure sugar with half the quantity of arrowroot used for the cream drops, and essence of wintergreen or mint to taste, rolled on a marble slab and cut out in disks the size of a quarter dollar. Confectionery is a pretty art for ladies and a very convenient one where there are children with the traditional sweet tooth. And what adds more repute to a hostess' table than that it is furnished with tempting fresh bonbons of her own making?

Harmless Colorings for Candies—Vegetable colorings are always to be used, the juice of blood beet for deepest red, cranberry juice tinging a delicate pink, and cochineal—the sole exception—giving a lovely rose. In coloring yellow, carrot juice or a very little yolk of egg answers better than gamboge. Spinach furnishes the best green, and is prepared by cutting fresh spinach into very small pieces and expressing the juice. A quarter oz. cochineal will color confectionery for a lifetime, and should be kept in a bottle closely corked. One bug is used at a time, pounding it and pouring on 2 or 3 teaspoonfuls of boiling water, after which the liquid is bottled and will keep three months, only a drop or two being needed for any common quantity of confectionery or frosting. Blue is rarely used, and the drop of indigo needed will not hurt any one. The petals of yellow roses, infused in boiling water, yield a delicate dye which is charming with old-fashioned rosewater desserts.

ICE CREAM, ICES, Etc.

Frozen Custard — One quart rich milk, 1 large cup sugar, 1 teaspoonful salt, yolks of 6 eggs, 1½ teaspoonfuls almond flavoring, 1 cup cream.

Let the milk come to a boil; beat the sugar, salt and eggs together, and add the milk, a few drops at a time; return to the double boiler and cook 5 minutes, stirring all the time. Set away to get cold, and freeze.

Grape Sherbet — One quart grape juice, obtained by boiling the grapes half an hour and straining through a jelly bag, juice of 8 good-sized oranges, 1½ cups sugar.

Mix the orange and grape juice, strain and pour into your freezer. Freeze for 5 minutes, pour out and add the whites of 2 well-beaten eggs; return to the freezer and freeze for 20 minutes. Remove the dasher and pack away for an hour, then serve.

Peach Ice Cream—Two quarts ripe peaches, 1 cup sugar, mix well and set away in a covered dish. Take one pint of milk and one of cream; let them come to a boil, mix together 1 cup sugar, 2 scant tablespoonfuls flour and a teaspoonful salt, beat the eggs well, mix all; then add the boiling milk and cream. Return to your kettle and boil gently 20 minutes, stirring often to prevent sticking. When quite cold stir in the peaches, which must be mashed fine, and freeze.

Lemon Water Ice — Half a box of gelatine, dissolved in 1 pint cold water. Take the juice of 8 lemons and mix with 1¼ lbs. white sugar, then pour 1 quart of hot water on the sugar and lemons; pour 1½ pints of boiling water over the gelatine, and when it is quite dissolved add to the rest of the ingredients. Strain and set away to cool; when cold whip 15 minutes, and freeze.

Caramel Ice Cream — Burnt sugar ice cream is a favorite dish in Virginia, and it is often called caramel cream on account of its peculiar color, though it requires neither chocolate nor vanilla. It is made by pouring boiled custard, a little at a time, over a frying-pan in which brown sugar has been burned until it is a dark brown color. Keep on adding the custard, stirring all the time until the whole is smooth and the pan is full, then pour the contents back into the main bowl of custard, which should be the color of strong coffee when it is all mixed. The art in making this cream is in burning the sugar until it is exactly right. If this is properly prepared you have only to freeze it like any other custard. For 1 gallon it requires 1 gallon of milk, 2 cups of white sugar, the yolks of 16 eggs, and 2 cups of brown sugar well burned.

Chocolate Ice Cream — Six tablespoonfuls grated chocolate, 2 breakfast cups cream, 1 of fresh milk, ½ lb. sugar.

Stir the chocolate into the milk, mixing well, add remaining ingredients and freeze.

Fruit Cream — One and one-quarter lbs. of any kind of preserved fruit, 1 quart cream, juice of 2 lemons, sugar to taste.

Take the whole of the ingredients, and work through a sieve. Then freeze in a freezing-can, and work until it is frozen. Then turn out and serve.

Ice Cream — One quart milk, 2 eggs, ¾ lb. sugar, 2 tablespoonfuls corn-starch or arrowroot, 1 qt. cream.

Scald the milk, yolks of eggs, sugar, and cornstarch or arrowroot, until it is of the consistency of custard. Then allow to cool. When cool add the cream whipped, and the whites of the eggs whisked to a stiff froth. Sweeten to taste, flavor, and freeze in the usual way.

Vanilla Ice Cream — Beat the yolks of 8 eggs with ¾ of a pound of sugar until very light. Put 1½ pints of rich milk on the fire to scald, highly flavored with vanilla. When the milk is scalded, stir it into the egg as soon as it is cool enough not to curdle. Now stir the mixture constantly until it has slightly thickened. Do not let it remain too long and curdle, or it will be spoiled. When taken off the fire again, mix in ¼ box of gelatine which has been soaked ½ hour in 2 tablespoonfuls of lukewarm water near the fire. The heat of the custard will be sufficient to dissolve it if it is not already dissolved. Cool the custard well before putting it into the freezer, however; stir it almost constantly until it begins to set; then stir in lightly a pint of cream, whipped. Stir it for 2 or 3 minutes longer, put it into a mould, and return it to a second relay of ice and salt.

Strawberry Water Ice — Boil 1 pint of water and 3 teacupfuls of granulated sugar for about 10 minutes, skimming carefully. Remove from the fire and allow it to grow cold, then add 2 pints of strawberry juice. Many people think the flavor is improved by adding a little currant juice. Beat the mixture well together and freeze. Red raspberry ice made in the same way is also excellent.

Orange Water Ice — Rub sugar on the peel of 2 oranges and 1 lemon. Squeeze and strain the juice of the lemon and 6 oranges. Dissolve the flavored sugar with a little hot water, and mix with ½ pint of syrup. If too sweet, add a little water. Strain into the freezing-pot, and finish as lemon water ice.

Crystal Palace Cream — A rich custard, ¼ oz. gelatine dissolved in a little boiling water, 2 sponge cakes, 2 macaroons, 2 tablespoonfuls milk.

Make the custard, dissolve the gelatine, and when it is nearly cold pour into the custard, which must also be cool; soak the cakes and macaroons in the milk (or, if preferred, any fruit syrup, which must be rich and sweet). Put the cakes into a mould and gently pour the cream over them; let it stand till cold. A few glacé cherries may be added.

Lemon Cream — One pint of thick cream, yolks of 2 eggs, 4 oz. fine sugar, rind of 1 lemon cut thinly, juice of the lemon.

Well beat the yolks and add to the cream, sugar and rind of the lemon; boil, and then stir it till almost cold; put the juice of a lemon into a dish and pour the cream upon it, stirring until quite cold.

Lemon Cream, Solid — Half a pint of cream, the juice of 3 lemons and the rind of 2, ¾ lb. loaf-sugar in small lumps.

Rub the sugar on the lemons, and lay them at the bottom of the dish, pour the lemon-juice over, make the cream a little warm; then, standing on a chair and with the dish on the ground, pour the cream on so as to froth it.

Lemon Cream (without cream) — Four lemons, 12 tablespoonfuls water, 7 oz. powdered white sugar, yolks of 9 eggs.

Peel the lemons very thinly into the above proportion of water, then squeeze the juice into the sugar. Beat the yolks thoroughly and add the peel and juice together, beating for some time. Then strain into your saucepan, set over a gentle fire and stir one way till thick and scalding hot. Do not let it boil or it will curdle. Serve in jelly glasses.

White Ribbon Cook Book.

Cherry Cream—Take 2 qts. cherries, heaping quarts, and bruise them without removing the pits, throw over them ¾ cupful sugar and let them stand in a cool place for 2 hours. Then strain. Sweeten the juice after straining, beat a pint of cream, gradually add the juice and the beaten whites of 2 eggs, continually whisking it till no more froth arises. The secret of success is to have cream and eggs all thoroughly chilled on ice, and in adding the juice a little at a time to prevent curdling.

Nesselrode Pudding—Make a custard with 1 pint milk, 8 tablespoonfuls sifted sugar, and yolks of 7 eggs (or use ½ pint milk and ½ pint cream); let the milk come to the boil, then mix it with the other ingredients; after stirring for some time put the mixture in a pan over the fire and go on stirring till it thickens, but it must not boil, or it will curdle; strain and flavor it with vanilla or any other flavor. Divide the custard in two separate basins; flavor and color the one to taste, partly freeze it, and add a small tumblerful of whipped cream, slightly sweetened with powdered sugar. Meantime brown, in ½ oz. fresh butter, 4 oz. blanched almonds and 1 oz. sifted sugar; pound this quite smooth, mix with the other half of the custard, strain and freeze. Mold the two ices in layers and freeze for 2 hours.

Tutti Frutti—When a rich cream is partly frozen, candied cherries, English currants, chopped raisins, or any other candied fruits, chopped rather fine, are added; add about the same quantity of fruit as there is of ice-cream. Mould and imbed in ice and salt. Serve with whipped cream.

Strawberry Ice Cream—Sprinkle sugar over the strawberries, mash them well and rub them through a sieve. To a pint of the juice add a pint of good cream. Make it very sweet. Freeze it in the usual way, and, when beginning to set, stir in lightly 1 pint cream, whipped, and lastly a handful of whole strawberries, sweetened. Put it into a mould which is imbedded in ice. Or, when fresh strawberries can not be obtained, there is no more delicious cream than that made with the French bottled strawberries. Mix the juice in the bottle with the cream, and add the whipped cream and the whole strawberries when the juice, etc., have partly set in the freezer.

Pineapple Ice Cream — Make a plain vanilla ice cream and when partially frozen stir in ½ can grated pineapple. Mix well and complete the freezing. The remainder of the pineapple may be converted into a most delicious trifle.

Pineapple Trifle — Line a pretty dish with stale sponge cake and spread upon it the grated pineapple. Whip 1 pint sweet cream, sweeten and flavor with vanilla; stir in 1-5 box Nelson's gelatine which has been previously soaked in ¼ cup cold water, then dissolved by adding ¼ cupful boiling water. Pour this over the cake and set on ice to stiffen.

Grape Sherbet — Lay a square of cheese-cloth over a bowl; put in a pound of ripe grapes; mash very thoroughly with a wooden masher; squeeze out all the juice; add an equal amount of cold water, the juice of 1 lemon, and sugar enough to make it very sweet. Freeze as usual.

Currant Ice — Boil 1 quart of water and a pound of sugar until reduced to a pint, skim it, take it off the fire, add a pint of currant juice; when partly frozen, stir in the whites of 4 eggs. Mould, and freeze again. A good ice for fever patients.

Lemon Sherbet — Soak 1 teaspoonful gelatine in ¼ cup cold water, and dissolve with ¼ cup boiling water. Add the juice of 6 lemons, 1 pint sugar, and 3½ cups water. Strain and freeze. If the lemons have become dry by being kept in the house, let them soak in cold water for a little time. A good way is to pour boiling water over the fruit, and then drop into cold water. This would destroy any insects which might be in the peel. Lemons may be kept in sour milk with good result. The gelatine is not used for nutriment, but to give a better consistency to the sherbet. If it is not convenient to use a freezer, the sherbet may be frozen in a pail. Put the lemon mixture in the pail and pack into a pail of ice and rock salt, using half salt and half finely-cracked ice in alternate layers. When it becomes hardened, scrape the sherbet from the side of the pail, and beat with a Dover egg-beater. Pack down again, and keep closely covered until ready to serve. If the sherbet is to be frozen in an ice cream freezer, use two-thirds of ice and one-third of rock salt, in alternate layers. Turn the crank very slowly, as the slower it is turned the faster the cream is frozen and the smoother it is. If the crank is turned rapidly, the liquid is stirred about so that it does not come in contact with the sides of the can long enough to freeze.

Peaches and Cream Frozen — Peel and quarter the fresh peaches; mix them with sugar and cream to taste. Arrange some of the quarters of the peaches tastefully in the bottom of a basin, then fill, and freeze the mass solid, without stirring. Turn it out to serve.

Iced Pudding — One and one-half pints of custard, composed of the yolks of 4 eggs, 4 tablespoonfuls of sugar, a flavoring of vanilla, 8 oz.

fruits, consisting of equal parts of dried cherries, pine-apple, dried pears, or apricots, all cut into very small pieces. These fruits may be selected, or perhaps it would be more convenient to purchase ½ lb. of the French preserved dried fruits; or add 1 oz. candied citron sliced, 2 oz. currants, 2 oz. stoned and chopped raisins, and ½ pint cream whipped. Freeze the custard in the usual manner, then mix in the fruits and whipped cream. Put into a mould, and place it on ice and salt. Serve whipped cream around it.

Frozen Custard with Fruit — Two pints milk, same of cream, 6 eggs, 3 teacups sugar, 1 pint berries, or peaches cut up small.

Let the milk nearly boil; beat the yolks of the eggs with the sugar and add the milk by degrees. Whip the whites of the eggs to a froth and add to the mixture; put all in a saucepan, stirring until it is a nice thick and smooth custard. When perfectly cold whisk in the cream and freeze. If the custard is allowed to freeze itself, stir in the fruit after the second beating.

Custard — One and a half quarts rich milk, 1 cup sugar, ½ box gelatine, 4 eggs, vanilla to taste.

Dissolve the gelatine in the milk; add the yolks and sugar; let it come to a boil, then remove from the fire. When cool, add whites of eggs, etc. Pour into mould. To be eaten with cream, if preferred.

Chocolate Custard — One quart milk, yolks of 6 eggs, 6 tablespoonfuls sugar, ½ cup grated vanilla chocolate.

Boil the ingredients until thick enough, stirring all the time. When nearly cold flavor with vanilla. Pour into cups, and put the whites of the eggs beaten with some powdered sugar on top.

PRESERVES.

FRUIT for preserving must be gathered in dry weather, and should be carefully selected, discarding all bruised fruit, and purchasing only that of the largest and finest quality. Use only the best white sugar. There is no economy in using common sugar, because it causes a greater amount of scum, which must of course be taken off. In making syrups the sugar must be pounded and dissolved in the syrup before setting on the fire; no syrups or jellies should be boiled too high. Fruits must not be put into a thick syrup at first. Fruits preserved whole or sliced may be boiled in a syrup made of two pounds of sugar to every pound of water, the quantity of syrup differing in some cases, but the general rule is one and a half the substance of fruit. The following has been found very good: To clarify six pounds of sugar, put into a preserving-pan, and pour into it five pints of cold spring water; in another pint beat lightly up the white of one small egg, but do not froth it very much; add it to the sugar, and give it a stir to mix it well with the whole. Set the pan over a gentle fire when the sugar is nearly dissolved, and let the scum rise without being disturbed; when the syrup has boiled five minutes take it from the fire, let it stand a couple of minutes, and then skim it very clean; let it boil again, then throw in half a cup of cold water, which will bring the remainder of the scum to the surface; skim it until it is perfectly clear, strain it through a thin cloth, and it will be ready for use, or for further boiling.

All unripe fruit must be rendered quite tender by gentle scalding, before it is put into syrup, or it will not imbibe the sugar; and the syrup must be *thin* when it is first added to it, and be thickened afterwards by frequent boiling, or with additional sugar; or the fruit will shrivel instead of becoming plump and clear. A pound of sugar boiled for ten minutes in one pint of water will make a very light syrup; but it will gradually thicken if rapidly boiled in an uncovered pan. Two pounds of sugar to the pint of water will become thick with a little more than half an hour's boiling, or with three or four separate boilings of eight or ten minutes each; if too much reduced it will candy instead of remaining liquid.

In making jams many cooks, after allowing the proper proportion of sugar, put the fruit into the preserving-pan without removing the stones or skins until after boiling, as the flavor is thought to be finer by adopting this method. Glass bottles are preferable to any other, as they allow inspection to detect incipient fermentation, which may be stayed by re-boiling. Copper or brass preserving-pans are the best kind to use, but they require a great deal of care to keep clean; the enameled are very nice and easily kept in order. Jams should be kept in a dry, cool place, and if properly made will only require a small round of writing-paper oiled, and laid on to fit, and tied down securely with a second paper brushed over with the white of egg to exclude the air.

Plum Jam — Allow $\frac{3}{4}$ lb. of white sugar to 1 lb. of fruit. It is difficult to give the exact quantity of sugar to be used in plum jam; in fact, it entirely depends upon the quality of the plums used; therefore your own judgment will be necessary. After weighing the plums halve them and remove the stones; then place on a large dish and sprinkle with the sugar; leave them thus for 24 hours; then put into a preserving-pan and let them simmer gently on the back of the stove for about 25 or 30 minutes, then boil very quickly for ¼ hour, skimming carefully, and stirring with a wooden spoon to prevent the jam sticking. It greatly improves the jam to put some kernels from the plum stones into it.

To Preserve Fruit in Syrup — To every lb. of fruit allow 1 lb. of lump sugar, ½ tumbler of cold water. Boil the water and sugar together until it thickens slightly, which will take about ½ hour if the sugar be good. Take off the scum as it rises. Add the fruit and boil for ½ hour (rather longer if stone fruit), stirring very slightly, or the fruit will break. Take off the scum as it rises, but if both sugar and fruit be good there will be very little. Put into jars and tie over.

N. B.—To keep well, fruit must be perfectly sound and dry when gathered.

Currant Jam — Three-quarters of a lb. of white sugar to every pound of fruit.

Let the fruit be very ripe, remove from the stalks with a silver fork; dissolve the sugar over the fire, then put in the currants and boil for 1½ hour, stirring and skimming all the time. Put into jars and cover air-tight.

Raspberry Jam — Allow 1 lb. white sugar to 1 lb. fruit, and ½ cup red currant juice.

Directly this fruit is purchased preserve it; if allowed to stand the jam and the flavor will not be so good; place in preserving-pan and allow to boil for ½ hour. Be particular to skim well, as this will make the jam nice and clear. When done, place in pots and cover in the usual manner.

Gooseberry Jam — Some fine full-grown, unripe gooseberries, their weight in sugar; to 1 pint of liquor allow 1 lb. of sugar.

Cut, and pick out the seeds of the gooseberries; put them into a pan of water, green, and put them into a sieve to drain; beat them in a marble mortar, with their weight in sugar. Boil a quart of them to a mash in a quart of water; squeeze, and add to the liquor sugar in the above proportions; then boil and skim it, put in your green gooseberries, and having boiled them till very thick, clear, and of a nice green, put them into bottles.

Damson Jam — Equal quantities of fruit and jelly.

Choose the fruit without blemish; remove the stones from the fruit, and put it and the sugar into your preserving-pan; stir slowly until the sugar is melted, and remove all scum. After the jam has begun to simmer, allow it to boil for an hour. It is necessary to stir diligently, or the jam will burn. When done, pot in the usual way.

Tomato Preserves — Select small, green tomatoes, wipe carefully and prick the skins in several places. To ½ peck of these take 4 lbs. sugar, juice of 6 large lemons, and 2 oz. green ginger root and 1 of mace; put on the rest of the ingredients and let them boil ½ hour, skimming carefully; then put on the tomatoes and let them cook gently. When the tomatoes are clear and can be pierced with a straw take them up and lay carefully on plates to cool, allowing the syrup to simmer on the back of the stove. Put the tomatoes into jars, pour over the syrup and seal. Small yellow tomatoes may be preserved in the same way.

Tomato Jelly—One peck yellow tomatoes cut into pieces and boiled until soft; strain through a jelly bag; put on the fire and boil 20 minutes; to every cup of juice measure one of sugar; set the sugar in the oven, being careful that it is only heated through, not scorched. At the end of the 20 minutes add the sugar and the juice of a dozen lemons which has been strained through your jelly bag; boil 15 minutes more, then pour into your jelly glasses. Have the glasses just washed in hot water and wiped dry, and put a teaspoon in each one as you are ready to fill it. This will prevent the hot liquid from breaking the glasses.

Quince Marmalade—Four lbs. peeled and thinly sliced quinces in 2 quarts acidulated water, 2 lbs. peeled, cored and sliced apples, 3 lbs. sugar.

Place the fruit on the fire to boil until soft; then add the sugar, and stir the marmalade with a clean wooden spoon over a brisk fire until reduced to a rather thick paste—running rather slowly off the spoon when lifted out of the pan; the marmalade must then be immediately removed from the fire and poured into pots.

Green Grape Jam—To 1 lb. grapes allow ¾ lb. sugar.

Pick the grapes carefully and reject any that are injured; wash them. Put the grapes into a preserving-pan, then a layer of sugar, then a layer of grapes. Boil on a moderate fire, stirring it all the time to prevent its burning, and as the grape stones rise take them out with a spoon, so that by the time the fruit is sufficiently boiled—

about 1 hour—the stones will all have been taken out. Put into jars and cover in the usual way.

Blackberry Jam—To every lb. of picked fruit allow 1 lb. loaf sugar and ¼ lb. apples peeled and cored and cut quite small. Boil the fruit for 10 minutes, add the sugar, boil, stir and remove all scum. It will take from ½ to ¾ of an hour.

Strawberry Jam—To 1 lb. fruit allow ¾ lb. or 1 lb. sugar; to 4 lbs. strawberries add 1 pint red currant juice.

Put the currant juice and strawberries on to boil for 30 minutes, and stir carefully all the time; then put in the sugar and boil up very quickly for 20 or 25 minutes, removing any scum that arises; put into your jars, covering air-tight. If a pound of sugar is used there will be more jelly.

Apple Marmalade—Pare, core and quarter some apples; put into a preserving-pan with sufficient water to prevent burning. Boil till it is a pulp. Take an equal weight of sugar in large lumps, dip in water and boil till it is a thick syrup; put it to the pulp, and simmer on a quick fire quarter of an hour. Grate in lemon-peel before it is boiled.

Apple Cheese—Dissolve 1 lb. sugar in ¼ pint water; add 1½ lbs. apples cut in quarters, and the rind of 1 lemon grated. Boil 3 hours; 10 minutes before that time add the juice of the lemon; stir all the time after the lemon is added, and boil quickly.

To Preserve Raspberries—To 1 lb. fruit, quite ripe, add 1 lb. finely-sifted sugar. Make the sugar as hot as possible without scorching, put it to the fruit, and stir till every particle of sugar is dissolved; put it in jars, and tie down with bladder. It will keep for a year, and looks just like fresh raspberries crushed with sugar.

Quince Jam — To 1 lb. quinces allow ¾ lb. sugar.

Peel and quarter the quinces, leaving the seeds in, as they readily impart their mucilage to the water and thus thicken the syrup. Put the fruit and sugar into a preserving-pan, and ½ teacupful water to moisten the bottom of the pan; stir the fruit and sugar frequently, and when it boils keep it boiling rapidly until the fruit is soft and of a clear red color. It will take about an hour, reckoning from the first boiling-up. Put into jam pots, and cover when cold.

Apple Jam — Allow to every pound of pared and cored fruit ¾ lb. white sugar, the rind of 1 lemon, and juice of ½ lemon.

Having peeled and cored the apples, weigh them, and slice them very thin. Place in a stone jar and surround with boiling water; allow them to boil until tender; when tender place in a preserving-pan, add the sugar, grated lemon and juice. Boil slowly ½ hour from the time it begins to simmer, remove the scum, and put into jars and cover in the usual manner.

Green Fig Preserves — Equal quantity of fruit and syrup, peel of 1 large lemon, a little ginger.

Lay the figs in cold water for 24 hours, then simmer them till tender; put them again into cold water, and let them remain for two days, changing the water each day. If not quite soft, simmer again, and replace in cold water until next day. Take their weight in loaf sugar, and with ⅔ of it make a syrup, in which simmer the figs for 10 minutes. In 2 days take the third of the sugar, pound fine, and pour the syrup from the figs on it. Make a rich syrup with the peel of the lemon and a little raw ginger, and boil the figs in it, then mix all together and put into large jam pots. The figs may be cut in half, if preferred, after they have simmered until soft.

Preserved Pumpkins — Equal proportions of sugar and pumpkins, 1 gill lemon juice.

Cut the pumpkin in two, peel and remove the seed, cut in pieces about the size of a 50-cent piece; after weighing place in a deep vessel in layers, first sprinkling a layer of sugar, then of pumpkin, and so on, until it is finished; now add the lemon juice and set aside for 3 days; now for every 3 lbs. of sugar add ½ a pint of water and boil until tender. Pour into a pan, setting aside for 6 days, pour off the syrup and boil till thick; skim and add the pumpkin while boiling; bottle in the usual manner.

Quinces Preserved Whole — Some ripe quinces; to every pint of water allow 3 lbs. white sugar.

Pare the quinces and put them into the preserving pan, three-fourths covered with cold water (if they should float while the water is being poured on them, press them down with a plate until you have gauged the exact height of the water); take out the quinces, measure the water and add the sugar. Let this boil rapidly in the preserving-pan for 5 minutes, and then put in quinces. The syrup should not cover them at first, but when they are half cooked it will then amply cover the fruit. Boil the quinces rapidly, until soft enough for a knitting-needle to pierce them easily, which should be in an hour and a half, reckoning from the first boiling-up. Take the quinces out carefully, so as not to break them, and lay them on dishes to cool. Run the syrup through a jelly bag, or a piece of new flannel, put in a gravy strainer; this frees it of all odd little bits that may boil from the outside of the quinces, and makes it clearer. Put the syrup back in the preserving-pan, and boil it rapidly until it will jelly when dropped on a plate; put the quinces into the boiling syrup, and let them simmer gently for 10 minutes. Place each quince carefully in wide-necked jars, pour the hot syrup over them, and when cold cover in the usual way.

Preserved Oranges—Any number of oranges, with rather more than their weight in sugar; allow rather more than ½ pint of water to each lb. sugar.

Slightly grate and score the oranges round and round with a knife, but not very deeply. Put them into cold water for 3 days, changing the water twice each day. Tie them up in a cloth and boil them until they are quite soft, that is, soft enough to be penetrated by the head of a pin. While they are boiling place the sugar on the fire with the water; let it boil for a few minutes, then strain it through muslin. Put the oranges into the syrup and boil till it jellies and is of a yellow color. Try the syrup by putting some to cool; it should not be too stiff. The syrup need not cover the oranges completely, but they must be turned so that each part gets thoroughly done. Place the oranges in pots, cover with syrup, and tie down with paraffine papers. This is an excellent way of preserving oranges or shaddocks whole. Only they should be looked at now and then, and boiled up again in fresh syrup, if what they are in has become too hard, which, however, if they have been properly done, will not be the case. They form a nice dish for dessert, or for serving, filled with whipped cream or custard, either cold or gently warmed through in the syrup in a stewpan.

To Cover Preserves — Cut a round of thin paper the size of your jar, brush it over with white of egg, and place on the preserve egg downwards. See that it lies flat so as to keep out the air. Cut a round of white cooking-paper rather larger than your jar. Snip round the edge. Brush well over with white of egg, place on your jar, and stick down the edges round the jar with a dry cloth. Let your jam be cold before done, and let the paper on the top dry well before putting away.

Apple Marmalade — Some good cooking apples, ¾ lb. fruit, ½ teacupful water to 6 lbs. sugar, a few cloves, cinnamon or lemon peel for flavor.

Peel, core and thinly slice the apples (apples that cook to a smooth pulp easily); put the sugar in a preserving-pan (a tin or iron saucepan will turn them black) with the water; let it gradually melt, and boil it for 10 minutes; then put in the sliced apple, and a few cloves, cinnamon or lemon peel to flavor, if liked. Boil rapidly for an hour, skim well, and put in jam pots; it should be quite a smooth pulp, clear, and a bright amber color. Will keep good for 12 months.

Grape Marmalade — Take 10 lbs. of nice ripe grapes and wash them carefully; squeeze the pulps into one dish and throw the skins into another, put the pulps through a colander to remove seeds, then put pulps and skins together with ¾ lb. sugar to 1 lb. of fruit and cook thoroughly until jellied.

Sweet Tomato Pickle — Three and ½ lbs. tomatoes, 1¾ lbs. sugar, ½ oz. each of cinnamon, mace and cloves mixed, 1 pint vinegar.

Peel and slice the tomatoes, sticking into them the cloves; put all together into a stewpan and stew an hour. When done pack in glass jars, and pour the syrup over boiling hot.

Sweet Peach Pickle — To 4 lbs. peaches allow 2 lbs. white sugar, ½ oz. each of mace, cinnamon and cloves mixed, and 1 pint of the best white vinegar.

Pour scalding water over the peaches and remove the skins with a butter knife; drop into cold water; stick four cloves in each peach. Lay the peaches in preserving-pan with the sugar sprinkled over them; bring gradually to the boil, add vinegar and spice, boil 5 or 6 minutes. Remove the peaches and place in bottles. Boil the syrup thick and pour over boiling hot.

How to Ice Fruit—Any desirable fruit may be iced by dipping first in the beaten white of an egg, then in pulverized sugar. Do this until the icing is sufficiently thick. Peaches should be pared and cut in halves, and sweet, juicy pears are treated in the same way. Cherries, strawberries and other small fruits are iced with the stems on, only the largest being chosen. Pineapples should be cut into thin slices and these again divided into quarters. Oranges and lemons should be carefully pared, and all the white skin removed. Lemons are cut into horizontal slices, and oranges are divided into quarters.

Salted Peanuts—Buy one quart of unroasted peanuts, break the shells carefully to prevent crushing; then drop the nuts into very hot water and rub gently until the red skin is off. Dry carefully, lay on flat tin plates and pour melted butter over them—a couple of teaspoonfuls will suffice; then set in rather quick oven until a nice brown; then take up and sprinkle liberally with salt, tossing them so that both sides will receive a coat.

CANNED FRUITS, ETC.

To Can Peaches — First prepare the syrup. For canned fruits, 1 quart granulated sugar to 2 quarts water is the proper proportion; to be increased or lessened, according to the quantity of fruit to be canned, but always twice as much water as sugar. Use porcelain kettle, and, if possible, take care that it is kept solely for canning and preserving — nothing else. Have another porcelain kettle by the side of the first, for boiling water (about 3 quarts). Put the peaches, a few at a time, into a wire basket, such as is used to cook asparagus, etc. See that it is perfectly clean and free from rust. Dip them, when in the basin, into a pail of boiling water for a moment, and transfer immediately into a pail of cold water. The skin will then at once peel off easily, if not allowed to harden by waiting. This, besides being a neat and expeditious way of peeling peaches, also saves the best part of the fruit, which is so badly wasted in the usual mode of paring fruit. As soon as peeled, halve and drop the peaches into boiling water, and let them simmer — not boil hard — till a silver fork can be passed through them easily. Then lift each half out separately with a wire spoon and fill the can made ready for use; pour in all the boiling syrup which the jar will hold; leave it a moment for the fruit to shrink while filling the next jar; then add as much more boiling syrup as the jar will hold, and cover and screw down tightly immediately. Continue in this way, preparing and sealing one jar at a time, until all is done. If any syrup is left over, add to it the water in which the peaches were simmered, and a little more sugar; boil it down till it "ropes" from the spoon and you have a nice jelly, or, by adding some peaches or other fruit, a good dish of marmalade. Peaches or other fruit, good, but not quite nice enough for canning, can be used in this way very economically. Peaches to be peeled as directed above should not be too green or too ripe, else, in the first place, the skin cannot be peeled off, or, if too ripe, the fruit will fall to pieces.

Another Way—After peeling and halving as above directed, lay a clean towel or cloth in the bottom of a steamer over a kettle of boiling water and put the fruit on it, half filling the steamer. Cover tightly and let it steam while making the syrup. When this is ready, and the fruit steamed till a silver fork will pass through easily, dip each piece gently into the boiling syrup; then as gently place in the hot jar, and so continue till all have been thus scalded and put in the jar. Then fill *full* with syrup, cover and seal immediately. While filling, be sure and keep the jars hot.

Pears—The skin will not peel off so easily as that of peaches by dipping them in boiling water, but it will loosen or soften enough to be taken off with less waste of the fruit than if pared without scalding. Prepare the syrup and proceed as for peaches. They will require longer cooking; but as soon as a silver fork will pass through easily, they are done. Longer cooking destroys the flavor.

Pineapples—Pare very carefully with a silver knife, as steel injures all fruit. With the sharp point of the knife dig out as neatly and with as little waste as possible all the "eyes" and black specks, then cut out each of the sections in which the "eyes" were, in solid pieces clear down to the core. By doing this all the real fruit is saved, leaving the core a hard, round, woody substance, but containing considerable juice.

Take this core and wring it with the hands as one wrings a cloth, till all the juice is extracted, then throw it away. Put the juice thus saved into the syrup; let it boil up 5 minutes, skim till clear, then add fruit. Boil as short a time as possible, and have the flesh tender. The pineapple loses flavor by over-cooking more rapidly than any other fruit. Fill into well-heated jars, add all the syrup the jar will hold; cover and screw down as soon as possible.

Plums — Plums should be wiped with a soft cloth or dusted, never washed. Have the syrup all ready, prick each plum with a silver fork to prevent the skin from bursting, and put them into the syrup. Boil from 8 to 10 minutes, judging by the size of the fruit. Dip carefully into the hot jars, fill full, and screw on the cover immediately. Cherries may be put up in the same way.

Strawberries (Canned) — Allow to each 1 lb. of fruit ¾ lb. of sugar.

Put berries and sugar into a large, flat dish and allow to stand about 3 hours, then draw off the juice and put into preserving-pan and allow to come to a boil, removing the scum as it rises; then put in the berries, and let them come to a boil. Put into warm bottles and seal quickly.

Cherries (Canned) — To every 1 lb. of fruit ½ lb. of sugar, 3 gills of water.

Put the sugar and water on the fire to heat, and as soon as it comes to a boil put in the cherries and allow them to *scald* for ¼ hour; put into bottles boiling hot and seal. A few of the kernels put in to scald with the fruit impart a fine flavor. Note — Be sure to skim well.

Preserved Crab Apples — Select large, fine crab apples, prick the skins in several places;

put into your preserving-kettle ¾ lb. of sugar to each pound of fruit and a cupful of water; let the syrup boil 20 minutes, skimming off the scum which rises to the top; then put in your fruit and cook gently until the apples can be pierced with a straw; then take them out and lay on plates; boil the juice ½ hour longer; then put the fruit in jars, fill up with juice and seal.

Fruit Jellies — The fruit should be placed in a jar, and the jar set in a stewpan of warm water, covered and allowed to boil until the fruit is broken; take a strong jelly bag and press a little of the fruit at a time, turning out each time the skins; allow 2 lbs. of sugar to 1 quart of juice, set on the stove to boil again. Many good cooks heat the sugar by placing in the oven and stirring now and then to prevent burning. When the juice begins to boil (watch that it does not boil over 25 minutes), then add the heated sugar; stir well and just bring to a boil, remove directly from the stove, dip the vessels to contain it in hot water, and set them upon a dish cloth wrung out of warm water, pouring the boiling liquid into them; cover in the usual manner.

Rhubarb Jelly — Soak 2 oz. gelatine in a pint of water with ½ lb. best lump-sugar; well wash and slice about 2½ lbs. of rhubarb of a nice bright color, put it into a stewpan to boil with a quart of water, leave it to get thoroughly stewed, but not long enough to let the juice get thick; strain the latter, and add 1½ pints of it to the dissolved gelatine, with the whites and shells of 3 eggs. Whisk it all quickly on the fire, pass it through the jelly-bag, and pour it into a mould and leave it to set.

Orange and Tapioca Jelly — Soak 6 tablespoonfuls of tapioca for 3 hours in 2 cupfuls of salted water; set in hot water and boil, adding 4 teaspoonfuls of sugar and a little boiling water if too thick. When like custard, add the juice of 1 orange. Cover the bottom of the mould with sliced oranges, and when the jelly is cool pour it over the fruit.

Quince Jelly — Ripe quinces, allowing 1 pint of water to each pound of fruit, ¾ lb. of sugar to each pound of juice.

Prepare the quinces and put them in water in the above proportions; simmer gently till the juice becomes colored, but only very pale; strain the juice through a jelly bag, but do not press the fruit; allow it to drain itself. Put the strained juice in a preserving-pan and boil 20 minutes; then stir in the sugar in the above proportions and stir over the fire for 20 minutes, taking off the scum, and pour into glasses to set. It should be rich in flavor, but pale and beautifully transparent. Long boiling injures the color.

Raspberry Jelly — Ripe, carefully picked raspberries; allow ¾ lb. of pounded sugar to every pound of fruit.

Boil the raspberries for 10 minutes, strain and weigh the juice and add the sugar in the above proportions and boil for 15 or 20 minutes. Skim and stir well.

Cherry Jelly — Maydukes or Kentish cherries (allowing ¾ pint of water to 1 lb. of fruit).

Boil the cherries in the water, strain the juice and proceed as for raspberry jelly.

Red Currant Jelly — Red currants; ¾ lb. of sugar to 1 lb. of juice.

Pick the fruit and simmer it in water for about an hour, or until the juice flows freely; strain, boil up the juice, add the sugar, and boil again, skimming and stirring well for 15 minutes. Put into small pots, and when cold and firm cover it.

Black Currant Jelly — Make in the same way, but use a larger proportion of sugar.

White Currant Jelly — Pick the fruit carefully, weigh it, and put into the preserving-pan equal quantities of fruit and sugar. Boil quickly for 10 minutes, and strain the juice into the pots; when cold and stiff cover them.

Blackberry Jelly — Make as directed for red currant, but use only 10 oz. of sugar to each pound of juice. The addition of a little lemon juice is an improvement.

Barberry Jelly — Barberries, a little water, ¾ lb. of sugar to every pound of juice.

Take ripe barberries, carefully reject any spotted or decayed ones, wash, drain them and strip off the stalks. Boil with a very little water till quite tender, press out and strain the juice, boil up the juice, add the sugar, and boil for 10 minutes, skimming and stirring as above.

Green Gooseberry Jelly — Carefully picked gooseberries, allowing to each pound of fruit ¾ pint of water; to every pound of juice allow 1 lb. of white sifted sugar.

Boil the fruit in the water, reduce to a pulp— it will take ½ hour—strain through a jelly-bag, weigh the sugar in the above proportions; boil up the juice quickly and add the sugar; boil till reduced to a jelly (about 20 minutes), skim and stir well; pour into pots.

Red Gooseberry Jelly — Make it in the same way as the green, but ¾ lb. of sugar will be sufficient for each pound of juice. In straining the juice be careful not to press the fruit. The surplus fruit, with the addition of some currant juice, can be made into common jam.

Mixed Fruit Jelly—Fruit, strawberries, currants, cherries, etc.; ¾ lb. of sugar to each pound of juice.

Take ripe fruit, strip off the stalks and remove the stones from the cherries, boil all together for ½ hour, strain the juice. Boil up the juice, add the sugar in the above proportions, stirring well till quite dissolved, boil again for 15 or 20 minutes till it jellies, stirring frequently, and carefully removing all scum as it rises.

Quince Jelly—Ripe quinces; to every pound of quince allow 1 lb. of crushed sugar.

Peel, cut up and core the quinces. Put them in sufficient cold water to cover them, and stew gently till soft, but not red. Strain the juice without pressure, boil the juice for 20 minutes, add the sugar and boil again till it jellies—about ¼ hour—stir and skim well all the time. Strain it again through a napkin, or twice-folded muslin, pour into pots or moulds, and when cold cover it. The remainder of the fruit can be made into marmalade with ¾ lb. sugar and ¼ lb. juicy apples to every pound of quinces, or it can be made into compotes or tarts.

Quince and Apple Jelly—Equal quantities of quinces and apples; to every pound of juice allow ¾ lb. white sugar.

Stew the fruit separately till tender (the quinces will take longer), strain the juice, mix it and add the sugar. Proceed as in quince jelly.

Apple Jelly—Some sound apples; allow ¾ lb. sugar to each pound of juice.

Peel, core and quarter the apples, and throw them into cold water as they are done; boil them till tender, then strain the juice from them through a fine sieve, and afterwards through a jelly bag—if necessary pass it through twice, as the juice should be quite clear; boil up the juice add the sugar, stir till melted, and boil for another 10 minutes; add the strained juice of a lemon to every 1½ lbs. of juice just before it is finished.

Apple Jelly (2) — One lb. moist sugar, 1 lb. apples, 1 lemon — the juice of the lemon to be used and the rind added, cut very fine.

Boil the whole until it becomes a perfect jelly; let it stand in a mould till quite firm and cold, turn it out and stick it with almonds; set custard round. If for dessert, use a small plain mould.

Orange Jelly — Put 1 package of gelatine to soak in 1 pint of cold water; when it is dissolved add 2 pints of boiling water and juice of ½ dozen oranges and 2 lemons, as well as 1 pound of sugar; when all is dissolved, strain through a jelly bag and set away to harden. Cider or other fruit juice may be substituted for the oranges and lemons.

Sago Jelly — Two lbs. picked red currants, 1 pint cold water, ½ lb. white sugar, a cupful of sago.

Put the currants into the water and boil till soft, pass them through a sieve; put the juice to boil again with the sugar; when quite boiling add the sago, previously soaked in cold water; boil 20 minutes until quite transparent, put into a mould, and when cold turn out. Serve with or without custard around it.

Currant Sponge — Cover ½ box of gelatine with cold water and let soak ½ hour; pour over a pint of boiling water, add ½ pint of sugar and stir over the fire for 5 minutes. Pour in ½ pint of red currant juice, strain into a tin pan, set on ice until the mixture begins to thicken, beat to a froth, add the well-beaten whites of 4 eggs, mix, and pour into a mould to harden. Serve with whipped cream.

DAIRY DISHES.

GREAT attention and cleanliness are required in the management of a dairy. The cows should be regularly milked at an early hour, and their udders perfectly emptied.

The quantity of milk depends on many causes; as the goodness, breed and health of the cow, the pasture, the length of time from calving, the having plenty of clean water in the field she feeds in, etc. A change of pasture will tend to increase it.

When a calf is to be reared, it should be removed from the cow in ten days at the farthest. It should be removed in the morning and no food given to it till the following morning, when, being extremely hungry, it will drink readily; feed it regularly morning and evening, and let the milk which is given to it be just warm; skimmed milk will be quite good enough.

The milk when brought in should always be strained into the pans. The cans containing the recently drawn milk should be placed in water about 56° F., which should rise a little above the level of the milk; the animal heat is thus reduced to between 56 and 58° F., and the milk will keep sweet for thirty-six hours even in the hottest weather. This temperature allows the cream to rise with greater facility and with less admixture of other constituents than can be obtained in any other way. Some butter-makers allow the milk to stand for thirty-six hours; others say that twenty-four hours is sufficient for all the cream to rise. After the cream has risen it is to be removed by skimming, and after standing a suitable time is placed in the churn. The kind of churn generally preferred by the best butter-makers is the common dash churn, made of white oak. Much depends upon the manner in which the operation is performed, even with the same churn. The motion should be steady and regular, not too quick nor too slow. The time occupied in churning 12 or 15 gallons of cream should be from 40 to 60 minutes. When removed from the churn, it should be thoroughly washed in cold water, using a ladle and not the hands. It should then be salted with about one-twentieth of its weight of the purest and finest salt, which should be thoroughly incorporated with it, by means of a butter-worker, or ladle, the hands being never allowed to touch the butter. Twelve hours afterwards another working should be performed and the butter packed in strong and perfectly tight white oak firkins. When filled they should be headed up and a strong brine poured in at the top. It should then be placed in a cool, well-ventilated cellar.

Dr. Ure gives the following directions for curing butter, known as the Irish method: "Take one part of sugar, one part of nitre, and two of the best Spanish great salt, and rub them together into a fine powder. This composition is to be mixed thoroughly with the butter as soon as it is completely freed from the milk, in the proportion of 1 ounce to 16; and the butter thus prepared is to be pressed tight into the vessel prepared to receive it, so as to leave no vacuities. This butter does not taste well till it has stood at least a fortnight; it then has a rich, marrowy flavor that no other butter ever acquires."

Preserving Butter—Two lbs. of common salt, 1 lb. loaf-sugar, and 1 lb. saltpetre. Beat the whole well together, then to 14 lbs. of butter put 1 lb. of this mixture, work it well, and when cold and firm put it into glazed earthen vessels that will hold 14 lbs. each. Butter thus preserved becomes better by being kept, but it must be kept from the air, and securely covered down. If intended for winter use, add another ounce of the mixture to every pound of butter, and on the top of the pans lay enough salt to cover them with brine.

Clouted Cream — In order to obtain this, the milk is suffered to stand in a vessel for 24 hours. It is then placed over a stove, or slow fire, and very gradually heated to an almost simmering state, below the boiling point. When this is accomplished (the first bubble having appeared), the milk is removed from the fire, and allowed to stand for 24 hours more. At the end of this time the cream will have arisen to the surface in a thick or clouted state, and is removed. In this state it is eaten as a luxury; but it is often converted into butter, which is done by stirring it briskly with the hand or a stick. The butter thus made, although more in quantity, is not equal in quality to that procured from the cream which has risen slowly and spontaneously; and in the largest and best dairies in the Vale of Honiton the cream is never clouted, except when intended for the table in that state.

Dairy Dishes.

Rennet — Take out the stomach of a calf just killed, and scour it well with salt and water, both inside and out; let it drain, and then sew it up with two large handfuls of salt in it, or keep it in the salt wet, and soak a piece in fresh water as it is required.

Maitre d'Hotel Butter — Two oz. fresh butter, juice of 1 lemon, white sugar and salt to taste, parsley blanched, freed from moisture and finely minced.

Put the butter in a basin with the other ingredients, incorporate the whole effectually and quickly, and put it by in a cool place until wanted.

Butter (to serve as a little dish) — Roll butter in different forms, either like a pine, making the marks with a teaspoon, or in crimping rollers, work it through a colander, or scoop with a teaspoon, and mix it with grated beef tongue or anchovies. Make a wreath of curled parsley to garnish.

Curled Butter — Procure a strong cloth, and secure it by two of its corners to a nail or hook in the wall; knot the remaining two corners, leaving a small space. Then place your butter into the cloth; twist firmly over your serving dish, and the butter will force its way between the knots in little curls or strings. Garnish with parsley and send to table.

Daisy Butter — Two tablespoonfuls white sugar, yolks of 2 hard-boiled eggs, 2 tablespoonfuls orange-flower water, $\frac{1}{4}$ lb. *fresh* butter.

Pound the yolks with the orange-flower water (in a mortar) to a smooth paste, then mix in the sugar and butter. Now place in a clean cloth, and force the mixture through by wringing. The butter will fall upon the dish in pieces according to the size of the holes in the cloth.

Melted Butter — Five oz. butter, 1 tablespoonful flour, 2 tablespoonfuls water, salt to taste.

Put all the ingredients into a stew-pan, and stir one way over the fire until all the ingredients are well mixed. Allow it just to boil, and it is ready to serve.

Cheese (to make) — Warm the milk till equal to new; but observe it must *not* be *too hot;* now add a sufficiency of rennet to turn it, and cover it over; let it remain till well turned, then strike the curd well down with the skimming-dish, and let it separate, observing to keep it still covered. Put the vat over the tub, and fill it with curd, which must be squeezed close with the hand, and more is to be added as it sinks, and at length left about three inches above the edge of the vat. Before the vat is in this manner filled, the cheese cloth must be laid at the bottom of it, and, when full, drawn *smoothly* over on all sides. The curd should be salted in the tub after the whey is out. When everything is prepared as above directed, put a board under and over the vat, then place it in the press; let it remain 2 hours, then turn it out, put on a fresh cheese cloth, and press it again 10 hours; then salt it all over, and turn it again into the vat; then press it again 24 hours. The vat should have several small holes in the bottom to let the whey run off.

Cheese (to preserve sound)—Wash in warm whey, when you have any, wipe it once a month, and keep it on a rack. If you want to ripen it, a damp cellar will bring it forward. When a whole cheese is cut, the larger quantity should be spread with butter inside, and the outside wiped to preserve it. To keep those in daily use moist, let a clean cloth be wrung out from cold water, and wrapped round them when carried from table. Dry cheese may be used to advantage to grate for serving with maccaroni.

Cream Cheese — Put 5 quarts of strippings, that is, the last of the milk, into a pan with 2 spoonfuls of rennet. When the curd is come, strike it down two or three times with the skimming-dish just to break it. Let it stand 2 hours, then spread a cheese-cloth on a sieve, put the curd on it, and let the whey drain; break the curd a little with your hand, and put it into a vat with a 2-lb. weight upon it. Let it stand 12 hours, take out, and bind a fillet round. Turn every day till dry, from one board to another; cover them with nettles, or clean dockleaves, and put between two pewter plates to ripen. If the weather be warm, it will be ready in 3 weeks.

Sage Cheese — Bruise some young red sage and spinach leaves, press out the juice, and mix it with the curd; then proceed as with other cheese.

Cheese Straws — Six oz. flour, 4 oz. butter, 3 oz. grated Parmesan cheese, a little cream, salt, white pepper and cayenne.

Roll it out thin, cut into narrow strips, bake in a moderate oven, and serve piled high and very hot and crisp.

Roast Cheese — Three oz. Cheshire cheese, yolks of 3 eggs, 4 oz. grated bread-crumbs, 3 oz. butter, a dessertspoonful of mustard, salt and pepper.

Grate the cheese, add the yolks, bread-crumbs and butter; beat the whole well in a mortar and add the mustard, salt and pepper. Make some toast cut into neat slices and spread the paste thickly on. Cover with a dish and place in the oven till hot through, then uncover and let the cheese color a light brown. Serve immediately.

Ramequins — Beat 2 eggs, whites and yolks separately; to the yolks of the eggs add 2 tablespoonfuls flour, 2 oz. melted butter and 2 oz. cheese, grated; to this add the stiff whites of the eggs. Mix well and bake in buttered gem-pans, in quick oven, about 15 minutes. Eat hot.

Cheese Dish — Quarter lb. good, fresh cheese, 1 cup sweet milk, $\frac{1}{4}$ teaspoonful dry mustard, a little pepper and salt, 1 tablespoonful butter.

Cut the cheese into thin slices, put it into a "spider" or saucepan, and pour over it the milk; mix in the other ingredients. Stir this mixture all the time while over the fire. Turn the contents into a hot dish and serve immediately.

Cheese Toast — Some rich cheese, pepper to taste, a beaten egg, with sufficient milk to make it of the consistency of cream.

Grate the cheese and mix with the other ingredients; warm the mixture on the fire, and when quite hot pour it over some slices of hot buttered toast. Serve immediately.

BEVERAGES

THE making of tea depends upon the brand. Always scald the pot just as you make the tea. A general rule is: "One teaspoonful for each person and one for the pot." Pour on a little boiling water to wet the tea. A minute or two later add a cup or two of boiling water. Allow to stand and add what boiling water is necessary for the amount of tea desired. This develops the stréngth of the tea and keeps it hot. Ceylon tea must not wait more than five minutes, as after that it takes on an unpleasant taste. Make a little, and often.

To make good coffee is the simplest and yet one of the most important things that pertain to cooking, but comparatively few know how to do it. For a family of five or six, take $\frac{1}{2}$ cup good ground coffee and mix with it the white of 1 egg and a little water; put it in the coffee-pot, and add to that about a pint of cold water. When it comes to a boil, set it on the back of the stove and add boiling water sufficient for use. This, with cream and sugar, makes most delicious coffee.

Remember in making coffee:

That the same flavor will not suit every taste, but that every one may be suited to a nicety by properly blending two or more kinds.

That equal parts of Mocha, Java and Rio will be relished by a good many people.

That a mild coffee can be made dangerously strong and still retain the mildness of flavor.

That the enjoyment of a beverage and slavish devotion thereto are quite different things.

That the flavor is improved if the liquid is turned from the dregs as soon as the proper strength has been obtained.

That where the percolation method is used the coffee should be ground very fine or the strength will not be extracted.

That if the ground coffee is put into the water and boiled, it should be rather coarse; otherwise it will invariably be muddy.

That a good coffee will always command a fair price, but that all high-priced coffees are not necessarily of high quality.

That, in serving, the cups and cream should be warm; the cream should be put in the cup before the coffee is poured in, but it is immaterial when the sugar is added.

That a level teaspoonful of the ground coffee to each cup is the standing allowance, from which deviation can be made in either direction, according to the strength desired.

Cocoa—Two tablespoonfuls cocoa, 1 breakfast cupful boiling milk and water.

Put sufficient cold milk in to form the cocoa into a smooth paste. Now add equal proportions of boiling milk and boiling water, mixing well. Great care must be taken that the milk does not burn, or it will impart a disagreeable flavor.

Chocolate—Allow 2 sticks of chocolate to 1 pint of new milk. After the chocolate is scraped, either let it soak an hour or so, with a tablespoonful of milk to soften it, or boil it a few moments in 2 or 3 tablespoonfuls water; then, in either case, mash into a smooth paste. When the milk, sweetened to taste, is boiling, stir in the chocolate paste, adding a little of the boiling milk to it first to dilute it evenly. Let it boil half a minute, stir it well and serve immediately.

Ginger Beer—One and one-fourth lbs. loaf sugar, 1 lemon, 2 oz. best white ginger, 1 gallon boiling water, 1 tablespoonful German yeast, and ½ oz. cream of tartar.

Peel the lemon; cut the inside in pieces. Crush the ginger, add the sugar and cream of tartar; pour over all the boiling water; stir well until the sugar is melted. Let it stand 24 hours to be quite cold, then stir in the yeast, which ought to be previously dissolved. Stir, and strain through a coarse cloth; then bottle, taking care the corks are secured. Keep in a cool place in hot weather.

Oatmeal Drink—(Dr. Parkes)—"The proportions are ¼ lb. oatmeal to 2 or 3 quarts water, according to the heat of the day and the work and thirst; it should be well boiled, and then 1 or 1½ oz. brown sugar added. If you find it thicker than you like, add 3 quarts water. Before drinking it shake up the oatmeal well through the liquid. In summer drink this cold; in winter, hot. You will find it not only quenches thirst, but will give you more strength and endurance than any other drink. If you cannot boil it, you can take a little oatmeal mixed with cold water and sugar, but this is not so good; always boil it if you can. If at any time you have to make a very long day, as in harvest, and cannot stop for meals, increase the oatmeal to ½ lb., or even ¾ lb., and the water to 3 quarts if you are likely to be very thirsty. If you cannot get oatmeal, wheat flour will do, but not quite so well."

Those who try this recipe will find that they can get through more work than when using beer, and that they will be stronger and healthier at the end of the harvest. Cold tea and skim milk are also found to be better than beer, but not equal to the oatmeal drink.

Lemonade (1)—Six large lemons and 1 lb. loaf sugar.

Rub the sugar over the rinds to get out the flavor, then squeeze out all the juice on the sugar; cut what remains of the lemons into slices, and pour on them a quart of boiling water; when this has cooled, strain it onto the juice and sugar, and add as much more water (cold) as will make it palatable.

Lemonade (2)—One oz. tartaric acid, 1 lb. loaf sugar, 1 pint boiling water, and 20 or 30 drops essence of lemon.

To be kept in a bottle and mixed with cold water, as desired.

Lemon Syrup—Boil until clear 1 pint lemon juice, strained, and 3 lbs. loaf sugar, stirring constantly, and add $\frac{1}{4}$ pint water to prevent its being too thick. The juice of a dozen lemons will give about a pint.

To Keep Lemon Juice—Buy the fruit when cheap, when not quite ripe; cut off the peels, and roll the fruit in your hand, so as to make them part with the juice readily. Squeeze the juice into a china basin, strain through a muslin which will not allow the least pulp to pass. Have ready $\frac{1}{4}$- and $\frac{1}{2}$-oz. phials (quite dry), fill with the juice so as to allow $\frac{1}{2}$ teaspoonful sweet oil in each. Cork tightly, and set them upright in a cool place. When wanted for use, wind some clean cotton round a skewer, and, dipping it in, the oil will be attracted. The juice will be quite clear; the rinds can be dried for grating.

Peppermint Cordial—One lb. loaf sugar, 1 pint boiling water.

Simmer 10 minutes, then stir in 1 tablespoonful honey; when nearly cold, add 30 drops essence of peppermint. Bottle for use. Four tablespoonfuls to a tumbler of cold or hot water makes a delicious drink. Essence of ginger can be used in the same way.

Raspberry Syrup—Fill a ½-gallon fruit-jar with ripe red raspberries, pour over them good cider vinegar; cover tightly, and set away in a cool, dark place for a week. Put on the fire and let come to a scalding point, strain through a jelly bag; to the juice add pint for pint of sugar. Boil gently about 20 minutes, skimming constantly. Bottle, seal, and keep in a cool place. Add a wineglassful to a glass of iced water. It is excellent.

Ginger Pop—Allow 4 quarts warm water, 1 oz. white ginger root, 2 lemons, 1 lb. white sugar, ½ tablespoon cream tartar, and ½ cup soft yeast. Cut the ginger root fine and boil in a little of the water; grate in the yellow rind only of the lemons, and put in the pulp and juice; when nearly cold, add the yeast. Put all in a stone jar in a warm place 24 hours, then bottle for use.

Currant Vinegar—Two quarts black currants, 1 pint best vinegar, 1½ lbs. white sugar.

Well bruise the currants and place into a basin with the vinegar; let it stand 3 or 4 days, and then strain into an earthen jar; add the sugar, set the jar in a saucepan of cold water and boil for an hour. When cold, bottle; it is the better for keeping.

Raspberry Vinegar—To 4 quarts red raspberries put enough vinegar to cover, 1 lb. sugar to every pint of juice.

Let the raspberries and vinegar stand for 24 hours; scald and strain; add sugar, boil 20 minutes, skim well, and when cold bottle.

Koumiss — Put 1 gill buttermilk into a quart of new, rich milk, and add 4 lumps white sugar; see that the sugar is dissolved. Put in a covered vessel, in a warm place, for 10 hours; it will then be thick. Pour from one pitcher to another, so that it may become uniformly thick, then bottle and set away in a warm place. It will be good in 24 hours in summer and 36 in winter. The bottles must not only be tightly corked, but the corks tied down. Shake the bottles well before opening. This is an excellent drink for people with weak digestion, and is also good for children.

Temperance Cup — Pare the yellow rind very thinly from twelve lemons; squeeze the juice over it in an earthen bowl, and let it stand over night, if possible. Pare and slice thinly a very ripe pineapple, and let it lie over night in $\frac{1}{2}$ lb. powdered sugar. If all these ingredients cannot be prepared the day before they are used, they must be done very early in the morning, because the juices of the fruit need to be incorporated with the sugar at least 12 hours before the beverage is used. After all the ingredients have been properly prepared, as above, strain off the juice, carefully pressing all of it out of the fruit; mix it with 2 lbs. powdered sugar and 3 quarts ice water, and stir it until the sugar is dissolved. Then strain it again through a muslin or bolting-cloth sieve, and put it on the ice or in a very cold place until it is wanted for use.

SICK-ROOM COOKERY

WITHIN the last few years great changes have occurred in the ideas entertained by the medical profession as to what is proper food for invalids. As a rule, patients are allowed to eat about what is desired, care being taken of course not to overload the stomach. There are cases, however, where there is little wish for food, and where the thoughtful nurse must look for something which is daintily appetizing as well as nourishing, and at the same time easy of digestion. To meet this want the recipes below are given.

Never set before the sick a large quantity of food; tempt with a very small portion delicately cooked and tastefully served. If not eaten directly, remove from the sick-room without delay, as no food should be allowed to stand there. Do not give the same food often, as variety is charming. Never keep the sick waiting; always have something in readiness — a little jelly, beef-tea, stewed fruit, gruel, etc. It will be found more tempting to serve any of these in glasses. If much milk is used, keep it on ice. Let all invalid cookery be simple; be careful to remove every particle of fat from broth or beef-tea before serving.

Beef-Tea — Take 1 lb. lean beef, 1 pint water, and ½ saltspoonful salt.

Cut the meat into very small pieces, carefully removing the fat. Put into a stone jar with the salt and water; cover with the lid, and tie over a piece of thick brown paper. Put it into a moderate oven, simmer slowly for 4 hours, and strain.

Beef Tea Custard—This may be served alone, either hot or cold, or a few small pieces can be put in a cup of beef-tea, which is thus transferred into a kind of *soupe royale*. Beat up an egg in a cup, add a small pinch of salt, and enough strong beef-tea to half fill the cup; butter a tiny mould and pour in the mixture. Steam it for 20 minutes, and turn it out in a shape.

Mutton Broth — Cut in small pieces 1 lb. of lean mutton or lamb, and boil it, unsalted, in 1 quart cold water, keeping it closely covered until it falls to pieces. Strain it and add 1 tablespoonful of rice or barley, soaked in a little warm water. Simmer for $\frac{1}{2}$ hour, stirring often, then add 4 tablespoonfuls milk, salt and pepper, and a little chopped parsley, if liked. Simmer again 5 minutes, taking care that it does not burn. Chicken broth may be prepared in the same way. Crack the bones well before putting them into the water.

Veal Broth—One and $\frac{1}{2}$ lbs. veal, 1 doz. sweet almonds, 1 qt. water, a little salt, 1 pt. boiling water.

Remove all the fat from the veal, and simmer gently in the water till it is reduced to a pint; blanch and pound the almonds till they are a smooth paste, then pour over them the boiling water very slowly, stirring it all the time till it is as smooth as milk; strain both the almond and veal liquors through a fine sieve and mix well together; add the salt, and boil up again.

Chicken Broth—An old fowl, 3 pints water, a pinch of salt, a blade of mace, 6 or 8 peppercorns, a very small chopped onion, a few sprigs sweet herbs.

Cut up the fowl and put it, bones as well, in a saucepan with the water, salt, mace, peppercorns, onion and sweet herbs; let it simmer very gently till the meat is *very* tender, which will take about 3 hours, skimming well during the time. Strain carefully and set aside to cool.

Egg Broth—An egg, ½ pint good unflavored veal or mutton broth quite hot, salt, toast.

Beat the egg well in a broth basin; when frothy add the broth, salt to taste, and serve with toast.

Beef Broth—One lb. good lean beef, 2 quarts cold water, ½ teacup tapioca, a small piece of parsley, an onion, if liked, pepper and salt.

Soak the tapioca 1 hour, cut in small pieces the beef, put in a stew pan the above proportion of water, boil slowly (keeping well covered) 1½ hours, then add the tapioca, and boil ½ hour longer. Some add with the tapioca a small piece of parsley and a slice or two of onion. Strain before serving, seasoning slightly with pepper and salt. It is more strengthening to add, just before serving, a soft poached egg. Rice may be used instead of tapioca, straining the broth, and adding 1 or 2 tablespoonfuls of rice (soaked for a short time), and then boiling ½ hour.

Scotch Broth — The liquor in which a leg of mutton, piece of beef or old fowl has been boiled, barley, vegetables chopped small, a cup of rough oatmeal mixed in cold water, salt and pepper to taste.

Add to the liquor some barley and vegetables, chopped small, in sufficient quantity to make the broth quite thick. The necessary vegetables are carrots, turnips, onions and cabbage, but any others may be added; old (not parched) peas and celery are good additions. When the vegetables are boiled tender add the oatmeal to the broth, salt and pepper to taste. This very plain preparation is genuine Scotch broth as served in Scotland; with any coloring or herbs, etc., added, it is not real Scotch broth. It is extremely palatable and wholesome in its plain form.

Broth (Beef, Mutton and Veal) — Two lbs. lean beef, 1 lb. scrag of veal, 1 lb. scrag of mutton, some sweet herbs, 10 peppercorns, 5 quarts water, 1 onion.

Put the meat, sweet herbs and peppercorns into a nice tin saucepan, with the water, and simmer till reduced to 3 quarts. Remove the fat when cold. Add the onion, if approved.

Mutton Cutlets (Delicate) — Two or 3 small cutlets from the best end of a neck or loin of mutton, 1 cupful of water or broth, a little salt, and a few peppercorns.

Trim the cutlets very nicely, cut off all the fat, place them in a flat dish with enough water or broth to cover them, add the salt and peppercorns and allow them to stew gently for 2 hours, carefully skimming off every particle of fat which may rise to the top during the process. At the end of this time, provided the cutlets have not been allowed to boil fast, they will be found extremely tender. Turn them when half done.

Rabbit (Stewed) — Two nice young rabbits, 1 quart of milk, 1 tablespoonful of flour, a blade of mace, salt and pepper.

Mix into a smooth paste the flour with $\frac{1}{2}$ glass of milk, then add the rest of the milk; cut the rabbits up into convenient pieces; place in a stewpan with the other ingredients and simmer gently until perfectly tender.

Meat Jelly (1) — Beef, isinglass, 1 teacupful of water, salt to taste.

Cut some beef into very small pieces and carefully remove all the fat. Put it in an earthen jar with alternate layers of the best isinglass (it is more digestible than gelatine) until the jar is full. Then add a teacupful of water with a little salt, cover it down closely. and cook it all day in a very slow oven. In the morning scald a jelly mould and strain the liquor into it. It will be quite clear, except at the bottom, where will be the brown sediment such as is in all beef tea, and it will turn out in a shape. It is, of course, intended to be eaten cold, and is very useful in cases where hot food is forbidden, or as a variety from the usual diet.

Meat Jelly (2)—A calf's foot, $1\frac{1}{2}$ lbs. neck of veal or beef, a slice or two of lean ham, 1 small onion, a bunch of parsley, a teaspoonful of salt, a little spice, 3 quarts of water.

Simmer slowly 5 or 6 hours, and strain. The above makes a strong but not highly flavored jelly. More ham or any bones of unboiled meat, game or poultry will improve it. The liquor in which chicken or veal has been boiled should, when at hand, be used instead of water. Meat jellies keep better when no vegetables are stewed in them.

Baked Hominy —To a cupful of cold boiled hominy (small kind) allow 2 cups of milk, a heaping teaspoonful of white sugar, a little salt, and 3 eggs.

Beat the eggs very light, yolks and whites separately. Work the yolks into the hominy, alternately with the butter. When thoroughly mixed, put in the sugar and salt, and go on beating while you soften the batter gradually with milk. Be careful to leave no lumps in the batter. Lastly, stir in the whites and bake in a buttered pudding-dish until light, firm and delicately browned. It may be used as a dessert.

Strengthening Blanc-Mange — One pint milk, ½ oz. isinglass, rind of ½ small lemon, 2 oz. sugar, yolks of 3 fresh eggs.

Dissolve the isinglass in the water, strain through muslin, put it again on the fire with the rind of the half lemon cut very thin, and the sugar; let it simmer gently until well flavored, then take out the lemon peel, and stir the milk to the beaten yolks of the eggs; pour the mixture back into the saucepan, and hold it over the fire, keeping it stirred until it begins to thicken; put it into a deep basin and keep it moved with a spoon until it is nearly cold, then pour it into the moulds, which have been laid in water, and set it in a cool place till firm.

Milk Punch — One-half pint new milk and 1 new-laid egg.

Set the milk in a clean saucepan over a moderate fire; while it is heating beat the egg to a froth in a basin or a large cup. When the milk begins to bubble, skim off the froth as it forms, and pour it into the whipped egg, quickly beating the milk in; *repeat* until the egg is well mixed (without curdling) with about half the now boiled milk. Pour the remainder from the saucepan into the mixture in basin, and quickly pour the whole back into the pan, then again into the basin, and so on until it is all frothy and well mixed. This cooks the eggs sufficiently. Add a pinch of salt, a lump or more of loaf-sugar, a few gratings of nutmeg or ginger according to taste, and serve in a tumbler, to be taken while hot. For cases of spasmodic pain from flatulency, or other cause, where brandy is often recommended, this is much safer to use.

A Fever Drink (1) — A little tea sage, 2 sprigs of balm, a very small quantity of wood sorrel, a small lemon, 3 pints of boiling water.

Put the sage, balm and wood sorrel into a stone jug, having previously washed and dried them, peel thin the lemon, and clear from the white; slice and put a piece of the peel in; then pour on the water, sweeten and cover.

A Fever Drink (2) — One oz. pearl barley, 3 pints water, 1 oz. sweet almonds, a piece of lemon peel, a little syrup of lemons and capillaire.

Wash well the barley; sift it twice, then add the water, sweet almonds beaten fine, and the lemon peel; boil till you have a smooth liquor, then add the syrup.

Apple Water — Some well flavored apples, 3 or 4 cloves, a strip of lemon peel, boiling water.

Slice the apples into a large jug (they need be neither peeled nor cored). Add the cloves and lemon peel, and pour boiling water over. Let it stand a day. It will be drinkable in 12 hours or less.

Currant Water — One quart red currants, ½ pint raspberries, 2 quarts water; syrup—1 quart of water, about ¾ lb. of sugar.

Put the fruit with the water over a very slow fire to draw the juice, for ½ hour. They must not boil. Strain through a hard sieve and add syrup. Other fruits may be used in the same way.

Sago Jelly — Boil a teacupful of sago in 4 pints of water until quite thick; when cold add a pint of raspberry juice pressed from fresh fruit, or half the quantity of raspberry syrup; add enough white sugar to sweeten to the taste, and boil fast for 5 minutes. Pour into the mould. Use a little cream with the jelly.

Flax-Seed Lemonade — Into a covered vessel pour 1 quart of boiling water upon 4 tablespoonfuls of flax-seed. Steep it for 3 hours, and then add the juice of 2 lemons and sweeten to the taste. If too thick, add cold water. Good for colds.

Bread Panada — Toast to a light brown several slices of stale baker's bread. Pile them in a bowl with sugar and a litte salt sprinkled between them. Cover with boiling water; cover tightly and set into a pan of boiling water, letting it simmer gently until the contents of the bowl are like jelly. Eat while warm, with a little powdered sugar and nutmeg.

Slippery-Elm Bark Tea — Break the bark into bits, pour boiling water over it, cover it closely and let it stand until cold. Put sugar and ice in for summer diseases, or add lemon juice for colds.

Rice Milk — Two tablespoonfuls rice, 1 pint milk, 1 tablespoonful ground rice (if wanted thick, 2 will be required), a little cold milk.

Put the rice into the pint of milk; boil it until done, stirring to prevent it burning. Put the ground rice with a little cold milk, mix smooth, and stir it in; boil for about 15 minutes.

Thick Milk may be made in the same way as "rice milk," only substituting flour for rice, thickening and sweetening to taste. Five minutes' boiling will do.

Chamomile Tea — One oz. dried chamomile flowers, ½ oz. dried orange peel, 1 quart boiling water.

Put the chamomile into a jug with the orange peel. Pour over it the boiling water, and stand in the back of the stove, just close enough to the fire to keep it simmering till the strength of the peel and flower is drawn out; then strain off for use.

Dandelion Tea — Six or 8 dandelion roots, according to size, 1 pint boiling water.

Pull up the dandelion roots and cut off the leaves; wash the roots well and scrape off a little of the skin. Cut them up into small pieces and pour the boiling water on them. Let stand all night; then strain through muslin. It should be quite clear and of a light brown color. About ½ glassful should be taken at a time. This decoction should be made only in small quantities, as it will keep fresh only two or three days.

Jelly Water—Stir a tablespoonful of currant or other jelly into ½ pint water; keep it cold and give as occasion requires. Excellent in fevers.

Toast Water—Toast a large slice of wheat bread so that it is a deep brown all over, but not blackened or burnt. Lay in a covered earthenware vessel, cover it with boiling water, and let it steep until cold. Strain it and add a little lemon juice, unless forbidden by the physician.

FOR CHILDREN.

For Diarrhœa — If the child has symptoms of diarrhœa or summer complaint, take the caul of mutton or lamb, and simmer in a pint of water, dusting in a little flour and a little salt. This soup is nutritious, and allays the irritation of the bowels.

Arrowroot, made quite thin, with a teaspoonful of sweet cream, is nutritious and harmless. Do not make the food for infants too rich.

Milk Porridge — Take 1 spoonful of Indian meal, and 1 of white flour; wet to a paste with cold water; put the paste into 2 cups of boiling water, and boil 20 minutes; add 2 cups of milk and a pinch of salt, and cook 10 minutes more, stirring often. Eat with sugar and milk stirred in while hot.

For Teething — Tie a teacup of flour closely in a cloth, and boil for 1 hour. When cold, grate fine — enough to thicken a pint of half milk and half water the consistence of porridge. **Add** a litte salt.

Barley Water — Pick over and wash 3 tablespoonfuls of pearl barley; soak it ½ hour in a very little lukewarm water, and stir, without draining, into 2 cupfuls of boiling water, salted a very little. Simmer 1 hour, stirring often. Strain, and add 2 teaspoonfuls white sugar. When milk disagrees with infants, barley water can often be used.

Digestion of Various Foods.

Easy of Digestion. — Arrowroot, asparagus, cauliflower, baked apples, oranges, grapes, strawberries, peaches.

Moderately Digestible.—Apples, raspberries, bread, puddings, rhubarb, chocolate, coffee, porter.

Hard to Digest. — Nuts, pears, plums, cherries, cucumbers, onions, carrots, parsnips.

TIME REQUIRED FOR DIGESTION.

	Hrs.	Min.
Apples, sweet	1	30
" sour	2	00
Beans, pod, boiled	2	30
Beef, fresh, rare, roasted	3	00
" " dried	3	30
" " fried	4	00
Beets, boiled	3	45

	Hrs.	Min.
Bread, wheat, fresh	3	30
" corn	3	15
Butter (melted),	3	30
Cabbage, with vinegar, raw	2	00
" boiled	4	30
Cheese (old, strong)	3	30
Codfish	2	00
Custard, baked	2	45
Duck, domestic, roasted	4	00
" wild, "	4	30
Eggs, fresh, hard boiled	3	30
" " soft	3	00
Eggs, fresh, fried	3	30
Goose, roast	2	00
Lamb, fresh, boiled	2	30
Liver, beef, boiled	2	00
Milk, boiled	2	00
" raw	2	15
Mutton, roast	3	15
" broiled	3	00
" boiled	3	00
Oysters, raw	2	55
" roast	3	15
" stewed	3	30
Parsnips, boiled	2	30
Pork, fat and lean, roast	5	15
" " " boiled	3	15
" " " raw	3	00
Potatoes, boiled	3	30
" baked	2	30
Rice, boiled	1	00
Sago, "	1	45
Salmon, salted, boiled	4	00
Soup, beef, vegetable	4	00
" chicken	3	00
" oyster	3	30
Tapioca, boiled	2	00
Tripe, soused, boiled	1	00

	Hrs.	Min.
Trout, fresh, boiled or fried	1	30
Turkey, domestic, roast	2	00
" wild, roast	2	18
Turnips, boiled	3	30
Veal, fresh, broiled	4	00
" fresh, fried	4	30
Venison steak, broiled	1	35

Fat, Water and Muscle Properties of Food.

100 PARTS.	Water.	Muscle.	Fat.
Cucumbers	97.0	1.5	1.0
Turnips	94.4	1.1	4.0
Cabbage	90.0	4.0	5.0
Milk, cows'	86.0	5.0	8.0
Apples	84.0	5.0	10.0
Eggs, yolk of	79.0	15.0	27.0
Potatoes	75.2	1.4	22.5
Veal	68.5	10.1	1.65
Eggs, white of	53.0	17.0	.0
Lamb	50.5	11.0	35.0
Beef	50.0	15.0	30.0
Chicken	46.0	18.0	32.0
Mutton	44.0	12.5	40.0
Pork	38.5	10.0	50.0
Beans	14.8	24.0	57.7
Buckwheat	14.2	8.6	75.4
Barley	14.0	15.0	68.8
Corn	14.0	12.0	73.0
Peas	14.0	23.4	60.0
Wheat	14.0	14.6	69.4
Oats	13.6	17.0	66.4
Rice	13.5	6.5	79.5
Cheese	10.0	65.0	19.0
Butter			100.0

Percentage of Nutrition.

Raw cucumbers, 2; raw melons, 3; boiled turnips, 4½; milk, 7; cabbage, 7½; currants, 10;

whipped eggs, 13; beets, 14; apples, 16; peaches, 20; boiled codfish, 21; broiled venison, 22; potatoes, 22½; fried veal, 24; roast pork, 24; roast poultry, 26; raw beef, 26; raw grapes, 27; raw plums, 29; broiled mutton, 30; oatmeal porridge, 75; rye bread, 79; boiled beans. 87; boiled rice, 88; barley bread, 88; wheat bread, 90; baked corn bread, 91; boiled barley, 92; butter, 93; boiled peas, 93; raw oils, 94.

Relative Value of Food (Beef par).

Oysters, 22; milk, 24; lobsters, 50; cream, 56; codfish, 68; eggs, 72; turbot, 84; mutton, 87; venison, 89; veal, 92; fowl, 94; herring, 100; beef, 100; duck, 104; salmon, 108; pork, 116; butter, 124; cheese, 155.

Percentage of Carbon in Food.

Cabbage, 3; beer, 4; carrots, 5; milk, 7; parsnips, 8; fish, 9; potatoes, 12; eggs, 16; beef, 27; bread, 27; cheese, 36; peas, 36; rice, 38; corn, 38; biscuit, 42; oatmeal, 42; sugar, 42; flour, 46; bacon, 54; cocoa, 69; butter, 79.

Foot-Tons of Energy per Ounce of Food.

Cabbage, 16; carrots, 20; milk, 24; ale, 30; potatoes, 38; porter, 42; beef, 55; egg, 57; ham, 65; bread, 83; egg (yolk), 127; sugar, 130; rice, 145; flour, 148; arrowroot, 151; oatmeal, 152; cheese, 168; butter, 281.

Loss of Meat in Cooking.

100 lbs.	raw beef............	=	67 lbs.	roast.
100 "	"	=	74 "	boiled.
400 "	raw mutton..........	=	75 "	roast.
100 "	raw fowl............	=	80 "	roast.
100 "	"	=	87 "	boiled.
100 "	raw fish............	=	94 "	boiled.

The Percentage of Starch

In common grains is as follows, according to Prof. Yeomans: Rice flour, 84 to 85; Indian meal, 77 to 80; oatmeal, 70 to 80; wheat flour, 39 to 77; barley flour, 67 to 70; rye flour, 50 to 61; buckwheat, 52; peas and beans, 42 to 43; potatoes, (75 per cent. water), 13 to 15.

The Degrees of Sugar

In various fruits are: Peach, 1.6; raspberry, 4.0; strawberry, 5.7; currant, 6.1; gooseberry, 7.2; apple, 7.9; mulberry, 9.2; pear, 9.4; cherry, 10.8; grape, 14.9.

Measures for Housekeepers.

Wheat flour........1 lb. is............1 quart.
Indian meal........1 lb. 2 oz. is........1 quart.
Butter (soft)........1 lb. is............1 quart.
Granulated sugar...1 lb. is............1 quart.
Powdered sugar.....1 lb. 1 oz, is.......1 quart.
Best brown sugar...1 lb. 2 oz. is.......1 quart.
Eggs...............10 eggs are.........1 lb.
Flour.............. 8 quarts are.......1 peck.
Flour.............. 4 pecks are........1 bush.

LIQUIDS.—Thirty-two large tablespoonfuls make a pint; 8 large tablespoonfuls, 1 gill. Four gills make 1 pint; 2 pints, 1 quart; 4 quarts, 1 gallon. An ordinary-sized tumbler holds half a pint; a wine-glass, half a gill. Thirty-five drops are equal to one teaspoonful.

BLANK PAGES
FOR
ADDITIONAL RECIPES.